MUSTANG !

The Complete History of America's Pioneer Ponycar

FORD
15M 644

MUSTANG!

The Complete History of America's Pioneer Ponycar

AN AUTOMOBILE QUARTERLY MARQUE HISTORY BOOK

BY GARY L. WITZENBURG

PRODUCED BY THE STAFF OF AUTOMOBILE QUARTERLY

AUTOMOBILE QUARTERLY PUBLICATIONS

•

Publisher and President: L. Scott Bailey
Editor: Beverly Rae Kimes
Senior Editor: Stan Grayson
Art Director: Theodore R.F. Hall
Assistant Art Director: Michael Pardo
Editorial Assistant: Grace Perrin Kimes
Production Editor: Mary B. Williams
Vice-President: Margaret Bailey
Business Manager: Kevin Bitz
Book Distribution Director: John Heffelfinger

•

Typesetting by Optima Typesetting, Inc., Kingston, New Jersey;
color separations by Lincoln Graphics Incorporated, Cherry Hill, New Jersey;
printing by Kutztown Publishing Company, Kutztown, Pennsylvania;
binding by National Publishing Company, Philadelphia, Pennsylvania

Second Printing

Library of Congress Catalog Number: 79-89754

ISBN 0-915038-13-7 Princeton Publishing Inc.

CONTENTS

FOREWORD

The Duke University campus is beautiful in spring, and one bright day in April 1964 that green and Gothic beauty was enhanced by the presence of the first real, live Mustang I ever saw. It was a fire engine red convertible, top down, and the April sunshine sparkling from its contours gave it the look of a giant red ruby resting proudly at the curb, awaiting its lucky owner. Little did I know then what a sensation this unique little car was causing throughout the country. Isolated as I was on a southern college campus and busy to the bone with "higher learning," I had not yet heard about the hordes of people crowding Ford showrooms just to catch a glimpse, and the high percentage of those waving checkbooks and clamoring to sign up. The car that Newsweek *had called a "jaunty, snub-tailed four-passenger cross between a sports car and a sedan" already was racking up sales records from Pittsburgh to Peoria to Portland and soon would set a major one as the best-selling new model in the industry's history to that date. Mustang Mania was sweeping the country. A whole new market segment had been created by Ford expressly for the swelling ranks of postwar babies, who were then beginning to move into the workforce and were seeking exciting new products on which to spend their new-found wealth in a booming mid-Sixties economy. "A market which has been looking for a car has it now," said* Car Life. *"It is a sports car, a* gran turismo *car, an economy car, a personal car, a rally car, a sprint car, a race car, a suburban car, and even a luxury car."* Car and Driver *called it "easily the best thing to come out of Dearborn since the 1932 V-8 Model B roadster." Mustang clubs and spin-off products proliferated, and soon the whole youthful generation was named for Mustang, first of the ponycars. As priorities changed, Mustang got very fast, then very big, and finally (soon after I started writing about cars for a living) very small. By the time* Automobile Quarterly *publisher Scott Bailey asked me to do this book, a fresh, exciting and beautifully designed new Mustang was about to replace the tired, old '78. Enthusiasts everywhere were busily restoring and preserving the now-legendary vintage models. The timing couldn't have been better.*

I have Karl Ludvigsen, author of numerous articles and books including several excellent histories in Automobile Quarterly*'s Library Series, to thank for recommending me for the job, Scott Bailey for acting on that recommendation, and editor Beverly Rae Kimes, art director Theodore R.F. Hall and the fine AQ staff for patiently and expertly putting it all together.*
Jim Bradley of the National Automotive History Collection of the Detroit Public Library was invaluable in helping with the research material, and Dave Crippen of the Ford Archives at Greenfield Village also graciously opened his files for the cause.
Owen Bombard, Bill Carroll, Linda Lee, Julie Mantho, Walt Murphy, Jim Olson, Paul Preuss and Larry Weiss are the Ford Public Relations people without whom this project wouldn't have gotten off the ground, let alone been completed.
Past and present Ford executives, engineers, designers and product planners who helped with interviews and crucial information include Nat Adamson, Gene Bordinat, John Bowers, Tom Case, Tom Feaheny, Howard Freers, Don Frey, Stu Frey, Joe Gilmore, Gail Halderman, Fran Hernandez, Ross Humphries, Lee Iacocca, Roy Lunn, Glen Lyall, Harold MacDonald, Fritz Mayhew, John Najjar, Jacque Passino, Don Peterson, Dick Place, Dave Rees, Connie Reuter, Gordon Riggs, Hal Sperlich and Jack Telnack.
Bill Buffa, Carole George and the rest of the Ford Photo Media staff handled the awesome task of producing hundreds of photographs from dusty, old negatives; and Ken Wagel of Ford Design Center Photographic assisted in the selection of a great many of those.
Dave Arnold of the Mid-Ohio Sports Car Course, Mike Hedge of Hedge Public Relations, Dennis Simanaitis of Road & Track *magazine and fellow auto writer Tony Grey provided additional photos and information, while Al Binder of* Ward's Automotive Reports, *Mac DeMere of the Sports Car Club of America and freelance writer Cindy Pries aided in researching and producing some of the comprehensive appendices. Finally, the able assistance and support of my very good friend Jill made completion of this ambitious project a lot less formidable than it might otherwise have been.*
Ford's Ponycar Pioneer approaches its sixteenth birthday as this is written, having survived infancy, early youth and a difficult puberty while the world around it changed at frightening speed. It enters the new decade a blossoming teen, confident of a proud and prosperous adulthood even as mounting fuel concerns once again cast a menacing shadow over the automotive industry and its customers.
Whatever the outcome, Mustang will remain one of the most important and best-loved cars of all time. Everyone has a fantasy, but too many are out of reach. For millions of people like you and me, Mustang has been so significant partly because it is not.

—Gary L. Witzenburg

Troy, Michigan
July 1979

1. GENESIS

Contrary to much of what has been written, the Mustang story does not begin with the Ford Motor Company's decision to build such a car late in 1962. Nor does it start with the promotion of Lee A. Iacocca to Ford Division general manager in November 1960.

No, the Mustang really has its roots deeply implanted in the middle of the previous decade—when Ford introduced the 1955 two-place Thunderbird roadster. Never intended as a true sports car, the original 'Bird nevertheless handily outsold Chevrolet's arch-rival Corvette during its three years of glory, tested the market for an American-built "personal" sportster and in the process created a legend which lives on today.

A few weeks before the 1955 Thunderbird was presented to the public—as product planner Tom Case remembers—Lou Crusoe, then Ford Division general manager, drove one home to see how it checked out on the road. Following a weekend with the new car, Crusoe called Case into his office on Monday morning.

"Tom," he said, "there is one thing wrong with the Thunderbird. It's a beautiful car, but we need a rear seat in it. Let's go to work and make a four-passenger 'Bird."

And so, not long after the original Thunderbird was launched, separate styling, planning and engineering groups were established within the division to lay out, design and develop a new, second-generation car which would presumably have a much broader market appeal than the two-seat version. The idea was to come up with the smallest possible four-passenger sporty car using the engine and powertrain components available at the time to get the performance desired. Out of this study emerged the four-place Thunderbird introduced in 1958.

Why wasn't it smaller and lighter, like the Mustang which would arrive some six-and-a-half years later? Because it was built around the rather heavy and bulky Ford high-performance V-8 engine of the period. It was not until Ford engineers had developed the thin-wall, small-block, 221-cubic-inch "Fairlane" engine in late 1961 that a Mustang-size sporty four-passenger car became possible. Says Tom Case, "The Mustang really was what the four-passenger Thunderbird would have been in 1958 if we had had the technology to fit the power we needed into that kind of package."

Maybe so, and maybe not. But as the T-Bird grew in size and price during the next several years, it became more a rich man's toy than a young man's fancy. True enough, the four-passenger 'Bird outsold its predecessor by more than three-to-one in its first year and continued to grow in popularity, but as a luxury car it contributed little toward attracting youthful buyers into Ford showrooms. Therein was the crux of a problem.

Meanwhile, sales of imported roadsters—MG's, Triumphs, Austin Healeys, Alfa Romeos, Fiats and the like, particularly those on the lower end of the price scale—were rising steadily, while Chevrolet's Corvette was carving its own niche as America's only true sports car. Soon Ford's offices were inundated with letters from owners and admirers of the original Thunderbird. They wanted a resurrection, and they wanted it fast.

But Ford in the late 1950's, like the other U.S. manufacturers, was far more concerned about the threat being posed by the mushrooming popularity of economical little VW Beetles and Renault Dauphines, and there was little time for frivolous thoughts of sports cars. As a result, the American public in the fall of 1959 was treated to Detroit's first serious attempt at economy cars: the Ford Falcon, Chevrolet Corvair and Plymouth Valiant. Ford's simple but solid Falcon was easily the star of this new car show, selling 417,174 copies—a new industry record—in its first year on the market. That performance nearly doubled the first-year sales of Chevy's more exotic rear-engined Corvair and it put a lot of smiles on executive faces in Dearborn, Michigan.

But still something was missing. Ford had built a solid reputation through the years as a maker of family cars—high-quality sedans and station wagons at affordable prices, plus a few convertibles and Thunderbirds—but as the fun-loving Fifties turned into the sexy Sixties, there was little in Ford showrooms to attract the attention of those whose automotive desires extended beyond practical transportation.

"We approached the decade of the Sixties at Ford with a rather stodgy, non-youth image," notes Lee Iacocca, who took over as Ford Division vice-president at the tender age of thirty-six. The son of a fiercely independent Italian immigrant, Iacocca was raised in Allentown, Pennsylvania, picked up an engineering degree (with an "A" average) at Lehigh University and a master's from Princeton, joined Ford as a trainee and completed an extensive business training

Competition winner, the Ford Studio's Cougar which, in twenty months, would be reproduced almost exactly as the production 1964½ Mustang.

FORD
002F-LOO
8-16-62
S-5638-1

FORD
002F-LOO
8-16-62
S-5638-5

Mustang styling heritage can be seen in long hood, short deck, low roof look of cars in the Ford stable. Below: Two- and four-seat T-Bird; above, the Lincoln Continental and Continental Mark II.

course—all by the time he was twenty-two. Dynamic, aggressive and hard-working, he had quickly pushed his way up through Ford's competitive sales organization to the position of marketing manager for Ford Division.

"You can work your tail off," he was fond of saying, "but you've always got to write down what your goal is." Iacocca's goal was simple: He merely wanted to be a Ford vice-president by the time he was thirty-five. He missed by exactly one year and eighteen days. It was November 1960.

Iacocca had long been keenly aware of his company's youth problem, but until then had not been in a position to do much about it. Once during the development of the Falcon, he had come across an experimental styling model sporting a roofline similar to that of the original small Thunderbird. "Later," he relates, "when I heard that the T-Bird roof had been discarded because it wasn't quote practical unquote, I could have cried." Although the Falcon was doing very well in the compact-car market, Iacocca and other young men at Ford couldn't help wondering how much better the new car might have sold had it been more attractive.

Now as leader of the Ford Division he had been handed a golden opportunity to try putting some of his many ideas into operation. On that fateful November day when Henry Ford II told him of his promotion, Iacocca recalls, "I walked out of Mr. Ford's office thinking of that good-looking little youth car."

Almost immediately he set up a committee of highly creative people to look into it. Iacocca himself headed this group, and among the men he brought in were product planning manager Don Frey and his special projects assistant, Hal Sperlich, market research manager Bob Eggert, public relations manager Walt Murphy, special projects (racing) manager Jacque Passino, marketing manager Chase Morsey, Jr. and advertising manager John Bowers. Ford's advertising agency, J. Walter Thompson, was also involved in the effort.

"Lee was trying to develop and convey a theme," Frank Thomas, a Thompson agency senior vice-president and supervisor of the Ford account, commented in a *Newsweek* article on the Mustang's introduction. "Now, I imagine you can say of Chrysler that engineering is its theme, and with GM, it's style and general excellence. But what was Ford's? Was it that Ford stood for basic transportation? Was it the 'Lively Ones' theme? Was it the safest-car-on-the-road theme? We found we were, as a team, going all over the lot. There were too many stop-and-go projects."

Rather than meeting in Ford offices, Iacocca chose to have his committee get together off the premises at the then-new Fairlane Motel in Dearborn, and thus it came to be called the "Fairlane Committee." As a result, many people thought these meetings were clandestine, that Iacocca didn't want his superiors in the corporation to know what he was up to. He denies it. "It was a convenient way to get together in the evening to discuss how we were going to attack this problem," he explains.

The Fairlane Committee, meeting weekly for fourteen weeks, gave birth to what Iacocca terms "a whole host of ideas," and primary among them was to "take a car called the Falcon and make something of it, and that became a thing called the Mustang." This youth-oriented car was to be the cornerstone of a whole new plan, a comprehensive marketing theme which later came to be termed "Total Performance." The other major thrust of this new direction became Ford's full-scale return to serious racing, which was carried out under the able leadership of Jacque Passino, while Iacocca and the rest of his hand-picked assistants busied themselves primarily with the task of making their "Mustang" a reality.

The Falcon's success, in spite of its austere looks and image, had convinced Iacocca that the growth market of the Sixties would be in the compact size class. But the really hot ticket would have to be something considerably different from the run-of-the-mill economy compact. Something very new and exciting. Something that would change the Ford image.

"In the Fifties," he explains, "we wrestled with getting cars so they wouldn't leak and rattle. We spent all our time working on resale value, durability, quality and reliability. But at that point it was time to step out. We had this committee, we put down a priority and we were off to the races, both literally and figuratively. It was a total program to attack what we considered one of our most difficult problems."

Several important criteria were laid down for the car they had in mind. It would be small, light and inexpensive—no more than 180 inches, 2500 pounds and $2500—but would carry four people; its styling would employ the sporty long hood, short deck, low profile look that made the original Thunderbird a modern-day classic; it would offer a choice of six-cylinder or V-8 engine, and would be versatile enough to be adapted to a wide variety of tastes.

"Work on this project began in late '61 or so," recalls Hal Sperlich, who had just been promoted to special studies manager in Ford Division's product planning group. "John Kennedy was President, and the country was taken by the enthusiasm of its youthful leader...the excitement, the promise...everything was upbeat and youthful at the time. Iacocca came in as head of Ford Division, and he was a vibrant kind of guy, a go-go type who wanted to make his mark, and he seemed to fit all of that. It was one of those wild times when the chemistry of people was right, the times were right."

On top of that, Ford had been doing a tremendous amount of research, all of which pointed to an impending explosion in the marketplace by the mid-1960's. The children of the postwar baby boom were turning eighteen in the early Sixties and would be voting age and self-supporting by mid-decade. The fifteen-to-twenty-nine age group was predicted to grow by nearly forty percent between 1960 and 1970, while the thirty-to-thirty-nine category would fall by almost nine percent.

Consumers as a whole, said the research, were becoming better educated, more sophisticated and more discriminating in their buying decisions, largely through the effect of television. There was tremendous growth in multi-car families as a result of increasing affluence, and the second cars were often smaller, specialized vehicles. Women were enjoying increasing influence in car purchasing decisions, and more and more of them were choosing the career route over marriage and family, at least temporarily. Importantly, this expanding number of female car-buyers, whether married or single, was generally attracted to smaller, more maneuverable cars, easier to handle and park.

Buyer preference surveys showed a surprising interest in sporty and performance-oriented options for a market that was supposed to be economy minded. This burgeoning army was moving as a group toward small and agile cars, both foreign and domestic, equipped with bucket seats, floor shifts and, whenever possible, the most powerful engines available.

Bearing this out, Chevrolet had greatly increased the popularity of its lackluster Corvair by introducing a sporty version called "Monza" in 1961, the significance of which did not escape the folks at Ford. "I remember seeing a red one before it was out," comments Sperlich, "and the damn thing had beautiful red bucket seats and good-looking wheel covers. I remember seeing it sitting there and thinking, son-of-a-bitch, the bastards have turned defeat into victory!"

Buyers of Ford's own compact Falcons were ordering such items as automatic transmissions, optional engines, dress-up kits and white-wall tires in significant numbers, prompting Iacocca to observe, "People want economy so badly they don't give a damn how much they pay for it." More and more it seemed that what Ford needed was a car with the flair and performance of a Thunderbird but the price tag of a Falcon.

And the researchers kept coming in with their facts, figures and predictions. Not only would there be more young people than ever before, but also the number of them with a college education would double—and people who go to college tend to earn more money and buy more cars than those who don't. Personal income would rise to the point where the number of households earning $10,000 or more would more than triple between 1960 and 1970.

As early as the summer of 1961, work was in progress in Gene Bordinat's Advanced Styling studio on variations of two-seater and 2+2 sports car concepts.

A special market test was conducted to see how people would react to a highly styled, small sporty car that was priced low enough for young wage earners to afford. So strong was the potential demand for such a car, according to the surveys, that the question seemingly became not *whether* to build it but how quickly it could be done.

"It was the eighteen-to-twenty-four group...the accumulators, the career starters, the trend-setters...that we wanted to get to," notes Iacocca. "We had to get into their minds even if they couldn't afford the car at first. Hell, we'd hit on such a good thing that we had to get moving on it before somebody else could come along and beat us to it."

The bottom line of all this research, possibly the biggest project of its kind ever conducted, was that at least one out of every two new cars sold in the 1960's would be bought by a customer between the ages of eighteen and thirty-four. The study also showed a strong correlation between Ford's lack of sporty products and the growing age gap between Ford and Chevrolet buyers. Clearly something had to be done.

The first reaction from the Fairlane Committee, the thing that could be done immediately, was to change the Division's marketing thrust, downplaying the previous safety and reliability focus and concentrating on "The Lively Ones." This new direction, according to *Newsweek,* "was turned over to a team of admen, engineers and designers working in the 'tomb'—a windowless room in an auditorium in the Ford Division office building where Iacocca imposed such rigid security that even the wastepaper was burned under supervision."

Out of the "tomb" came a whole new image program for Falcon, plus some fresh touches—vinyl-covered roofs and four-speed floor shifts—for the stodgy standard-size Fords and the new intermediate Fairlane line for mid-year 1962. Falcon got a new sporty series called "Futura" in coupe and convertible versions, complete with bucket seats and floor shift to counter Chevrolet's Monza, plus—at last—the T-Bird-styled squared-off coupe roof that Iacocca had liked so much several years before. With the addition of a Fairlane 221-cubic-inch "V-8," these Falcons became mini performance models called "Sprints." And by this time the marketing theme had shifted again, to the bolder "Total Performance" tack which Iacocca referred to as an all-out "crossed flags" campaign.

Some within Ford had reservations about trying to "sporty-ize" their compact car. "Doing that to the Falcon was like putting falsies on Grandma," says product planner Dick Place. "It just was out of character. Falcon was not a sporty car and couldn't be made into one."

Nevertheless, encouraging sales figures in the fall confirmed the soundness of the trend and strengthened Iacocca's resolve to bring a brand-new car to market as quickly as possible. He had the small V-8 engine. He had the Falcon suspension and powertrain components, all of which had been strengthened for the V-8; and there were plenty of other pieces available from the new Fairlane series if necessary.

"We had some pretty good hunks of hardware," he relates, "but we didn't have the wrappers to put them in. Everybody was Thunderbird nuts at that time, and I felt we should have a poor man's T-Bird, a T-Bird for the working girl."

Iacocca was more convinced as day passed day. By now he had been exploring the idea for more than a year and a half, trying to put together the right combination of package size, styling and price. In mid-1961 he had instructed styling chief Gene Bordinat to assemble every Ford and Chevrolet product then available for comparison purposes. "Usually when he came over to discuss something, he'd already been thinking about it for a long time," recalls Bordinat,"...so we took all the cars that Chevy had and all the cars that we had and put them out in the court area, lined up against one another. And there was a void." It was right where Iacocca knew it would be. It was

Design center concept of Falcon-based sports car from September 1961. Iacocca finally got the fancy Falcons he wanted in '62 model year. Futura convertible offered "sports car size" and choice of bucket seats, three- or four-speed manual transmission and "six different performance packages." Sports Futura got "clubby" T-Bird-style roof with optional vinyl, standard bucket seats and optional four-speed transmission—all this to provide competition for Chevrolet's popular Corvair Monza.

opposite the Corvair Monza.

It so happened that Bordinat had something to show the young Ford Division boss that day. "We work on cars around here of all kinds that are exploratory," the styling chief explains, "without any given program. Things that we anticipate might be required or useful in the marketplace or might give our management a new opportunity."

Code-named "Allegro," this particular project had been created, according to Bordinat, "in a rather clandestine fashion in the bowels of this organization by our advanced studio under Bob Maguire. We were trying to figure out what kind of styling 'cues' we could come up with that would connote sort of a personalized sports-type car. Not having anything but ordinary mechanicals to work with, we had decided that a long hood wasn't all that bad...there's something about a long hood that says, 'there's a lot of engine here'...a modestly compressed rear seat wasn't all bad, and low overall height and so forth. Allegro was our first car of that general configuration."

It was also exactly what Iacocca had in the back of his mind. Not that the car's actual styling turned him on so much, but it did ably demonstrate the viability of such a package for production.

"It was an interesting car," Bordinat adds, "and perhaps if it had been put into production it could have done as well as the Mustang did, but we'll never know."

Iacocca wanted to see more variations on the theme, and so a group of advanced designers and clay modelers was put to work for the next nine months coming up with several more small, sporty package concepts...two-seaters, 2+2's and four-passenger cars with varying rear-seat room.

Meanwhile, the new Ford Division boss had one of his key product planners investigating a completely different avenue. A lot of people at Ford still wanted to resurrect the original T-Bird, and Tom Case, who had moved from Thunderbird to Falcon planning manager in early 1958, remembers Iacocca asking him late in 1961 to check out the possibility of doing a new four-place car based on the old two-seater body.

"So I got an office with a lock on it and a secretary, and I worked about six months building a car on paper," Case recalls, "...dimensions, value objectives, cost estimates, price and profit programs, the whole job. And one of the things I did, as an alternate idea, was go back to Budd Company, which had supplied the original T-Bird bodies, to see if the old tools were still available and how much they thought it would cost to bring them up to date and make them usable again. They got very excited about the program and came up with a proposal to take the Falcon and put the Thunderbird body on it."

Budd Company actually constructed a prototype vehicle using a modified '57 T-Bird body on a cut-down '61 Falcon underbody, and called it "XT-Bird—a sporty, popular-priced roadster in the original Thunderbird concept." It had a tiny jump seat in the back, suitable for children when the convertible top was up, and looked something like a stretched '57 T-Bird but with no characteristic fins or hood scoop. Budd estimated that tool, jig and fixture costs for the XT-Bird would be no more than $1.5 million versus $6 million or so for an all-new body, and said it could begin shipping complete bodies in six months from the date of authorization. The company also did some market research of its own, concluding that "there is a ready-made market for a two-seater such as the XT-Bird."

But to Ford management it looked more like a Falcon than a Thunderbird, it was a bit too expensive and it was still basically a two-passenger car, which would have limited its volume. "I remember I was dead set against it," says Iacocca. "They wanted a two-passenger car and I couldn't see the total market for that at more than 50,000 at the time. We were talking about a sports car for the masses, and our research said it better have 2+2 or four-seat capability. We could have gotten the car quicker with the Budd idea, but it didn't take long before we decided to go with a whole new car instead."

By this time, early 1962, Tom Case also had completed the four-passenger sports car concept as requested by Iacocca and was promoted to head up the Ford and Lincoln-Mercury special vehicles office. Product planning manager Don Frey and his special studies assistant, Hal Sperlich, were assigned the responsibility of creating this affordable sports car, code-named "Special Falcon."

"So how do you work from that platform and make an exciting car?," Sperlich asks. "We started putting together different ways to approach it, working with styling, and a lot of the initial thrust was really with modestly-changed Falcons. We looked at a whole bunch of alternatives that involved some skin change on the Falcon as ways to go, but finally decided we needed a whole new skin."

Meanwhile, Iacocca still had Gene Bordinat's advanced styling people working on half-a-dozen different sporty-car concepts, and

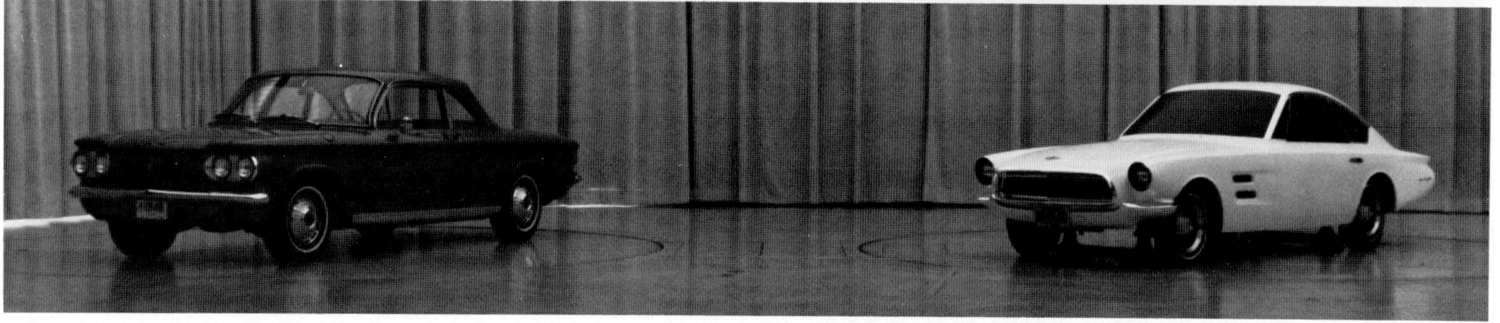

Top: Although not photographed until June 1962, the Allegro was a four-passenger sporty-car package that Bordinat and DeLaRossa had been working on for over a year; the first Ford Advanced Styling effort to incorporate the long-hood, short-deck, low overall height look that would later characterize the Mustang, it was the car Bordinat showed to Iacocca in mid-'61 as a possible answer to the sporty Corvair Monza. Above: The Avanti, or Median, another four-seat sporty-car concept developed to compete with Chevy Monza. Below: Avanti "sport car seating" illustrated; and the Avanti, now called Avventura, in fiberglass model form by July 1962, complete with interior, controls and instrumentation. Page opposite: Budd Company's 1962 proposal for a low-priced T-Bird resurrection, a stretched and modified '57 body on altered Falcon underbody, rejected in favor of doing a whole new car that became the first Mustang.

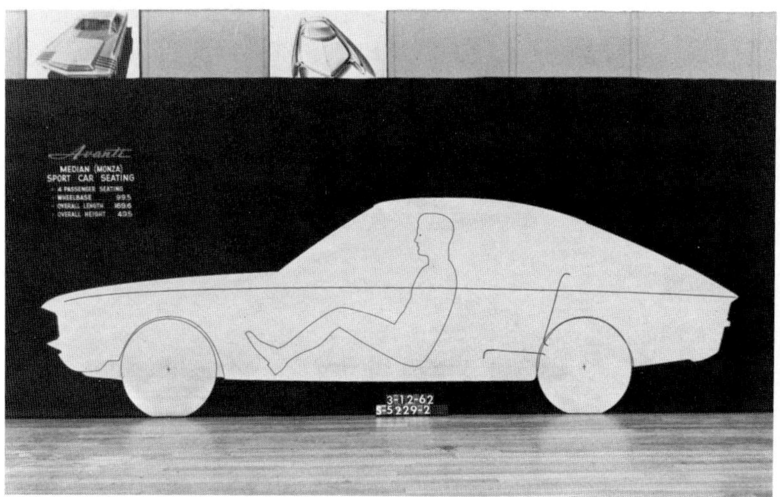

By mid-July of 1962, a handsome fastback version of the Allegro sported a hood scoop, rear deck vent and large, round taillamps.

Frey recalls happening across one of those clay models one day that had the styling flair he wanted. "I remember bringing Lee over to the studio," he says, "to show him this car. But it was a two-seater, and he said it ought to have four seats to broaden its market appeal and give the people with kids a usable back seat. He was right, of course, so at this juncture we got a little more serious about it and started laying out four-seater package drawings...recognizing that it would be a bit more difficult to make it sporty enough with four seats."

In mid-1962, the idea was first presented as a formal program proposal, called a "Blue Letter," but was rejected. "There was not much top management interest," says Frey, "and still not much interest coming even from styling." Bordinat recalls wryly that "after spending some nine months going through all these studies trying to determine how much of a back seat it should have, it was finally determined that a car just about on that original Allegro dimensionally was the kind of car we were talking about."

The styling chief also remembers showing some of this small sporty car work to Henry Ford early in 1962: "He was cold toward the whole idea, and we couldn't understand it because he's a car buff. But he wasn't having any part of this at all. In fact, he said, 'I'm leaving,' and he walked out of the meeting. I had never seen him so cold to a car. It turned out that when he left, he went straight down to Ford Hospital and spent the next few months down there with mononucleosis. Of course he wasn't interested in the car...he wasn't interested in anything that day, because he was feeling terrible!"

Once the seating package was fairly well set, according to Sperlich, "there was a ton of work done trying to get a styling design that made sense, with one failure after another. Until finally Lee called for a competition."

Iacocca was by now impatient with the lack of progress in coming up with a viable exterior design for his pet project and in mid-summer Bordinat was directed to produce a half-dozen new clay models in a big hurry. "I was given something like two weeks to turn all the troops loose in this place to come up with other candidates," he says. "We had three major elements at the Design [Styling] Center working on these cars, and each turned out two models in two weeks...a phenomenal performance. This was after Mr. Ford was out of the hospital and was feeling a hell of a lot more inclined to listen."

The three studios involved were Corporate Projects (Advanced), Ford and Lincoln-Mercury. Each was given the package dimensions and asked to engage in open competition. "The challenge sent a wave of enthusiasm through the studios," according to official Ford history. Designers who normally shared ideas were locking their studios, refusing to let their rivals in. They all wanted to win that competition.

History also records that the clear winner was a design called

The six designs competing for approval were shown to Ford Division management in mid-August of 1962. Above: The notchback Allegro again, now with wide, ribbed, horizontal taillamps. Below: Another entry from Advanced Styling, with racy front fender sculpturing and large horizontal taillamps.

"Cougar" that was submitted by Dave Ash, assistant to Ford studio head Joe Oros. Oros had had to leave town during the contest but had left Ash in charge of putting together the contest cars. "To save time," said Oros, who usually gets credit for the design that later became the production Mustang, "we worked up a list of do's and don'ts and tacked it up on the wall before we started sketching. We didn't want the car to look like any other car. It was supposed to be unique."

The Cougar was, in Bordinat's words, "the car that jumped out of this group. Some were sheer and some were soft, but this one seemed to have the greatest distinction. It was the one selected by management and the one we went on to produce."

Not coincidentally, it was also the one which had the most Thunderbird and Lincoln Continental Mark II heritage in its roofline and profile, while other candidates tried too hard to look Italian or to mimic the round-cornered Corvair. The fact that Iacocca (and other Ford executives) were self-confessed Mark II and four-seat Thunderbird fans was apparently not lost on Oros and Ash.

Iacocca remembers it a little differently, however. According to him, the favored candidate at first was a sleek little number from the Ford studio called "Stiletto." "The Stiletto was by far the one we wanted to go with," he recalls, "but when we priced it out we found it would have been too expensive to build. Cougar was the compromise candidate, and today that Stiletto still looks a lot more modern in concept than the Cougar design. There were a whole host of others in the running too, but they didn't have the leanness. They didn't have youth written all over them. They were a little too heavy-fat."

In any case, the Cougar must have set some sort of design record in the closeness of its relationship to the final Mustang design. Its European-style rounded rectangular headlamps, of course, became round in production, the side sculpturing was straightened out some, and the decorative side louvers simplified. There were small changes in roof height, front and rear details and lower body dimensions, but

Above: Looking like a performance coupe of the later 1960's, the Stiletto was the design Iacocca and others preferred at first, but it would have been too expensive to sell for the $2500 price he had in mind. Center: This Lincoln-Mercury Studio entry had tall, curved rear fins, Studebaker Avanti-like taillamps and quad exhausts protruding through rear body panel. Below: Another Lincoln-Mercury concept featured "flying buttress" rear pillars, deep side sculpturing from headlamps to wrap-around taillamps. Page opposite: The competition-winning Cougar clay model's left side featured the wide sculpture and louvers that were to become a Mustang trademark, while the right side had a humped-fender, air scoop treatment that would ultimately be rejected.

otherwise the Cougar went from clay model to assembly line with astonishingly little alteration.

What took a little more doing was convincing the corporate powers that the car should be produced at all. "By this time," says Don Frey, "we were on the second or third Blue Letter proposal to management, and it still was not approved. Then Lee went back to Mr. Ford and got him to come back and look at it again. He agreed to bring it to a corporate product approval meeting and at that time finally gave Lee his own tentative approval...sort of 'Okay, I'll approve the damn thing just to get you guys off my back.' "

There were three strikes against Lee Iacocca when he went in to sell his program on September 10th, 1962. For one thing, the cost-conscious and conservative Ford corporate management was not yet assured of the need to spend much money on this so-called "youth market" that was just beginning to emerge in force. For another, they were wary of any new-car project, having recently been terribly embarrassed and financially burned by their Edsel's inglorious demise—and remarkably, the Edsel, like the Mustang, had been a car for which all the market research spelled instant success. Finally, the corporation was already committed to spending a tremendous amount of money retooling the regular Ford line for 1965, with some $250 million earmarked for Ford Division alone.

Always the practical type, Ford Motor Company president Arjay Miller had ordered his research chief, George Brown, to come up with the expected incremental volume of this proposed little sporty car. In other words, he wanted to know how many more cars Ford could expect to sell *with* the new car added to its line than without it, recognizing that it would certainly cut into Falcon sales and possibly damage the new Fairlane series as well. Brown had come back with an annual figure of 86,000 units—not enough to justify the expenditure. According to Don Frey, however, Brown privately advised individual members of the planning committee to use their own judgment. "You're car men," he said. "You make the decision."

On the positive side was the fact that Henry Ford liked the idea—and, as has so often been said, his name is on the building. Iacocca also had an exciting and attractive design in the Ash/Oros Cougar that could be put into production quickly and with a minimum dollar investment using Falcon componentry. Also, he and his people had done their homework well, having gone through an exhaustive amount of product planning, packaging, feasibility and cost versus profit studies.

"There was a lot of cost work done on it," Hal Sperlich relates, "and a lot of hard selling, because we had to sell it to a management that didn't really understand it and didn't want to do it. The first planning volume for the car was 75,000 units, and that's where the program was finally sold."

When Lee Iacocca came out of that September meeting with a reluctant corporate blessing and a modest $40 million with which to tool and develop his Mustang, he remarked that he had never been through such a tough selling job in his life—a significant comment from a man who had risen through the very tough ranks of Ford's sales organization.

The car would be built at Ford's Dearborn plant, and the first one, "Job One," was scheduled to roll off the assembly line on March 9th, 1964, with public introduction some five weeks later. Normal gestation period for a new car from approval to production is about three years. Iacocca and his team had not quite eighteen months to put their dream into reality.

2.

THE FIRST MUSTANG

Early in 1957, Carroll Shelby visited Enzo Ferrari in the Commendatore's Modena, Italy, office. Equipped with the thick, curly hair, broad smile, ten-gallon hat and striped bib overalls that had become his trademarks, plus a fair share of raw nerve and driving talent, the slender Texan had won nearly every stateside sports car race he had entered the year before in an privately-owned Ferrari, and now Ferrari himself was considering taking him on as a factory driver.

But Shelby was not about to settle for the meager pay and second-rank status Ferrari had in mind, and he walked out of the meeting. "I'll blow your ass off someday," he was quoted as saying in Leo Levine's Ford racing history, *The Dust and the Glory.* That season, Shelby was named sports car driver of the year by *Sports Illustrated* magazine, and in 1959 he added the legendary 24 Hours of Le Mans to his impressive list of victories.

Just two years later, however, his driving career was cut short when doctors discovered he had developed a minor heart ailment, and at the age of thirty-eight he took to running a Goodyear racing tire business and a high-performance driving school to pass time and earn a living. But in "Old Shel's" fertile mind was a crazy idea, an idea that had been tried before with little success by men with far more money and high-placed contacts than he enjoyed.

The plan was to combine a powerful, mass-produced American engine with a lightweight European roadster body and chassis to create an exciting hybrid sports car that would be equally at home on the street and on the race track. Turned down by General Motors, the smooth-talking Texan next approached Ford Motor Company to see if he could work out a deal for some of Ford's upcoming lightweight 221-cubic-inch V-8 engines. Little did he know how ripe the Ford Division management was at that time (August 1961) for just such a scheme.

How they happen: Ford Motor Company traces a sporting evolution.

Lee Iacocca's Fairlane Committee had met and emerged with excitement and youth appeal at the top of its shopping list. A revitalized racing program, beginning on the stock car circuits, was in its infancy under Jacque Passino—though still under the table due to the Automobile Manufacturers' Association (AMA) ban on factory-backed competition. The seeds of the production Mustang were just starting to germinate in the newly-fertilized creative soil at Ford. The catch words "Total Performance" had been coined and embraced by the Ford marketing forces.

Initially, in September, two engines were shipped to Shelby's modest garage. By January Ford was helping with expenses, and on January 30th, 1962, the first Shelby Cobra prototype was tested at the Silverstone race course in England. Days later the car was crossing the Atlantic by sea and Shelby was showing movies of the successful test to enthusiastic Ford executives in Dearborn. On February 5th, according to Levine, an agreement was signed stipulating that Ford would supply engines and other mechanical components in exchange for the affixing of "Powered by Ford" labels on every car Shelby produced. This was the first official paperwork establishing the fruitful partnership that would produce not only the exciting Cobra sports cars and Shelby Mustang conversions but also numerous road racing victories in sports cars, prototypes and Mustang sedans in the ensuing years.

To say the enthusiast press writers were turned on by the Cobra when they saw it later that month would be gross understatement. Shelby's creation soon graced several major car magazine covers, this in an era when Ford rarely received anything more than an interior story. The division's modest investment in his wild idea already was paying off several-fold in publicity and much-needed image boost. Iacocca was delighted, and the spirited public reaction to the car at Ford's New York auto show exhibit only served to strengthen his belief in the relationship.

Contracts were signed in early August establishing Ford's virtual ownership of Shelby American Inc. in return for financing the car's development and production as well as the planned extensive racing operation. What had begun as an idea to simply drop the V-8 engine (now up to 260 cubic inches) and a four-speed transmission into the handsome British A.C. roadster body had evolved into a major testing and development program to ready the car for production, with able assistance from race driver Dan Jones.

Coincidentally, the Cobra's competition debut came at the same time as Chevrolet's introduction of the revolutionary independent-rear-suspension, four-wheel-disc-brake Corvette Sting Ray. At Riverside Raceway in California that October, Billy Krause's Cobra led the new Corvettes with ease until a broken hub carrier handed

THE EVOLUTION OF FORD MOTOR CO. EXPERIMENTAL AND SPORTS PROTOTYPE VEHICLES

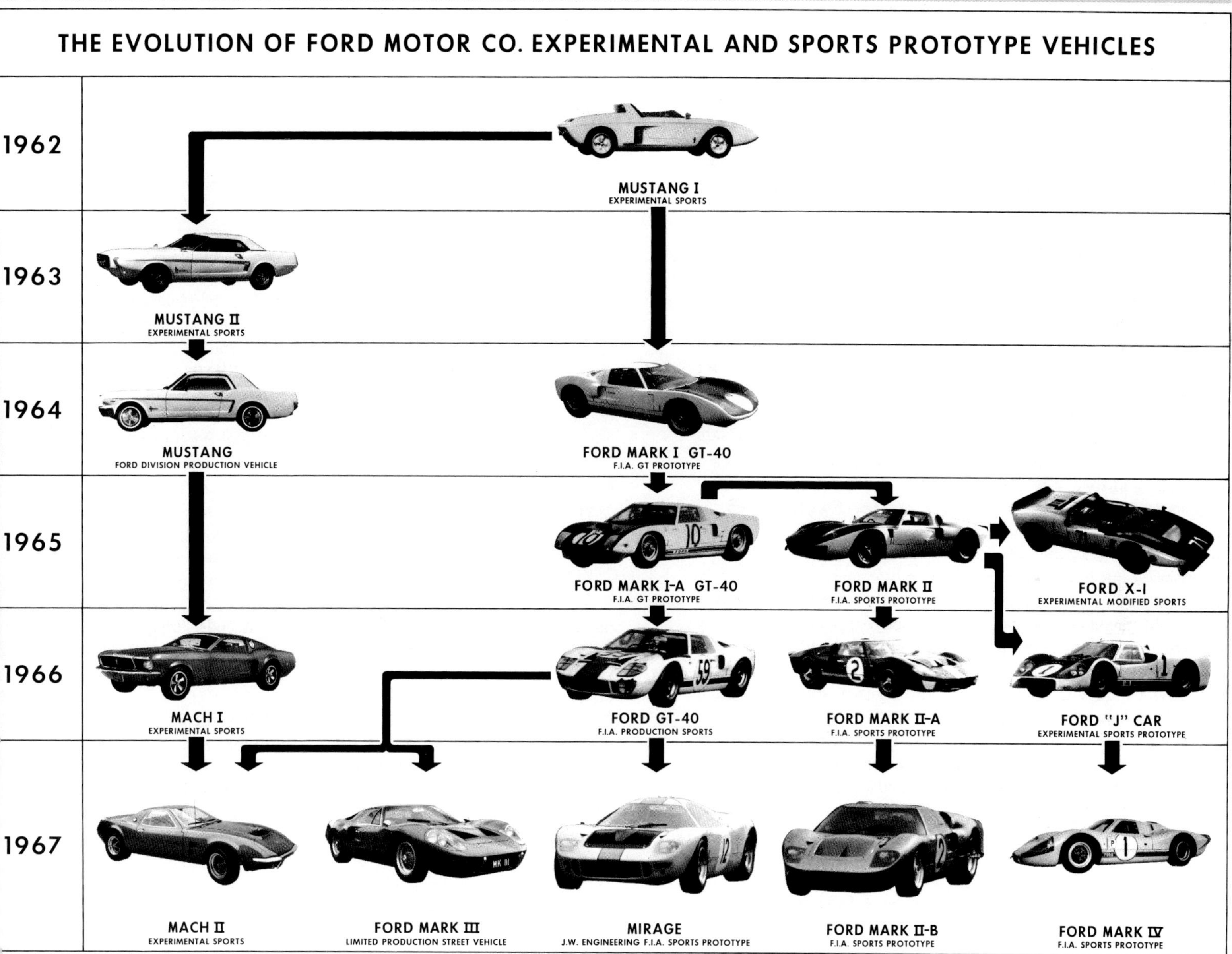

A smiling Texan named Shelby, Ford racing boss Jacque Passino.

round one of what was to be a long and hard-fought racing rivalry to Chevrolet. Before the '62 season was over, however, a Riverside SCCA regional race provided the first Cobra victory with a one-two sweep by sports car aces Dave MacDonald and Ken Miles.

Meanwhile, another association and another key image boosting program had been taking shape deep within Ford Engineering. In 1961, Jack Brabham had driven an underpowered rear-engine Cooper-Climax European formula race car to an inauspicious ninth-place finish at Indianapolis. Few took serious note of this rear-engine debut; but the following year a tall, handsome and enormously talented American driver named Dan Gurney—who was then a factory Formula One Porsche pilot, had won the fledgling Daytona Continental road race earlier in the year and then had been impressive in his first stock car ride (in a Holman-Moody Ford) in the Daytona 500 until the engine had blown—got a chance to run Indy in a Mickey Thompson Buick V-8-powered rear-engine car. His ride lasted until the car's transmission failed at less than half-distance, but it had been enough to convince both Gurney and British race car builder Colin Chapman (in attendance at Gurney's request) that they could win Indianapolis with one of Chapman's rear-engine Lotuses, provided it was equipped with the proper engine.

Less than two months later, on July 23rd, Gurney and Chapman walked into planning manager Don Frey's office armed with their detailed plan for winning the prestigious 500-mile race. All they needed, they said, was a lightweight, reliable engine producing about 350 horsepower. By remarkable coincidence, the Ford men were already at work on that very thing! It happened that Frey and Dave Evans, Passino's right-hand man in the reborn racing department, also had attended the same Indy race, had been interested in the new rear-engine machinery and on their way home had hatched a scheme to build a Ford Indianapolis engine. Gurney and Chapman had come to the right place.

And what would any red-blooded American "Total Performance" program be without stock car racing? The question really answers itself, but to put the situation into perspective we should backtrack to 1957. Ford's factory NASCAR effort had just begun to gather steam when, in June that year, the AMA imposed its ban on manufacturer-sponsored activity as well as performance-oriented advertising and promotion. Despite warnings from youth-minded executives and engineers that the ban might be a General Motors plot to knock Ford out of a competitive position, that the company's youth appeal would suffer and product development would stagnate, Henry Ford himself ultimately issued the order for his car divisions to get out of racing.

The next two years proved the skeptics right. While first-rate privateer campaigners such as Holman-Moody and Smokey Yunich kept the Ford name in both NASCAR and USAC stock-car winners' circles through the second half of the '57 season, it was obvious that the marque would soon lose its leadership position without factory assistance. The beneficiary of most of the factory's parts and equipment after the pull-out, Holman-Moody hung together and kept its Fords running and even winning with some regularity during the next few years, but the GM divisions (Chevrolet, Pontiac and Oldsmobile) continued to grow in strength. Yunich had quit in disgust in September 1957; worst of all for the privateers' fortunes, the nearly-developed Ford 390-cubic-inch race engine project had been shelved in dutiful respect for the AMA ban and would not surface again until some four years later.

True to the fears of the Youth Turks at Ford who were chafing under the no-competition edict, evidence mounted that the GM divisions were cheating on the spirit if not the letter of the ban. According to author Levine, Chevrolet was helping build cars on the sly, and Chevy high-performance parts remained readily available through its catalogue. Pontiac was busy preparing a full-scale effort "in case someone else is caught cheating," and several GM dealers were sponsoring efforts that appeared far too expensive for dealers alone to support without under-the-table factory money. Some Ford people wanted to respond in kind, but division general manager Robert MacNamara, interpreting the AMA order literally, said "no deal." Complaints against the GM activities were lodged with AMA, and Ford once even took the matter directly to Chevrolet, by letter, although to no avail.

English A.C. body and Ford 260 V-8 combined for first Cobra, 1962.

Ford managed to outsell Chevrolet in 1957, but then fell behind in recession-year 1958. There were many factors involved—the Edsel was not a Ford Division product incidentally, but the first product of the new and separate Edsel Division, and therefore not a factor in Ford versus Chevrolet divisional competition—but the fact that Ford was pushing safety while Chevy stressed power and excitement certainly had a lot to do with the dismal situation. Slowly the attitude began to change among Ford managers as they watched closely what the competition was doing on and off the track.

For the '59 model year Chevy came out with its "batwing" styling monstrosity; Ford's sales improved accordingly. This in turn generated more money to spend, and evidence was mounting that some should be spent on performance. "Heavy duty" parts began to show up in Ford catalogues, and by the '60 season Holman-Moody was selling fully race-prepared cars complete with new 352-cubic-inch engines.

Still, this "limited re-entry" was not enough. The few first-rate Ford cars managed to win more NASCAR races in 1960 than any other make, but the top ten finishing positions were thoroughly dominated by Chevrolet. Undisputed kings of the new high-banked superspeedways (Daytona, Atlanta and Charlotte), however, were the fast-rising Pontiacs. A good look at a Pontiac racing engine late in the year gave the struggling Ford people a clue as to how this game was played: The killer Pontiac motor, in Levine's words, "not only was totally non-stock from the cylinder block on, but it violated at least fourteen NASCAR rules."

That fall, John Fitzgerald Kennedy was elected President of the United States, and he selected MacNamara, the newly-appointed Ford Motor Company president, to serve as his Secretary of Defense. Aggressive engineer-turned-salesman Iacocca had been moved into the Ford divisional managership in November; and once the anti-performance MacNamara left in January, the coast was clear for Iacocca's Fairlane Committee meetings and the division's Total Performance marketing effort that resulted late in '61. Iacocca had to shore up Ford's sagging image with youthful buyers as quickly as possible, and he wanted to go racing in a serious way—not only with stock cars but on all fronts, which is where the Shelby Cobras and the Gurney/Chapman Indianapolis program came in.

Henry Ford, disgruntled with Chevrolet's and Pontiac's blatant back-door involvement, gave the green light, and the stage was set for what would become the most formidable factory racing effort in industry history. Holman-Moody, after a lackluster 1960 season, already was looking for greener pastures, but Iacocca's racing ("special vehicles") manager Jacque Passino talked them into sticking with Ford, and Moody hired talented hotshoe Fred Lorenzen (himself badly discouraged and ready to quit) to be his driver. The 390-cubic-inch engine was taken off the shelf and readied to do battle with the mighty 389 Pontiacs; while the budget was limited, and the effort still had to remain undercover in token observance of the AMA pact, Ford nevertheless entered the '61 stock-car wars with high hopes.

Only to see them shattered. Pontiac dominated the season, winning an unprecedented thirty races and often filling the first several rows of the starting grids. Ford did manage seven wins (three by Lorenzen) to Chevy's eleven, Plymouth's three and Chrysler's one, but by year's end it was clear that a better-organized effort and a lot more money would be needed to regain equality, let alone superiority.

By early 1962, the racing program was shifted into third gear. The efforts of Iacocca, Frey and Passino to get top management interested were paying off; a great force of internal engineering talent was giving its all; Holman-Moody and the other Ford stock-car team, the racing Wood Brothers, were making good progress; Shelby was already on board with his prototype Cobra; and the likes of Gurney and Chapman were about to venture into the Ford camp and go to work on the Indy-car front. But there was still that troublesome AMA ban to be dealt with.

Henry Ford did not want to be first to openly break with the anti-racing pact for fear of damaging his company's reputation with the non-performance public as well as increasingly safety-conscious forces within the government. But when a more realistic agreement could not be worked out among the manufacturer members (the GM senior executives' answer to criticism of the Chevy and Pontiac

produced in Germany for America, Europe and other world markets. Called the Cardinal project, it was an austere little shoebox of a car but fairly sophisticated under the skin, sporting front wheel drive and a compact V-4 engine. It was scheduled for introduction in 1962, and its costly development in 1960 and early '61 was one reason the rejuvenated racing program could not get the money it needed at that time.

But Iacocca was dead set against MacNamara's Cardinal for the U.S. market, since such a basic transportation car would run counter to everything he wanted to accomplish with his Total Performance theme. Almost as the door swung closed on MacNamara, the new Ford Division boss made it his personal campaign to kill the Cardinal. He went to Ford of Germany and told them not to count on the projected 300,000 units for the U.S. market, then convinced Ford's board of directors to write off the $35 million already invested.

"I'm the guy who personally killed that Cock Robin," Iacocca says. "It was a nothing. It was a front wheel drive program, but it was done by committee—and before we knew it we had a little car that had gotten too big, didn't get enough fuel economy and had all sorts of problems. It would have been a disaster in this country. It would have followed the Edsel and would have been worse than the Edsel. We had to kill it before we could start doing the program we wanted to do. It was what I considered the avoidance of a great disaster for this company."

The Cardinal was ultimately tooled and produced in Germany as the Taunus 12/15 M; some 2.5 million units were sold in the European market between 1962 and 1970. "The success of the 12/15 M was immense," says retired engineer Frank Theyleg, who had overseen the car's transaxle, steering, and front-drive system developed at Ford's Livonia, Michigan transmission and chassis facility. "It was the first car that made a significant dent into the VW on that car's home market, and it should be noted that Renault, and later even VW, adopted front-wheel drive, with Renault copying most of the Cardinal's transaxle features."

The Cardinal, thanks to Iacocca, never made it to U.S. soil, but it's obvious that Mr. Theyleg and others were justifiably proud of some of its design features, especially the sophisticated transaxle, which he glowingly described in a letter to Les Henry, former curator of the Ford museum at the Greenfield Village complex in Dearborn: "The transaxle had direct drive combined with a hypoid ring gear/pinion for noise reduction reasons. It was internally interchangeable for three- or four-speed shifting, and was designed to be installable into right- or left-hand column shifted cars. And it was designed in both metric and U.S. custom measurements, on the same drawing and interchangeable with each." (Remember, this was circa 1959.)

One day in 1960, according to Theyleg, he and English-born chassis engineer Roy Lunn—both sports car enthusiasts—were discussing "spin-off" possibilities of the Cardinal drivetrain, and they hit upon the idea of mounting the little V-4 engine and transaxle behind the passenger compartment of a lightweight, two-seat sports

First car to wear the Mustang name and insignia, and the Cardinal from which the Mustang I's driveline was borrowed, a cutaway shown page opposite.

car. But their idea didn't get any farther than conversation between themselves until after the U.S. Cardinal had been killed and the Total Performance campaign launched.

It was early in 1962, when Iacocca and styling chief Gene Bordinat were casting about for a viable production sporty-car concept, that the mid-ship sports car idea suddenly gained some support. Bordinat had been charged with the responsibility of exploring various two- and four-passenger sporty packages, and he assigned Bob Maguire (exterior) and Damon Woods (interior) as chief stylists over the project. Under Maguire and Woods, respectively, were executive stylists John Najjar and Jim Sipple, and it was the team led by this pair which ultimately turned out the lean and lithe little beauty that would incorporate the Cardinal drivetrain amidships.

"We did this drawing on a blackboard and showed it to Maguire and Bordinat," Najjar recalls. "They sort of liked what they saw and authorized us to start some work on a full-size clay model. About that time, also, Dan Gurney came through at Mr. Iacocca's invitation. He had looked at some of the other two-seater clay models and thought they were too big, heavy and cumbersome. Then he saw this layout and said, 'that's more like it.' Then we started doing our clay model."

At about the same time, corporation engineering vice-president Herb Misch and his public relations man, Cog Briggs, were looking for a real show-stopper concept vehicle to knock the socks off the enthusiast press at their 1963 model introduction that fall. Bordinat suggested the little Najjar/Sipple mid-ship car, Misch went for it, and

The Najjar/Sipple mid-ship sports-car package drawing ultimately leading to Mustang I; an "F-modified" road racing car brought to the studio for study.

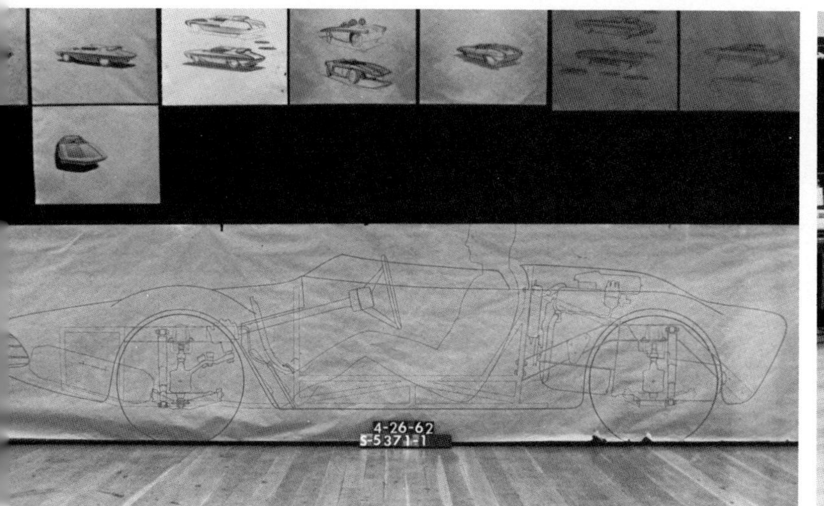

Mustang I takes shape in clay in the studio in late May 1962, with chassis development following in late September. Seated in the running prototype is Engineering vice-president Misch, while Styling's Gene Bordinat looks on. The second car was a mock-up for automobile show use.

F O R D

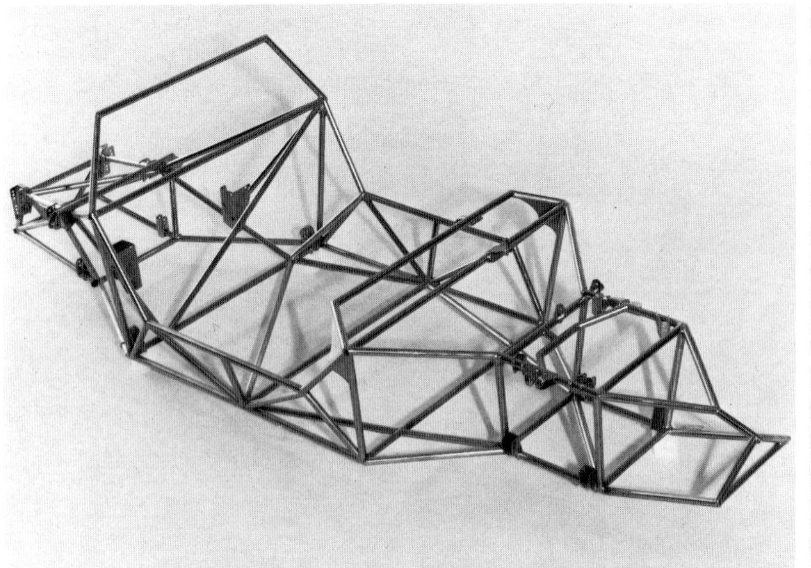

Parts that made up the Mustang I whole: birdcage chassis, V-4 Cardinal engine

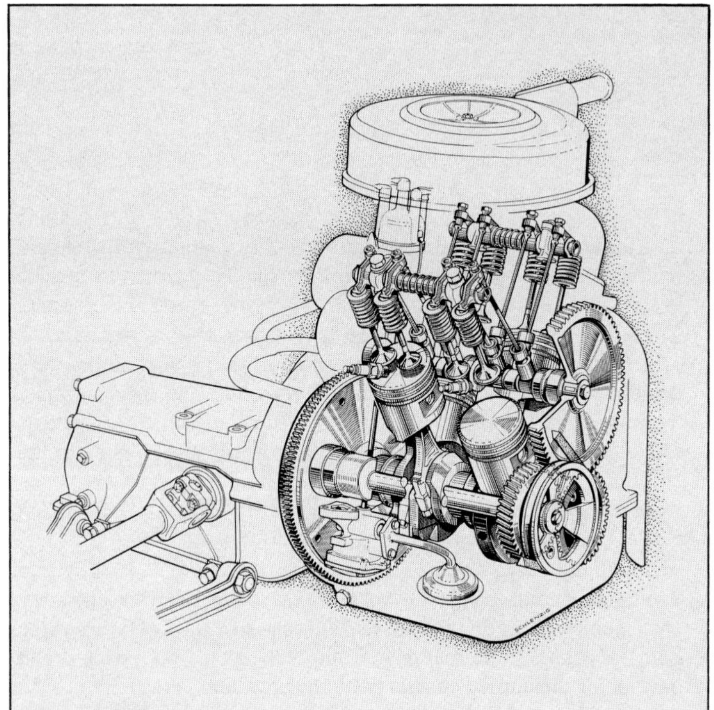

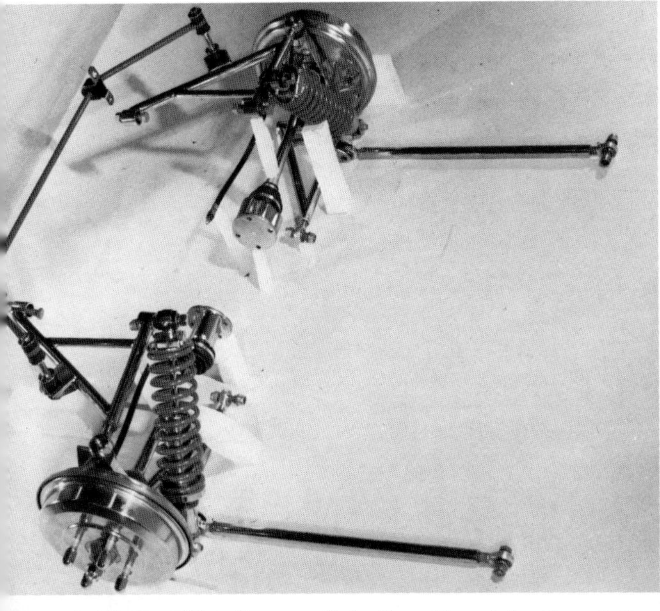

uspension layout, T-handle-controlled adjustable pedal unit, cockpit.

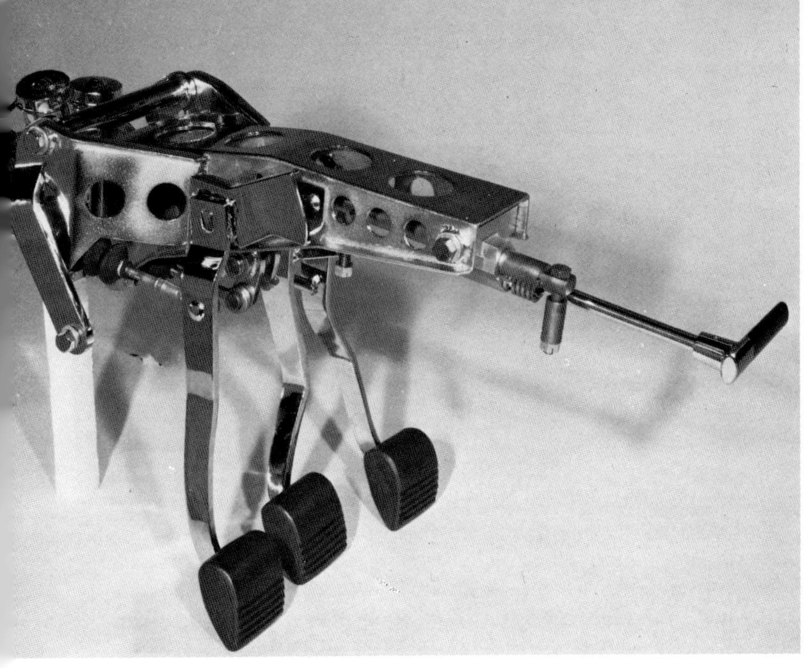

the first "Mustang" was literally off to the races.

Mid-ship enthusiast Roy Lunn received the assignment of putting the components together into a driveable vehicle. On May 9th, 1962, the formal program study was initiated, and two weeks later Lunn was meeting with Troutman-Barnes, a Culver City, California custom car building firm, to discuss the building concept. The job had to be done in just four months, and he was looking for expert outside help to do it. The following day, May 24th, the build program was launched.

A week later, exterior drawings taken from the clay model were completed by styling, and by June 4th they had been approved and transferred to Troutman-Barnes by Lunn's Vehicle Concepts Department. On June 9th, a plastic body form was shipped to the builder, and four days after that Lunn sent layout drawings of the interior, frame, fuel tank, exhaust system and hardware details. On June 20th, a dummy engine/transaxle unit was dispatched.

By August 23rd, the last mechanical component had been sent to Troutman-Barnes, and just two short weeks later Lunn took delivery of the completed body and chassis. Now came the task of finishing the body, plugging in the real powertrain (called the "ponypack") and developing the untried chassis (with the able help of race driver Dan Jones). Advanced Engine Engineering supplied the modified Taunus

FORD MOTOR COMPANY
ENGINEERING AND RESEARCH STAFF — COMPARISON VEHICLE SPECIFICATIONS — RELEASE OCTOBER 7, 1962

Make Model	Alfa Romeo Giulietta Spyder	Fiat 1500 Cabriolet	MG 1600 Mark II	Porsche 1600N	Sunbeam Alpine Mark II	Triumph TR4	Ford Mustang
Dimensions (Inches)							
Wheelbase	86.6	92.1	94.0	82.7	86.0	88	90.0
Tread, Front	50.6	48.5	47.5	51.5	51.2	49.0	48.0
Tread, Rear	50.0	47.9	48.8	49.3	48.7	48.0	49.0
Length	152	158.7	156.0	158.0	155.2	156.0	154.3
Width	62	59.8	58.0	65.6	60.5	57.5	61.0
Height	52	51.2	50.0	52.4	51.7	50.0	39.4 (At roll bar) 28.8 (At cowl)
Engine							
Position	Front	Front	Front	Behind Rear Axle	Front	Front	Fwd of Rear Axle
Type	4-Cyl. In-Line Water Cooled DOHC	4-Cyl. In-Line Water Cooled DOHC	4-Cyl. In-Line Water Cooled OHV	4-Cyl. Hor. Opp. Air Cooled OHV	4-Cyl. In-Line Water Cooled OHV	4-Cyl. In-Line Water Cooled OHV	60° V-4 Water Cooled
Displacement	1290 cc	1491 cc	1622 cc	1582 cc	1592 cc	2138 cc	1500 cc 1500 cc
Gross HP/RPM	92/6000	90/6000	93/5600	70/4500	85/5000	105/4750	89/6600 109/6400
Torque/RPM	79.6/4000	77/4000	97/4000	82/2800	94/3800	128/3350	89/3600 99/5200
Transmission							
Number of Speeds	4	4	4	4	4	4	4
Number of Synchro	4	3	3	4	3	4	4
Tire Size	155-15	155-15	5.60-15	5.60-15	5.90-13	5.50-15	5.20-13
Seating Capacity	2	2	2	2+2	2	2	2
Curb Weight	2040	2200	2050	1980	2150	2240	1500
P.O.E. Price	3150	3650	2444	4195	2595	2849	
Top Speed	100	105	105	100	100	110	108 117
Standing $\frac{1}{4}$ Mile	19.2 sec.	18.5 sec.	18.7 sec.	19.4 sec.	19.3 sec.	17.8 sec.	NA NA

Specification comparison compiled by the Ford Motor Company between Mustang I and its supposed competition indicated good market potential if the price was right.

V-4 on September 18th, and Transmission and Chassis Division followed with a working transaxle on the 21st. Styling delivered the painted and trimmed body on the 23rd, and the next nine days were spent on final assembly with the finished and trimmed components, plus Jones' chassis development work. On October 2nd the completed car was shown to Ford management and later that same day it was shipped to Watkins Glen, New York, for its first public showing in conjunction with the October 7th United States Grand Prix race.

Five months from authorization of the clay model to finished, working sports car...a remarkable achievement for Bordinat, Lunn, Troutman-Barnes and everyone concerned. With no time to proceed through normal sluggish channels, most of the components were either fabricated from scratch or "bootlegged" by enthusiastic supporters of what they thought could turn into a real, live production Ford sports car program at long last. According to transaxle engineer Frank Theyleg, "the engine people 'made one Cardinal prototype engine too many,' and I, by that time in Cologne, Germany, to help put the Cardinal into production, built 'one transaxle too many,' sent it to Bob Krithers in Sterling (Michigan) where he put in a 3.3:1 ring gear/pinion set and applied a super paint job. I also found a rack-and-pinion steering gear, left over from a previous project, the front half-shafts and some other goodies needed."

John Najjar takes credit for the name...but he borrowed it not from the horse, as one might surmise, but from the legendary World War II fighter plane, for which he confesses a strong passion. Najjar suggested the Mustang name to styling public relations man John Breeden, who was working on the publicity program with Cog Briggs, and Breeden submitted it to the Ford legal staff. Breeden also planted a teaser in a popular Detroit newspaper about Ford having a new horse in its corral called Mustang.

"About three days later," Najjar chuckles, "I got a call from Chuck Jordan at GM Styling asking if it was true that we were going to introduce a new car called Mustang. I told him yes, it was true, but I didn't tell him anything about it. 'Damn,' he said. He told me they had just finished a special vehicle for [GM styling chief] Mitchell that they called Mustang—with the horse and everything on it—'and here you guys do it. Don't you have any other names?' I said, yeah, we could use 'Stud' or 'Mare,' and we both laughed."

Although the name originally had been inspired by the plane, the major justification for using it came out of a desk-top dictionary, and its definition of a "hardy, wild horse of the American plains." Najjar had designer Phil Clark draw up a galloping horse with a red, white and blue "tie-bar" behind it, and from that drawing evolved the famous Mustang logo. "We wanted to get the red, white and blue into it," he explains, "and we liked vertical bars because they counteracted the running horse."

The Mustang I, as it later came to be called, had a tubular steel space frame structure under the formed and welded aluminum body, which was secured by "blind" rivets. An integral roll-bar conforming to then-current racing specifications was supported by the birdcage frame structure and aerodynamically integrated into the body. A low-drag windshield was fitted, but design consideration was given to using a removable hardtop in case the car eventually was produced. Engine cooling radiators sat behind air scoops on each side of the body, complete with decorative louvers (which also reduced turbulence in the entering air) and electric fans that switched on thermostatically when needed.

Besides conforming to both SCCA and FIA sports car road racing requirements of the day, the sleek Mustang I also incorporated everything necessary for street driving. Headlamps popped up manually, park and taillamps were faired into the body front and rear, the front license plate folded into a covered recess "for competition work," and a license bracket was provided at the rear. The two seats were formed aluminum buckets upholstered with leather-covered foam rubber.

The 1500 cc 60-degree V-4 pushrod engine was boosted from its normal 89 hp to a more fitting 109 hp via increased compression (11:1), special intake manifold, high-performance camshaft, high-rate valve springs and dual Weber carburetors. The shift lever was a stub-type, console-mounted affair connected to the four-speed axle by aircraft-type control cables, and the clutch was hydraulic.

The front suspension had upper and lower A-frame arms of welded, tubular steel construction supported by racing-type integral coil spring/tube shocks, adjustable for camber and caster as well as toe. The rear suspension used tubular A-frame upper arms, inverted semi-trailing lower, fore/aft strut rods, and coil-over shocks. Adjustment was provided for rear-wheel toe and camber changes, and unique wheel spindles were used with double rows of ball bearings in the hubs. Anti-sway bars were incorporated to control body roll both front and rear. Brakes were front disc, rear drum with dual master cylinders and a quick-release park lever in the console. Tires were 5.30x13 racing type on 13x5-inch cast magnesium wheels.

Both steering wheel and pedals were adjustable to fit the driver, since the seats were fixed in place in the structurally rigid passenger box. "Ray Smith came up with the adjustable steering column and pedals, as well as the flushed-out license plate," says Najjar. Instrumentation was complete including speedometer, tachometer and gauges for fuel, oil pressure, water temperature and amps. Interestingly, both horn button and choke lever were located in the console for convenience.

For packaging and weight distribution, the thirteen-gallon fuel tank, as well as the spare tire and battery, were mounted in the front compartment. The electric fuel pump and fuel gauge sending unit were submerged in the tank, and a large-diameter fuel filler pipe was provided for racing purposes. The exhaust system consisted of separate pipes from each dual cylinder bank connecting to a single transverse muffler and dual megaphone tailpipes extending through the rear body panel, all of which was mounted on the engine/transaxle "ponypack" unit.

Obviously, the Mustang I's creators were serious about the feasibility of production, even though Iacocca and his product planners were by this time already locked in on a four-seater coupe package rather than a limited-volume two-seater sports car. There was apparently never any serious top management thought given to producing the little Mustang mid-engine car, and its creation was intended solely to whet the public's appetite until the four-passenger Mustang could be rushed into production. This first Mustang, says Iacocca, "was rigged up to go to Watkins Glen to show the kids that they should wait for us because we had some good, hot stuff coming."

Nevertheless, Roy Lunn had his people prepare a feature-by-feature chart comparing their concept car to other popular sportsters on the market, such as the Fiat 1500, MGA 1600, Porsche 1600, Sunbeam Alpine, Triumph TR-4 and Alfa Romeo Spyder. Compared to its theoretical competition, the 90-inch wheelbase, 1500-pound, 39-inch-high, 89-hp (in street trim) Mustang was truly revolutionary in styling, engineering and concept...but it never could have been built at a competitive price as designed, and even in diluted form it might have been too expensive for the mid-Sixties sports car market. Still, it's nice to dream of what might have been.

Unveiled at Watkins Glen with considerable fanfare, it was described by Ford as "a high-performance personal automobile which could fit the mass sports car market" and "the first car built by a major American manufacturer which fits into the European-dominated popular sports car class." Press kits and brochures were distributed by the ton. "The Mustang," they boasted, "is the development of Ford Motor Company engineers and stylists—men who have a genuine fondness for motor cars—men who experience each day the excitement and satisfaction of creating, in much of their variety, the

The Mustang I is introduced. Below: Test driver Dan Jones is seated in car, Roy Lunn and Bob Negstad are fourth and fifth from the left respectively. Right: Dan Gurney prepares to demonstrate the car at Watkins Glen, October 7th, 1962, as Negstad (cigarette in hand) and Lunn (hands in pocket) look on.

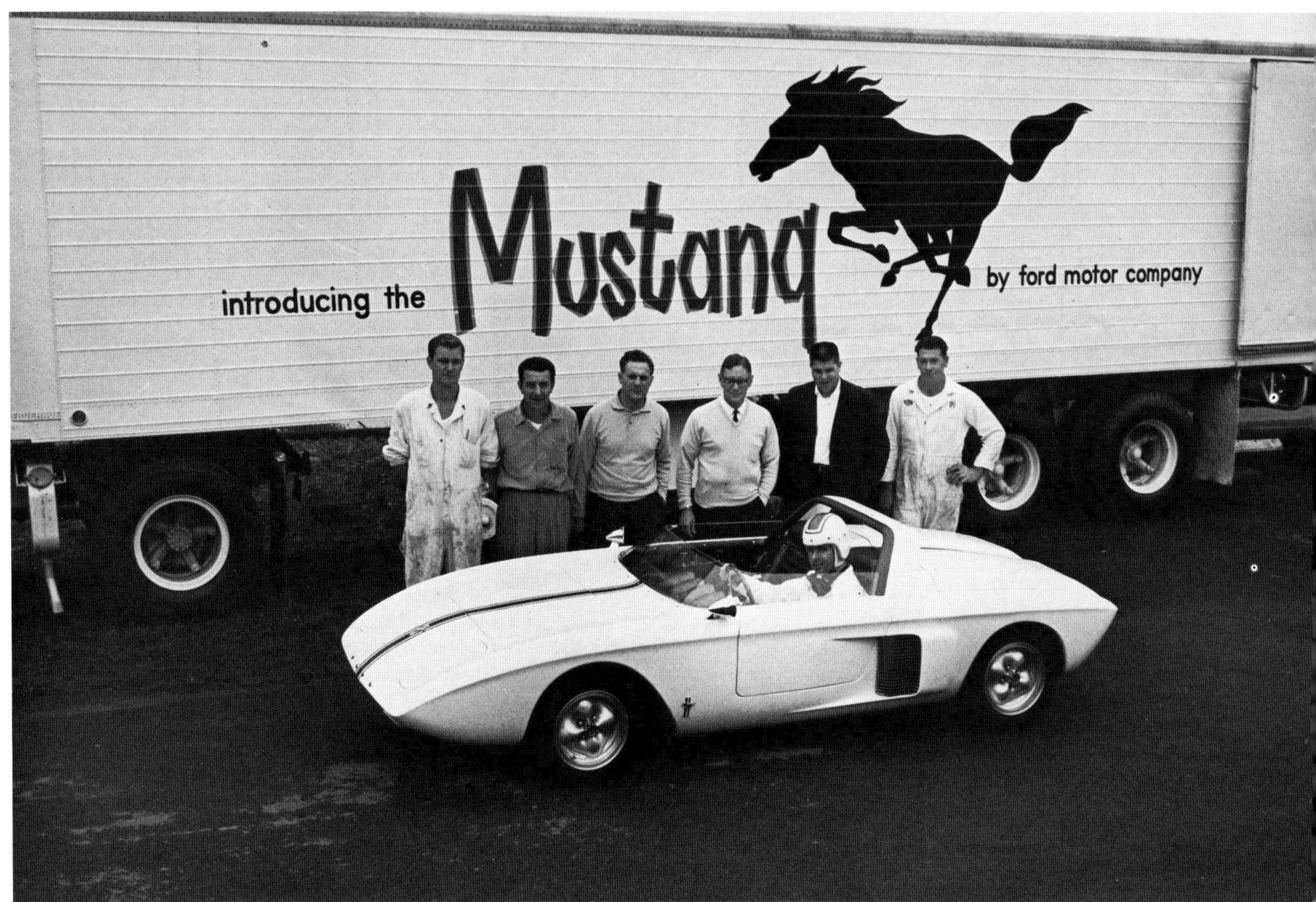

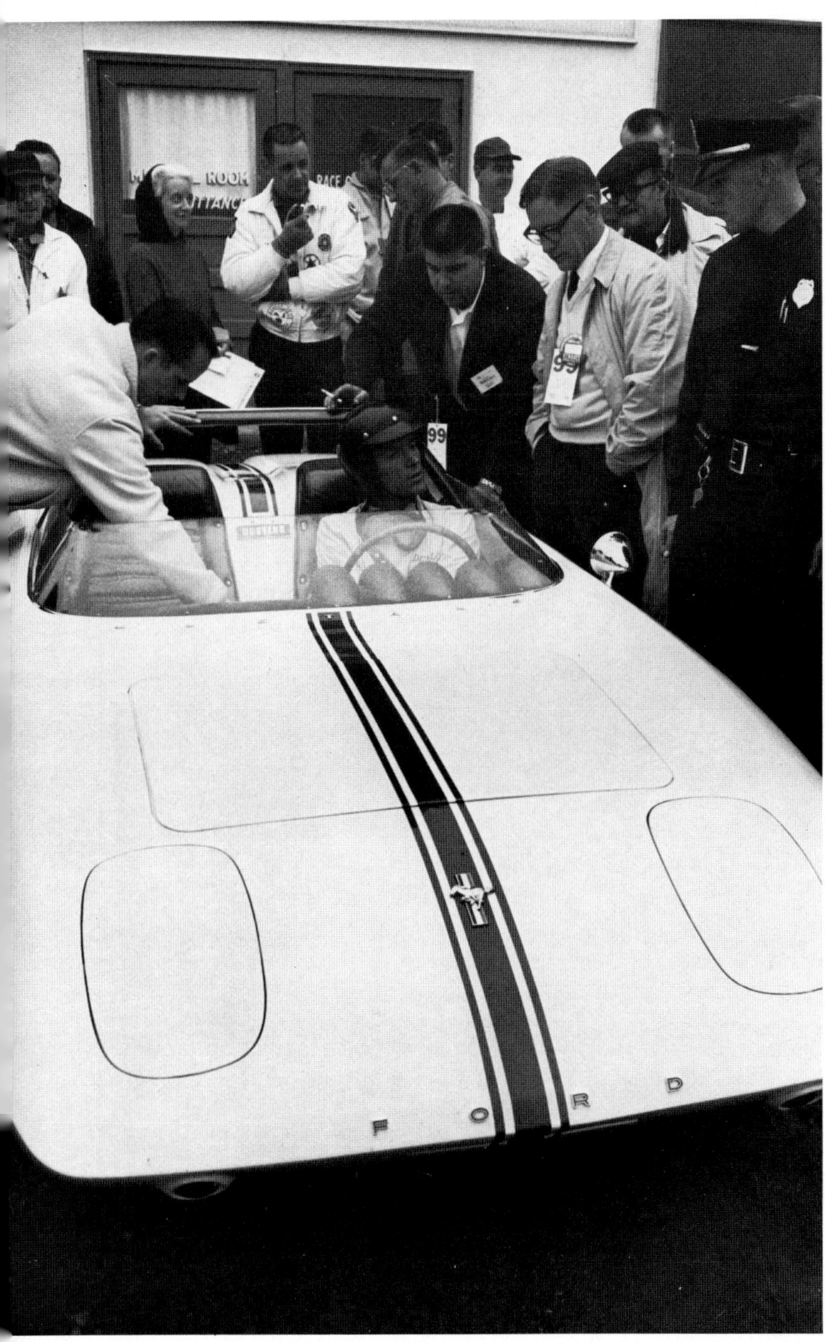

cars on the American road. And the particular team which designed this car has a professional interest in sports cars.

"In the Mustang are represented their best talents—their ideas of what the American sports car should be—the spirit of the wild Mustang bred into a fine machine, a car with manners, a superb performer on road or track, a proud possession."

For all the Watkins Glen crowd knew, this car was on the verge of introduction, and they went crazy over it. They watched Dan Gurney drive it quickly and smoothly in a demonstration ride around the Grand Prix course ("before anyone could stop him, he was doing about 120 mph," enthuses Theyleg), they watched it in the parade lap preceding the race, and those who were lucky enough to get close literally drooled over it all weekend long.

Handily overshadowing Chevrolet's mid-engine, Corvair-based Monza GT experimental sports car (which also turned up for public display at Watkins Glen), Ford's Mustang graced the December-issue covers of almost every major automotive magazine in the country. Demonstration rides were given reporters and some lucky journalists were allowed to test it in street form. "The car handles magnificently," said *Car and Driver*'s Jan Norbye. "One of the most exciting cars I have ever ridden in," raved Barrie Gill of the *London Daily Herald.* "Comfort and performance match some of the best sports cars Europe can offer...acceleration and handling are superb."

"I believe that the Mustang is quite the most exciting vehicle of its class that has appeared for years," said fellow Englishman Maxwell Boyd of the *London Sunday Times.* "I am certain that its advanced specification, pioneering several important novelties of design, will rapidly drive British sports car designers back to their drawing boards."

"Ford's much-rumored Mustang, the most pleasant surprise of 1962. The first true sports car to come out of Dearborn," added *Car and Driver.* "Performance and public reaction will determine whether Ford will market the Mustang."

Only a handful of insiders then knew what Ford really had up its sleeve for public introduction some sixteen months later, but the first Mustang had served its purpose. It had provided Iacocca, for the second time, the enthusiast press attention he craved—and just a few months after Shelby's Cobra had garnered Ford's first magazine covers in years. And it had indeed whetted the car enthusiast's appetite for something exciting from Dearborn.

Until the real Mustang's introduction in April 1964, the Lunn/Bordinat creation toured the country with Jacque Passino, whetting more appetites at car shows and on college campuses as part of a Total Performance traveling road show. A second fiberglass model was decked out (*sans* powertrain) as purely a show car so the

Mustang could be ogled in two places at once, even as its mid-ship concept was providing continued inspiration for Roy Lunn, who was now at work on the GT-40 endurance racing car.

Frank Theyleg in his letter to Les Henry waxed poetic on the original Mustang I's fate: "The customers clamored for its production, which never happened. Instead the M-1 became the conceptual forerunner and basis for the Ford GT-40 and then disappeared into oblivion. It would have wound up in a blast furnace, had it not been for Morris Garter, Chuck Gumushian and myself, who literally stashed it around the company, hiding it from various budget-happy executioners. Occasionally the car served as a show piece here and abroad, helping to build traffic or transport a homecoming queen, but after that the hide-and-seek game began and the car began to quietly rot. Until Morris and I decided on our secret 'save the Mustang' mission, which was to last more than fourteen years and included complete restoration of its paint and upholstery, as well as replacement of the

The Mustang I's cockpit, and a lucky (though unidentified) journalist tries the car.

badly corroded magnesium wheels.

"Throughout these years, we tried to interest the company in producing the car as Ford's answer to the various European sports cars. As time went on, Morris and I realized that our 'save the Mustang' efforts would come to an end, partly because we ran out of hiding ideas, partly because some over-interested party had tried to 'acquire' it by hiding it in a barn under a load of hay, hoping that it would not be missed, but mainly because both Morris and I were heading for our retirement, which occurred at the end of 1974. So we decided to have the car 'museumized'."

On November 3rd, 1975, the Mustang I sports car was officially donated by Ford Motor Company to the Edison Institute for display in the Henry Ford Museum in Dearborn, Michigan. Created for public relations purposes by the talented minds and hands of Lunn's Vehicle Concepts group, Bordinat's Advanced Styling Studio and Troutman-Barnes' West Coast shop, it had paraded with Grand Prix pilot Dan Gurney at Watkins Glen and had become the instant darling of motoring journalists and sports car aficionados in this country and abroad. Its svelte good looks graced magazine covers and brightened auto shows, while its sophisticated chassis and mid-engine powertrain delighted student and professional auto engineers alike.

Put out to pasture in the hoopla surrounding the four-seater that took its name, saved from the glue factory by an intrepid pair of its dearest in-company fans, once stolen and recovered, it had finally come to rest in a place safe from both cold-hearted accountants and the rotting effects of time. It had preceded the mid-ship Porsche 914 by nearly a decade and the still-popular Fiat X1/9 by more, and who knows where it could have gone had it been produced.

But Iacocca was content to leave the 50,000-unit two-seater sports car market to Chevrolet and the imports. He was after much bigger game. By year's end, 1962, his Ford Division people were already hard at work on the perfect bait.

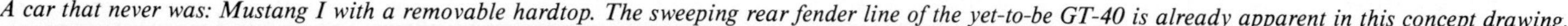

A car that never was: Mustang I with a removable hardtop. The sweeping rear fender line of the yet-to-be GT-40 is already apparent in this concept drawing.

3. MUSTANG TO MARKET

By the time Iacocca received the corporation's reluctant approval to go ahead with his pet project, he had set a near-impossible goal for himself and his people. The first car was to roll off the assembly line on March 9th, 1964, just one day short of eighteen months from the day he got the green light.

Luckily, the car's simple but effective styling was already fairly well set. There were details to be worked out—seats, interior trim, the instrument panel design, wheel covers, grille texture, side louvers, insignia and decorative exterior trim items—but everyone seemed satisfied with the basic size, shape and major design characteristics of the Oros/Ash Cougar as it sat. The oblong, European-style headlamps would have to go in accordance with federal requirements, and the side sculpturing would have to be straightened somewhat for ease and economy of production, but that was about it.

Little more than a week after the approval meeting, full-size renderings were completed which looked almost exactly like the car that would be publicly introduced one-and-a-half years later. Any modern car that comes out looking very much like the designer's original sketches and models is an industry rarity, and one that emerges as a near-exact reproduction of what he had in mind is almost unheard of. There is always the battle between stylists and engineers. The former are talented artists with very creative ideas as to how an automotive masterpiece should look. They are designing three, five, even ten years into the future, trying things that haven't been tried before, setting trends, leading public taste and fashion, confident it will follow. It is not their job to worry about how it goes together in production or how much it costs to sweep a fender line this way or that; their chief concern is how it works on paper and in the sculptor's clay.

Engineers, on the other hand, are by-and-large a cold-hearted lot.

This drawing, dated September 21st, 1962, showed the convertible model Mustang almost exactly as it would be introduced a year-and-a-half later.

Instead of seeing art in a designer's sketch or a sculptor's model, they see a potential pile of nuts and bolts, screws and washers, sheet metal, plastic and glass, tolerances, dimensions and "fits." It is their job to translate the designer's imagination into hard reality and build it for ten cents a pound. To them, a handsome grille is something that must let enough air through to cool the engine, the crease of a fender is something that must be tooled and stamped out of flat metal, a sexy roofline is something that must be smoothly joined to the lower body. Chassis and suspension components must be designed and developed to carry the stylist's work around; and engines, transmissions and axles must propel it in proper fashion. Their work is no less an art than the stylists' but it is art of a very different sort. Their creations are sculptures born of practicality and function, structural and mechanical pieces that must move and flex and transmit forces to do a specific job.

Generally speaking, the stylists and engineers find themselves on opposite ends of the philosophical scale. Artists by nature are jealous of their work and don't like it tampered with. If the engineer has to straighten a line, alter a form or simplify a shape to make it easier to tool and less costly to produce, he's often made an instant enemy of the designer, who is convinced that his artwork is ruined by even a slight alteration. On the other hand, the engineer is equally convinced that stylists live in a dream land, couldn't know or care less about production realities, and are prone to coming up with million dollar designs for thousand dollar products—thereby increasing the difficulty of his job with every stroke of their pencils.

Somewhere in the middle of these warring factions sits the product planner, charged with the responsibility of combining the efforts of both into attractive, appealing, functional real-life products that will sell in record numbers. He knows that each is partially right and that each is equally important. Ugly cars don't sell, but neither do those which don't work as they should. He's no artist and he's probably no technical genius, yet he must keep a hand in everyone else's pie to make sure the finished product comes out as planned — a well-conceived and well-executed compromise between creativity of form and practicality of function.

These three diverse human elements in the creation of an automobile must work together in relative harmony if a really successful product is to be the end result. The worst automotive creations are usually "committee cars," on which everyone had to have a say and no one could agree on much of anything. Sadly, too many of the products of such massive industrial organizations as the Ford Motor Company are turned out in this way: They are crushingly ordinary, bland and uninspired, offensive to few but exciting to no one.

Fortunately for the Mustang, however, it had several important

9-21-62
5-5730-48

factors going for it throughout that year-and-a-half between approval and production. First, it had the powerful leadership of Lee Iacocca, who considered it his own personal product and guided its development every inch of the way. Second, it had the strong cohesive force of an excellent initial design; everyone who was involved with it loved it, and no one wanted to see it changed in any major way. Third, it was a fairly small and insignificant project in the corporate scheme of things, done largely out of the mainstream by a small group of enthusiastic people while most everyone else was too busy with other matters to be constantly looking over their shoulders as the car progressed. Finally, the time and money factors themselves worked in the Mustang's favor; with only a small budget and eighteen months to get the job done, there just wasn't time or money enough for mistakes, disagreements, or slow, committee-type decision making.

"This car was peculiar," one Ford Division man recalls. "It excited everybody who worked on it. Everybody wanted to preserve the design." Oros has stated that to his knowledge, no car had ever been so little changed from original design to production model. Quoted in *Road & Track* at the car's introduction, Bordinat said: "We demanded—and received—engineering flexibility and inventiveness," meaning his stylists wouldn't give an inch when it came down to the traditional battle of the inches.

But there were some problems with the styling, the most well remembered being the high, "mouthy" grille opening. "We were intent on giving the feel of the silhouette, at least, of the expensive sports cars of old," Iacocca remembers. "We had arguments about

Left: The four-headlamp idea in January never made it into clay; auxiliary lamps in grille (later to appear on GT version) were tried in February.

the mouthiness of the grille. We wanted the mouth to come out beyond the fender line to give it a growly, long look. All the $25,000 cars I'd seen in Italy had that pointed, mouthy appearance."

"It was sort of a tough car to put together with that high mouth in the front end," recalls Bordinat, "because we didn't have the advantage of plastic fronts in those days. We had a lot of 'joinery' problems and things like that. It took a lot of noodling, but it was worth the effort. It wasn't a terribly sophisticated sort of design, but it sure as hell made a statement."

Several slight variations on the frontal design were tried, including at least one with quad headlamps, but the Oros/Ash nose and single round headlamps soon won out. Round, driving-type auxiliary lights just inside the grille opening were also given a try on one early model but were ultimately saved for the later GT package option. The caged Cougar in the center was reversed in direction (folklore claims that it was changed to face the grandstands on the outside of an American counterclockwise race course, but Bordinat says he ordered the change simply because he's right-handed and liked it better that way), and slim vertical and horizontal chrome bars were added to divide the grille opening into four quadrants.

It's interesting to follow the insignia designs in the grille, on wheel covers, steering wheel hubs, instrument panels and exterior trim as the car's name changed from month to month. First it was just "T-5," then "Cougar" after the original model, then it reverted back to a special "Falcon," then "Torino" and finally "Mustang." As late as January 1964, there were at least three different horse emblems still

Below left: Emblems designed when car was still a "Special Falcon." Below: Horizontal grille bars added and the "caged Cougar's" direction reversed.

under consideration before a running Mustang on a red, white and blue tribar, much like that on the Mustang I two-seat sports car, ultimately won out. "There was a variety of horses done," Hal Sperlich recalls. "The symbolism may have had its birth with the Ferrari prancing horse (it was about this time when Ford tried to buy Ferrari), and Lee had a thing about horses, too. Also, the red, white and blue thing was a late add."

Joe Oros, whose studio (led by executive stylist Dave Ash) had created the original design, was adamant that the car be called "Cougar." That name was well-liked by many and was used as a code name for the project throughout the early stages of development. He forwarded notes to Iacocca asking that the car never be called by any other name, and later sent the full-size grille ornament from the original clay model with a hand-lettered card on the back: "This is to make you remember what we should have called the car," it read, according to Iacocca, who has kept it ever since. When Lincoln-Mercury Division eventually did its version of the Mustang, the Cougar name and cat logo were revived, "I think because they had all the cats already designed," Iacocca chuckles. "Picking a name is the toughest part of making a new car. It gets very emotional at times."

About mid-year 1963, the J. Walter Thompson ad agency people set about producing a film as a communications vehicle for introducing the car to the press, Ford dealers and ultimately to the public. As recounted in an internal marketing publication:

> Ford agreed to van the first fragile, costly prototype to the Michigan Proving Ground at Romeo, with Ford personnel riding in cars ahead and behind. JWT met the van with a crew of twenty-five artists, writers and photographers.
>
> For three days they shot the secret film around the clock and around the car. The photographic safari produced 5000 feet of movie film and 1000 still shots.
>
> The movie was entitled "Torino," for that name had become a front-runner for the new offering. It was reasoned that the car had an "imported" look. Italian fashions were in vogue, and Italian car makers were producing some of the finest coachwork in the world.
>
> Sample advertisements were prepared. Some headlined: "Torino by Ford," others, "Torino by Ford—brand new import—from Detroit," and another variation, "Torino by Ford—only 1,478,000 lire?"
>
> At this point, however, the subject of names was reopened. "We wanted to sell it as an American car," said Petersen.

Also, it was rumored, the name "Torino" was favored by some within the division as a bit of flattery to Iacocca's Italian heritage; but

Iacocca wasn't having any of that. He had no clear favorite himself, but he felt that "Torino" sounded too European. Henry Ford II, for his part, wanted to call the car "T-Bird II," but could muster no support from his top executives on that one. "It was kind of amusing," recalls Bordinat, "because Mr. Ford is very sensitive to car names, and there's only one word beginning with an 'F' that he'd like to see on all cars. So we always had a hassle with him on names."

"Every time you need a name," Bordinat continues, "you pull out a dictionary and make a long list. Then you eliminate it down to a half dozen or so, then go out and survey those. This is usually an ad agency's commission." So John Conley, a J. Walter Thompson account executive who had twice before researched bird names for Ford's Thunderbird and Falcon, was duly dispatched to the Detroit Public Library. He produced some 6000 candidates, which eventually were culled to a handful that included Cougar, Bronco, Puma, Cheeta, Colt and Mustang. Of these, Mustang kept rising to the top of the surveys and was ultimately picked "because it had the excitement of the wide-open spaces and was American as all hell," according to the Thompson agency's Frank Thomas.

While all this was going on, the designers, engineers and product planners were struggling with more pressing matters. Some instrument panel ideas with both two and three large, round gauge forms were tried, but the design soon came around to a slightly modified version of the basic (and inexpensive) Falcon cluster and panel, featuring twin optional "rally" gauges on either side of the steering column. Trim materials, colors and detail designs had to be worked out for all three interiors—base, sporty and luxury. One innovation was the use of stamped sheet metal inner door panels, developed at Najjar's request, that were textured to have a soft, vinyl-like appearance. Such seemingly minor details as ignition keys and gearshift handles (both manual and automatic) had to be carefully designed to contribute to the all-important look and feel of the final product. Vinyl top variations for the luxury coupe were studied, and both a removable hardtop and a fiberglass tonneau cover for the convertible were tried but rejected because of cost and manufacturing complexity.

Body engineers found they could save both weight and cost by shaving one inch from the car's overall width, but they had to use slightly curved glass (at a cost premium) in the side windows to increase interior space. A problem with ankle fatigue was reported by test drivers, and minor redesigns of the accelerator pedal pad, the linkage spring and the floor mat were tried. Finally, as late as January 1964, the costly decision was made to move the seat, relocate the pedal and change both its angle and its pivot point "to improve the driver's relationship with the accelerator pedal."

C. N. Reuter was a development engineer under executive engineer

In June of '62 the car was called "Torino," but by November it was the "Mustang T-5" with running horse and "Tri-bar" design similar to the two-seat experimental sports car of year previous. The sextet of wheel cover designs shows name changes from "Cougar" to "Torino" to "Mustang."

Jack Prendergast, who worked for Bert Andren, chief engineer on the project. Reuter remembers the difficulty he had getting help from some of the supplier divisions: "The introduction of this program created a $40 million investment problem overnight," he relates, "and there was no money to do it. Nevertheless, we were told, 'do it!' Our problem in the vehicle development group was that we had to deal with the different divisions and get them to do work for us. For instance, we had to get axles out of the Transmission and Axle Division, get engines out of Engine Division and deal with the other various areas to get everything together in order to build prototypes and component cars for the test program."

At one point he called the axle people and asked for eight different prototype rear axles to try various ratios. The answer was, "No financial authorization, forget it." Finally, after some haggling, they agreed to build a couple of them. Exhaust people were supposed to design the car's exhaust systems, order parts, put them in prototype vehicles and test them. But they had too much other work to do and refused to help at all. Prendergast and Reuter ended up doing the exhaust system layouts themselves, at night, because the drafting tables were all in use during the day. They came up with an innovative system with the muffler mounted transversely under the rear pan, "because we couldn't figure out any other way to get all the stuff under there," Reuter says.

But as the program progressed, people began to realize the car was going to be a winner, and they wanted to be associated with it. Slowly, the uncooperative attitudes were revised. "They changed from not even answering the phone to calling and asking what they could do to help us," says Reuter, "but it took about a year before it began to be apparent that the car would be a seller. I'll never forget when that exhaust guy who had refused to talk to me called one day out of the blue and asked if he could be of help."

Much of the program involved adapting basic Falcon componentry for use in the smaller, sportier car, changing things ever so slightly or not at all to keep the cost down, yet creating an end product with a very different character. "It was the age-old problem of the automotive industry," Reuter explains, "...fix it but don't change it, because change can be pretty damned expensive. The basic structure was patterned after the Falcon but not identical. Suspension was almost identical but with enough changes to get the thing into a sporty atmosphere. The steering linkage was changed slightly, both to improve the handling and to make it easier to put the V-8 engines in."

Spring and shock rates and sway bar sizes were different, and the car had a wider tread than the Falcon both front and rear. It was also much lower, requiring that the floor pan be sunk down around the drivetrain. This resulted in a high center tunnel, but that was no

Several horse emblems were considered before the final, famous running horse was adopted. The first instrument panel proposals used large, round gauge forms,

problem in a car intended for bucket seats only. "Doing that," says Reuter, "you can get the passenger lower, the roof goes lower, and then you've got yourself a sporty image car. We also wanted the cowl height lower, which meant we had to come pretty darn close to the engine with the hood lines. This accounted for some of the sculpturing in the hood." Another innovation involved getting rid of the structural "torque box" in the Falcon's floor pan by tying the transmission tunnel structurally up into the dash panel and windshield ("A") pillars. This idea was brand-new in car construction so far as the Ford people knew at the time, and it resulted in a savings of both cost and weight.

Reuter, who took over responsibility for the program when Prendergast was reassigned elsewhere, speaks for everyone directly involved when he describes his group's team spirit: "As a small group, we were so enthusiastic that we got ourselves identification pins and other such things. We weren't going to take 'no' from anybody!"

When they completed the first prototype, he remembers, "it came closer to meeting the image we had for the car even at that point than any car I have ever run into. Perhaps one reason was that we were so short of time that we were not willing to make any compromises. If you have a little extra time, you'll try different things; but when you're faced with seventeen months from styling approval [a month after Iacocca's green light] to Job One, you do it the way you think it's going to work out the first time, because you don't have any room for alternatives. And, in spite of the short lead time, when we got finished with the car it came in at something like $21 under the cost bogey and forty-odd pounds under the weight. That is pretty rare."

Product planning chief Don Frey recalls, "We did the car 'on the cheap,' basing it on the Falcon and using many common components. We also tried to keep it simple, because we wanted to maintain the Falcon's reliability. And it was a 'happy car,' easy to develop and build, one of those once-in-a-lifetime things where everything went together right the first time in spite of the short seventeen-month gestation period."

Reuter relates some good stories about taking prototype Mustangs out on the road for ride and handling evaluation trips during the winter of 1964: "The enthusiasm we got from people who saw the car on these trips was fantastic. Once we stopped for coffee at a place in Kentucky that was attached to a liquor distillery, and people in the office wanted to buy one. Later we were in a motel near Drake University and took one of the cars to dinner. By the time we had finished eating, there was a crowd of about 200 people around that car—and we had parked it in a secluded spot, hoping no-one would notice it. But here was this tremendous crowd of kids, just vibrating over the car. When we pulled out, they jumped in their cars and followed us, and we never did shake them. Back at the motel, we tried to hide the car, but at one or two o'clock in the morning there was still a crowd of people out there making enough noise that we had trouble sleeping.

"The next day we were driving down the road in Virginia, when all

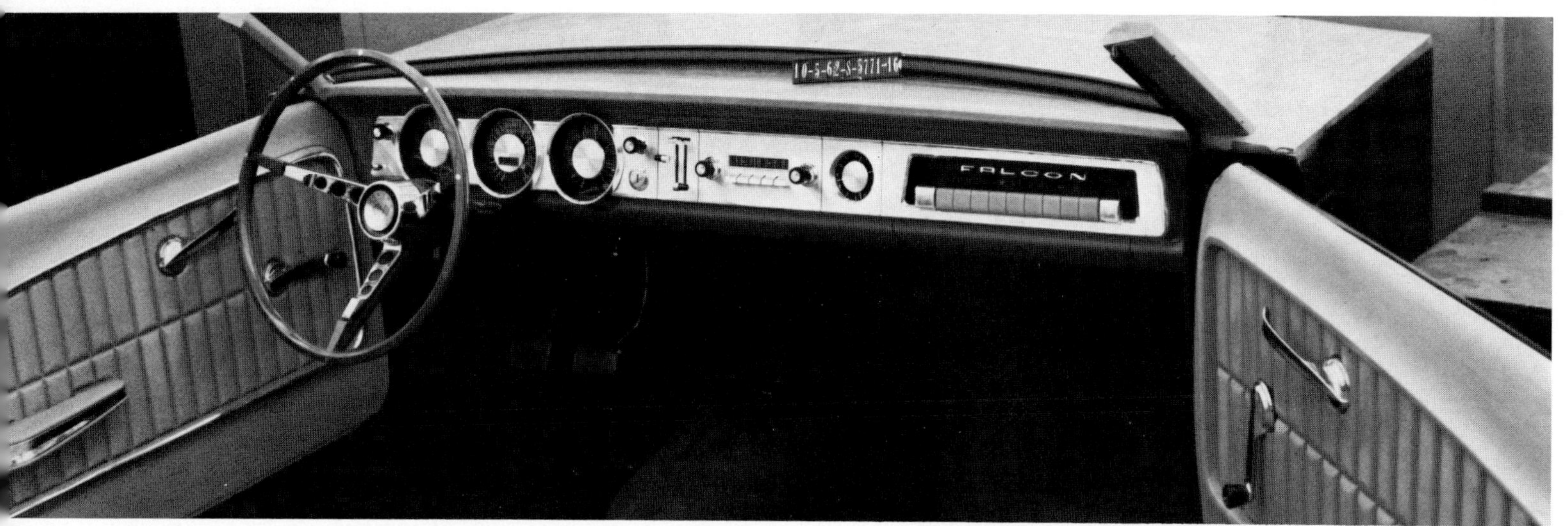

but a simpler, less expensive design nearly identical to that of the Falcon won out. At this point, November 1st, 1962, the car was still a "Special Falcon."

of a sudden this guy in a big sedan pulled up beside me and started waving furiously for me to pull over. I thought something was wrong, so I pulled over and stopped. The guy was acting like a cop, but he didn't have a police car. Turned out he was from Texas. 'Is that Henry's pony car?' he demanded. 'I've been hearing about that.' I said it was just an experimental car that might or might not go into production. He said, 'Don't kid me, that's Henry's pony car. I want to buy it!' I said you didn't ask how much it costs. He said, 'I'm not interested in how much it costs, I want to buy it!' I said, well maybe it will be in production shortly and he could buy one then. He said, 'No, no, I want to buy *that* car.' And he wouldn't go away. I told him that it probably had cost $110,000 to build that prototype and that we couldn't possibly duplicate it. He said, 'OK, I'll buy it.' He was serious. He wanted to buy the car and he didn't care what it cost."

Massive consumer research, clinics and survey programs had helped prove that there was a tremendous market out there just waiting for a product to satisfy it, and now more research was telling the Ford men that this was indeed the right sort of product for that market. "We did a hell of a lot of research," says Iacocca, "a hell of a lot. It was all good, wherever we went, which was the reason we knew we had a winner with this one. The key question we asked was, 'OK, now you've seen it, you've sat in it...how much would you pay for it?' And there wasn't anybody under $2500...I mean nobody. As I recall, the average was around $3500-3800. We were also trying to find out if there was any point of controversy that maybe we should fool

around with. But the Mustang had nothing controversial...nothing!"

"It was interesting," says styling vice-president Bordinat. "We were doing surveys, not on the variants but on the way the car finally went out...sort of a confirmation survey to see whether our judgment was right. We had them put a price tag on it, and they came up with some phenomenal prices. Some were up around $7000-8000, thinking in the Ferrari category. Maybe the horse did that."

More research followed checking the peoples' feelings about various options and features, as well as the styling; and there were pricing studies and more pricing studies throughout 1963 while the car was being prepared for production. In the fall, a special clinic was held to recheck design decisions. The subjects of this study were fifty-two couples with pre-teen children who owned a single standard-size car—not likely prospects for a small, sporty coupe. They were shown the car in small groups in the Ford Styling showroom, and their reactions were enthusiastic, but most said the car was impractical for them as family people. Asked what they thought the price of such a car might be, the couples overestimated by $1000 or more. When they were told that the price would be about $2380 or even lower, a strange transformation took place in their attitudes. They went back and looked again, and then they began to think of reasons why the car might be practical for them after all.

"For a new product, that's magic," says planning manager Hal Sperlich. "If people overestimate the price of a car compared to what

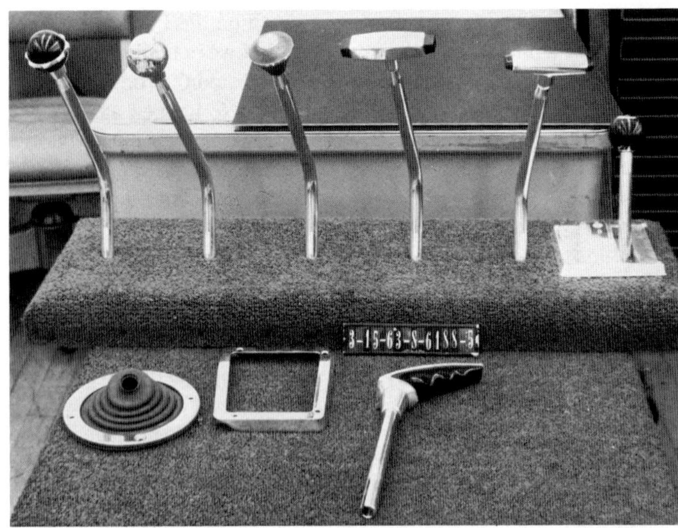

Varieties of gearshift handles were carefully designed for maximum effect.

it's going to be, you've got a winner. If the reverse is true, you're in real trouble. That was dynamite, and from that research came the advertising idea of just showing the car and the price."

Enthusiasm for the car kept growing within the company, and sales estimates grew along with it. The stylists, to begin with, were crazy in love with this perky little creation, to the point that Bordinat began to worry. "I kept waiting for a bomb to fall," he told a *Newsweek* reporter. "But the car has 'lived' well with us. If it tires us, the same thing will happen in the marketplace."

Planning volume, initially set at a modest 75,000 units for the first year, was doubled soon after and had climbed to well over 200,000 by mid-1963. It would take more than one plant to build that many cars, so Iacocca convinced corporate management to take the considerable risk of converting a second plant to Mustang production. The San Jose, California facility was chosen, boosting theoretical annual capacity to some 360,000 Mustangs. By the time the car was introduced, so confident were the Mustang people of its success that another plant at Metuchen, New Jersey was already being converted to produce it.

Product planner Dick Place, who had gone to work for Sperlich after the project had received approval, recalls: "At first we thought we needed one plant, and then you could feel the well-spring of excitement about this product building within the company. Another plant was added, and a third was on the way by the time the car was introduced. The company had been burned on the Falcon. We had planned for a much lower volume than what we actually could have achieved, and we suffered a great deal. We couldn't produce enough cars to meet the demand. That wasn't going to happen again."

Says Bordinat, "It took great faith to commit three plants to production of this car before it was even introduced. That's a lot of dedication of facilities, and I admire Iacocca for that."

Iacocca was between the proverbial rock and the hard place. The only crime for someone in his position worse than building a losing car is to come up with a winner and then not be able to build enough to satisfy the market demand. "It does little good to look back on a 100,000 year and say, 'If I'd been smart enough to build 200,000, I could have sold them,' " he told *Newsweek*, "by that time, you're out on your can."

He remembers vividly the first time he went back to management to propose increasing the car's volume: "I haven't sold a car yet, and I walk in and ask them to put their big glasses on and think about increments. They say, 'If you feel that strongly about it, go ahead. That's your job.' I don't know how tolerant they'd be if it flopped, but you have to make up your mind. You can't go home and ask your wife."

And things were not all wine and roses in the early stages. "I remember the program dying several times," recalls Hal Sperlich. "There were a couple of times when one or another financial disaster

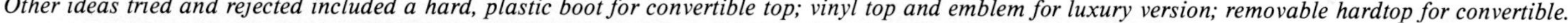

Other ideas tried and rejected included a hard, plastic boot for convertible top; vinyl top and emblem for luxury version; removable hardtop for convertible.

Shelby's Ford-powered Cobra and Jim Clark in "Lotus powered by Ford" at Indy in 1963 helped the division's performance reputation, as did the '63½ fastback

struck, and the program was no longer palatable from the financial standpoint. Each time, some major surgery had to be done on the financial side to bring it to life again. It was a terribly tough program to do financially, because a lot of top management was against it at first, and if it ever fell out of favor it was going to die before it got to market. As a result, there had to be a lot of compromises made, so it wasn't a very fancy car."

And *because* the budget discipline was so strict, the car ended up coming in slightly under the cost target, and some extra value could then be tacked on. The selling price of $2368 had long been determined, and ads using that figure were already in progress, so why not add some stuff to make the car even more appealing?

A major part of the marketing strategy was to have as well-equipped a car as possible within the cost ceiling. Says Iacocca: "One thing we decided at the beginning was that the car would never have little hubcaps...it would have full wheel covers, a paint stripe...that sort of thing all was to be standard. In those days—the Japanese hadn't taught us our lesson yet—everybody got a stripped car at base price, and there were certain value items that people knew they had to pay extra for. Then this car came out at that price and it was not a stripped job. We didn't put that much in it...bucket seats, carpeting, wheel covers...a few cues like that, and people said, 'My God, that car's equipped!' But those items separately would have gone for maybe $150."

Ford (two pictured here at Daytona Beach, 1963), and the 1963 assault on the prestigious Monte Carlo Rally with four-wheel-disc-equipped '63 Falcons.

One decision that was made by the marketing people was to stay with a single series and just one name, rather than trying to glamorize the more luxurious and sporty versions with special designations as was the custom of the time. The basic Mustang was to be sharp inside and out: color-keyed, all-vinyl interior and wall-to-wall carpeting; foam bucket seats; sport steering wheel; three-speed manual floor shift; front arm rests; cigarette lighter; automatic door courtesy and glovebox lights; wrap-around front bumpers and bumper guards front and rear; full wheel covers; padded instrument panel; self-adjusting brakes and more—all standard. So there was high perceived value even in the lowest-price version, and then a nearly limitless selection of options to let the buyer tailor his or her car to suit his or her individual needs.

It was Iacocca who came up with the idea of "the three faces of Mustang": the sound, good-value, base Mustang; the plush, "mini-T-Bird," luxury Mustang; and the macho, performance-oriented sporty Mustang. Thus the car could be almost anything to nearly anyone—male and female, young and not-so young, swinging single and suburban family type alike. It was infinitely adaptable, its fresh and youthful styling was equally at home at the dragstrip or at the country club, and all these factors would combine to make it one of the most successful new cars in industry history.

Speaking on the car's overall design, Iacocca says: "You've got to make a statement in the marketplace. You've got to have some reach.

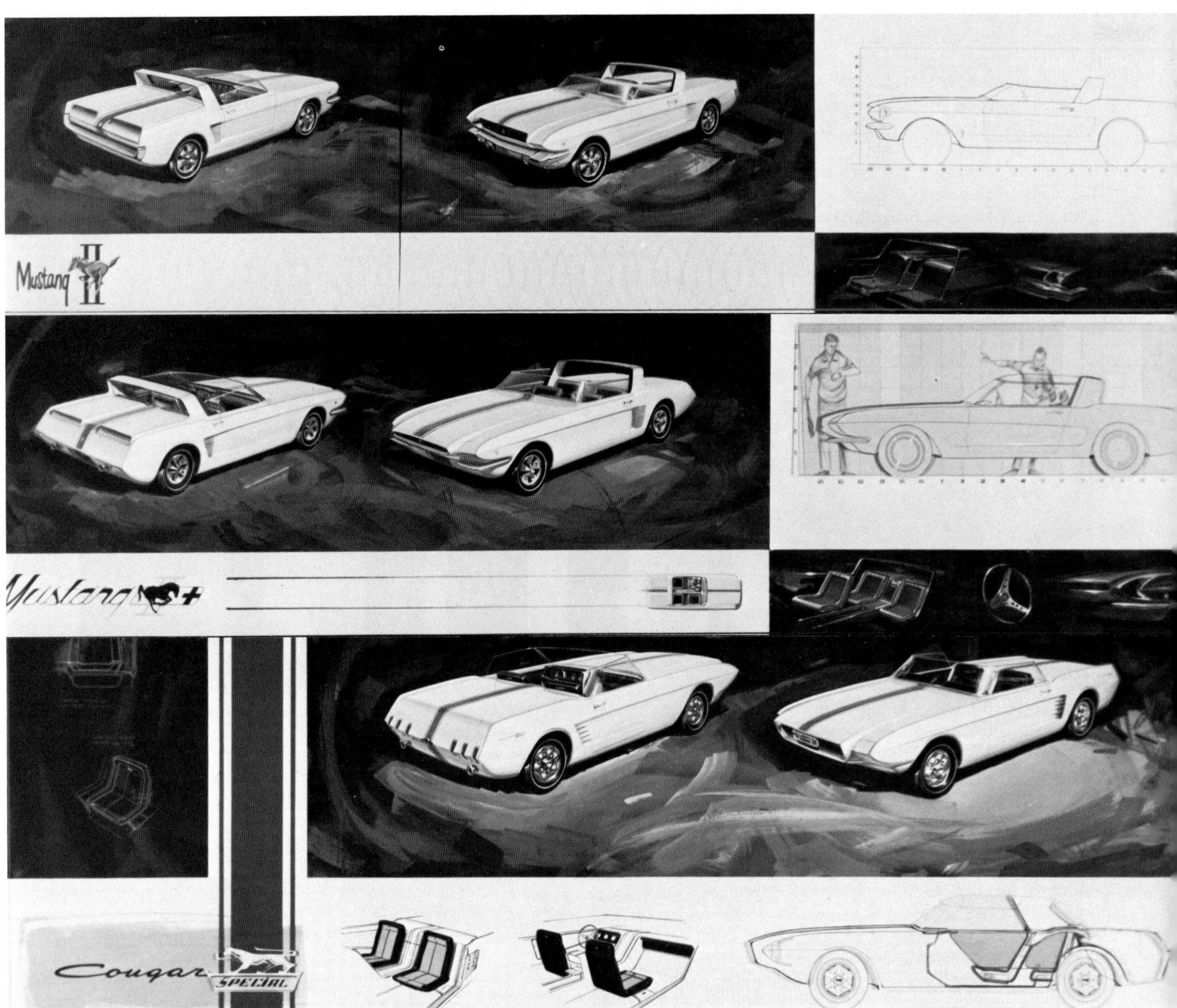
Mustang II
Mustang +
Cougar
SPECIAL

Four-door sedans and wagons will always look about the same because the package fairly well dictates the shape. But with a two-door sporty coupe, you've got to shock 'em a bit at first. You can't make it too far out, but if you make it too bland you get caught from behind, and people will say it's just like another little sedan from Toyota. There are certain images...cues, we call them in styling...that can turn people on or off instantly.

"With the Mustang, it was dangerous because it was so different. That's why there was flack from some of the top management people. Even when it seems you have a certain winner, people are going to

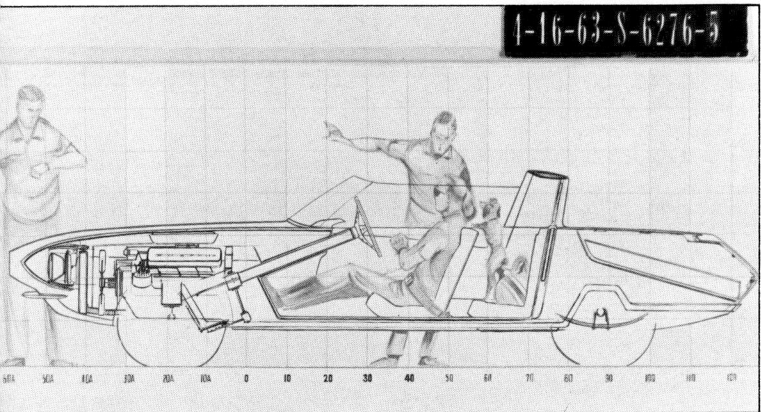

Left: Early concept sketches of the Mustang II show car. Above: April 16th blowup of Mustang II layout shows proposed interior and exterior details, including suitably-sized rear-seat occupant. Below: Najjar's final mid-May sketch is very close to the way the production-based show car turned out.

worry just because it's different. Do they really want to put that much money behind it? What if it's a fad and runs out of gas in a hurry? If it's a fad, you're going to sell maybe 50,000 and that's it."

As it turned out, the Mustang was sort of a smaller four-seat Thunderbird in its basic look, but Bordinat says it was not projected that way by his people. "It was kind of funny," he recounts, "because here we were, we thought, inventing this whole new set of ground rules...the long hood, etc. ...and here we had it sitting in front of us all the time. A lot of people probably thought it was done as a poor man's version of the T-Bird, but that was not the intent. We looked at it afterward and said, 'Hey, you know what we've just done? We've just done a T-Bird in a different scale.' Sometimes we get credit or blame for things that don't really happen that way at all."

Meanwhile, the racing people and the public relations forces were busy setting the stage for Mustang's debut. Shelby's road-racing Cobras, after a slow start, had won nearly everything in sight in both amateur and professional events during the 1963 season, and a British-entered Cobra had even finished an impressive seventh (behind six Ferraris) at the Le Mans 24-Hour.

When Mr. Ford had told the world he was going to go racing, he meant he was really going to go *racing*. In the spring, he had even tried to buy Ferrari, a move calculated to put the Ford name right on top of international racing in a big hurry. The plan was to form two separate companies in Italy, Ford-Ferrari and Ferrari-Ford, one to build cars and the other (under Ferrari himself) to race them. "But the Old Man wouldn't go for that," says Hal Sperlich, who was one of the Ford men involved, and the negotiations fell through.

Then Ford decided they would do it themselves. Top talent was hired (Eric Broadley of Lola fame and John Wyer from Aston Martin, to name two) and with Roy Lunn they set to work building a car (the GT-40) that could win at Le Mans. A limited-production version of the car was also planned to eventually replace Shelby's Cobra as an image booster to do for Ford what the Corvette was doing for Chevrolet.

Ford's stock-car program had begun to roll again late in '62, and in mid-1963 the famous "fastback" body style (designed expressly for high-speed ovals) appeared and began winning races in the hands of Fred Lorenzen, Fireball Roberts, Tiny Lund, Dan Gurney and many others, complete with a brand-new 427-cubic-inch, 450-hp engine. The Indianapolis Lotus-Fords had debuted impressively, qualifying well in the hands of Gurney and Scottish Formula One star Jimmy Clark, running one-two for a while and finishing with Clark second (in his rookie appearance) behind Parnelli Jones and Gurney seventh in spite of several lengthy pit stops due to excessive tire wear and other problems. And other high-dollar efforts were also helping Iacocca to win the excitement he wanted with Ford and Ford-powered cars in forms of the sport as diverse as drag racing, the Pikes Peak hill climb, international performance rallying and open-wheel formula car racing in Europe and elsewhere.

One interesting technical development was that Ford became the U. S. industry's disc-brake pioneer as a direct result of the Falcon rallying program. As Iacocca remembers it: "We put the V-8 in the Futura, but Holman-Moody said they couldn't stop the thing with drum brakes. 'We'll never make it around the curves,' they said. 'We'll lose it.' So we ordered 10,000 sets of front disc brakes for the '63 Falcon just so we could get them on the Monte Carlo rally cars, which launched disc brakes on production cars in the U. S. Most people here had never even heard of disc brakes until then, when we got forced into it."

Ford had gained a ton of publicity the year before by taking the exotic mid-engine Mustang I sports car to Watkins Glen, so the decision was made to do it again with another special car in 1963. By then, the Mustang's styling was pretty well settled, and the plan was to duplicate a ploy often used by General Motors. They would cobble up a pre-production prototype Mustang to look like a show car so people would get the impression that the soon-to-come production model had been derived from the show version. It was to be decorated much like Lunn's little sports car (white with blue stripes) and would serve as a bridge between the two-seater and the production Mustang.

"We took a steel prototype body, made it a convertible, took the bumpers off, restyled the front and back and did a lot of things to pick up cues from that Lunn-mobile," Hal Sperlich remembers. Bordinat takes credit for the idea, having been inspired by all the GM show cars

The beautiful Bordinat-created Cobra/Cougar II (below) and the Allegro based on the old Avventura clay model (above right) were shown widely during 1963 and early '64. T

that bore such a striking resemblance to later production models.

Executive stylist John Najjar, then in charge of the production Mustang's interior design, recalls Bordinat visiting the studio and chatting about needing a connecting link between the sports car and the real Mustang. "So I had a man working for me by the name of Jimmy Sherbourne turn out some drawings that were a blend of the two vehicles. We had the bumpers tucked in, we still had the roll-over bar and we were beginning to play with a retractable, stowable roof and dropped rear window. As it went along it got more of an abstract look, but also got closer to the production car. I quickly did later sketches myself, and they ended up as the Mustang II that was shown at Watkins Glen in October."

Two other idea cars had been shown during the year: the Allegro, which was really the old Avventura fastback with a futuristic interior

running Mustang II show car began as a pre-prototype stock Mustang body (below).

and a steering wheel that could be swung over a central hub for easy adaptation to either right- or left-hand drive; and the Cougar II, a sexy two-seater that was coded Cobra II in development and was Bordinat's personal project, featuring a unique plastic laminate body and a zippered convertible top (made from waterproof diving suit zippers) that came apart into sections for easy stowage.

At an afternon press conference the day before the Watkins Glen Grand Prix, Iacocca told newsmen: "The Mustang II is one of a series of recent idea or show cars Ford Division and Ford Motor Company have built to test public reaction to styling and functional innovations... Showing these vehicles to people like you—and to large segments of the public at auto shows and other special events—gives us a pre-test of likely customer response to styling and mechanical innovations we may be considering for future production models."

With that, he unveiled the car which, except for its lack of bumpers, lowered roof, an extra five inches of hood length, sexier head- and taillamps and other details, was the same as what was scheduled for public introduction a half year later. The newsmen applauded; and the Mustang II soon appeared on the CBS television network and in newspapers and magazines all over the world. It was a masterful teaser for both the name and the car that were to come.

Back in Dearborn, the engineers, stylists and product planners were now faced with a mere six months to make their final decisions and iron out what problems remained. Hal Sperlich, who was by then the light-car planning manager (responsible for both Mustang and Falcon) under Don Frey, recalls a handling problem that came up during the development program. "There were a lot of meetings over at the track," he relates, "driving the cars with the engineers, trying to sort out the problems and fix them. It was a car with basically bad weight distribution with the V-8, typical of a rear-drive car with a relatively heavy front engine and a minimum of overhang. That's one of the toughest kinds of cars to make handle well at high speeds. But we developed a handling package and made it available as part of the so-called 'sporty' face of Mustang, and it worked fairly well."

Although nearly everything went together and performed as designed in a minimum of time, there were still some problems remaining right up to the last minute. Development engineer Reuter tells of working a lot of nights and weekends as the Job One date approached, and on the Sunday before production was to begin the following Monday morning—March 9th, 1964—he and his men were working frantically on a mysterious resonance in the exhaust system. "We were changing exhaust hangers furiously trying to get rid of a 'moan' at about 1800 rpm with the 260 V-8 engine. You would get to a certain period and the thing would sound like a sick cow. At the last minute we took some hangers off the 390 c.i.d. Ford exhaust system,

Above: Mustang II in clay on May 16th, still bearing Torino name and Cougar grille piece. Right and below: The real thing as shown at Watkins Glen in October.

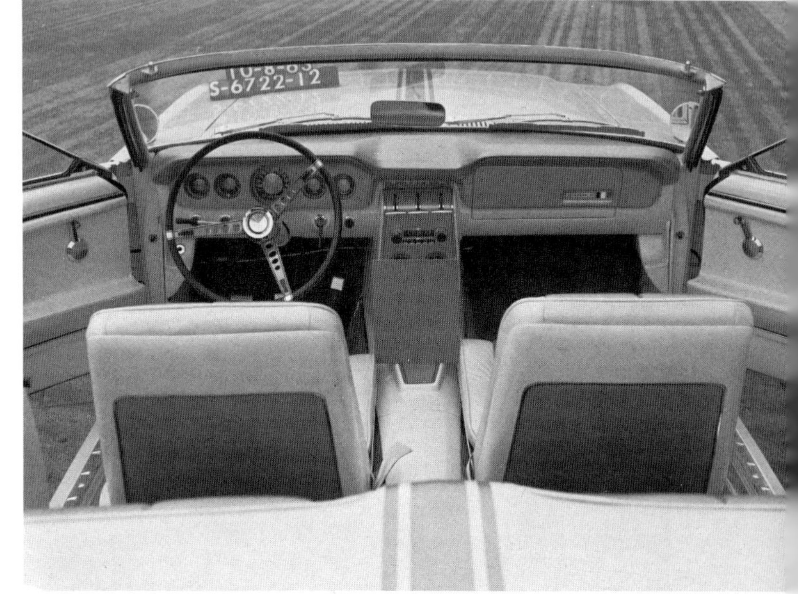

mounted them in a different location and managed to make an emergency fix to get the thing going. After that we were scrounging up pieces and taking them by hand to the plant, instructing the people where to put them."

In the end, such frantic effort and long, high-pressure hours were well worth the trouble. "It was an interesting program," says Reuter, "and if it hadn't been so short, I think we would have made more mistakes." Product planner Dick Place puts it even more enthusiastically: "It was a genuine thrill to be involved in that program," says he echoing the sentiments of almost everyone who was there at the time.

Surprisingly, there was still some doubt and resistance from upper management people even very late in the program. Reuter describes an incident when he was asked to show the car to one vice-president who had been hearing a lot about it and wanted to see for himself what it was like. "We took our best prototype and let him drive it around the track, and I rode with him," Reuter recalls. "I was so enthusiastic about the car that I was just bubbling. But as he drove it, his face grew grimmer and grimmer. 'This thing is nothing but a buckboard,' he told me, 'and nobody is going to buy it.' I felt like somebody had poured

Both interior and exterior are modified from production version to follow in the spring, but it worked as planned as a tremendous teaser for Mustang styling and name.

cold water on me. I was proud of that car. But he was the older type of person who was not really tuned in to what the younger people would want."

Chief product planner Don Frey recalls what Bill Mitchell, GM's famed, outspoken and controversial design vice-president, had said when he got a look at the Mustang II "idea" car at the Detroit Auto Show. "It looks like a Hamtramck Falcon," he told Frey (Hamtramck is an area in Detroit largely inhabited by people of Polish descent.) "That's exactly what we intended," Frey shot back.

As introduction date neared, it was obvious that Iacocca was risking everything to make his little pony car a success. Ford's investment had increased from the initial $40 million to some $65 with the addition of two more plants, and that was not counting all the money being spent on racing, idea cars, advance publicity and other peripheral activities. If the Mustang bombed, if it was mildly successful but less so than predicted...above all, if it lost money for the company, Iacocca's tenure as division vice-president might have been a very short one. "Lee, of course, has brass balls" is the way design chief Bordinat succinctly puts it. "It took a lot of guts. He was putting his whole damn career on the line with this car."

4. OFF AND RUNNING

In the fall of 1963, Ford Division invited a number of national magazine writers to Dearborn for exclusive, confidential, day-long briefings on the upcoming Mustang. Included were top staffers from the likes of *Time, Newsweek, Life, Look, U. S. News and World Report, Business Week, Esquire* and *Sports Illustrated.* Planning manager Hal Sperlich gave them prepared presentations on the growing youth market, the trend toward higher education, women's and young people's influence on purchases and other factors behind the new car's creation. This marked the beginning of what became the biggest and most effective public relations effort ever conducted in the automobile industry.

"I remember the slide presentations," says Sperlich. "The whole thrust of the program was that this was a lot more than just a new car. It was the youth market emerging, a whole, big demographic change going on. I think that turned the magazines on."

Ford Division boss Lee Iacocca then made his own presentation, emphasizing the increasingly youthful character of the market and the fact that this new car had a lot of the Thunderbird's sporty personality and appeal, but at a much lower price. Those two factors alone, he stressed, should make the Mustang an unqualified success.

"One strange thing about the program," said Sperlich later, "was that, as close as we were to it, I think we missed one extraordinary fact. We thought we were doing a small, economical sporty car; but as I look back on it, I think what we really created was the first 'nice' U.S. small car. By that I mean there were a lot of small cars around, but small was cheap and big was luxurious. I think there was a tremendous appetite among people to buy a small, economical, *really nice* car. A sexy, interesting car."

Ford Division public relations prepared a sixteen-page Mustang "white paper," press kits were mailed in advance of introduction to 11,000 North American newspapers and magazines, and foreign language versions were widely distributed abroad. Live stage shows and presentations were held for dealers in thirteen key cities, and an hour-long film was shown to salesmen in thirty-seven other locations throughout the country. Thus the Ford people's enthusiasm was systematically spread like salvation gospel across the country in anticipation of Mustang's public unveiling in April.

The Mustang goes to market. Lee Iacocca (left), Don Frey (right), the new Mustang sporting a license plate indicating its sales target.

A few weeks before introduction, 200 top radio disc jockeys were invited to Dearborn to test drive the car. Those who accepted were given fact sheets and asked to translate their impressions into ad-lib radio commercials. As extra inducement, each was loaned a Mustang for his own personal use for one week by his local Ford dealer. Some were so impressed with the car that they left advance deposits to buy their own Mustangs.

Looking for a novel and effective way to introduce Mustang to key print, radio and TV news people, Ford PR came up with the idea of linking the car's press introduction to a preview of the company's New York World's Fair pavilion. On Monday, April 13th, some 125 media heavies from the United States, Canada and Puerto Rico gathered on the World's Fair grounds at Flushing Meadows, Queens. Most had ridden through the Walt Disney-created Ford exhibit and viewed the latest Ford products (except Mustang) the previous day.

Lee Iacocca began the presentation by pointing out youth-oriented market trends and emphasizing that the day's activities were part of Ford's first-ever international introduction, since Mustang was also being presented on that date to two-thousand press, radio and TV newsmen throughout Western Europe. He told how compact-car buyers were dressing up their purchases with every conceivable option, "and their tastes," he added, "reflected youth and fun and liveliness and pizazz." He said that the car would be built at Dearborn and San Jose (the third plant was still being converted), and revealed that Ford planned a "heavy program" of Mustang participation in competition events both here and abroad.

At that point, the Mustang was revealed in the flesh, and a ten-minute film on its features followed. The group then moved to Westchester Country Club for lunch and the start of a 750-mile road rally to Detroit. Ak Miller, best known for his winning runs at the Pikes Peak hill climb in Colorado, had been hired to prepare the cars and conduct the rally, and his crew did their jobs so well that not one major mechanical problem was encountered by anyone. Naturally, this performance led to the hoped-for accounts of Mustang's durability and reliability in press reports on the trip. And much to the Ford people's delight, the cars attracted crowds everywhere they went. Sports car drivers tagged along and wanted to drag with the newsmen at stoplights, and Ak Miller himself was once challenged to a race by

417 BY 4-17

state troopers...but declined.

On Thursday evening, April 16th, 1964, Mustang monopolized TV advertising during the key 9:30 to 10:00 p.m. time slot on all three major networks, the first time such television saturation had ever been realized. Conservative Ford estimates were that the company rode Mustang into twenty-nine million households that night. Over the weekend and throughout the week that followed, full-page ads proclaimed Mustang's arrival in twenty-four national magazines and 2600 major newspapers. Iacocca and his creation simultaneously graced the covers of both *Time* and *Newsweek,* an almost unheard-of stroke of fortune for any commercial product, and feature stories appeared in *Life, Look, Esquire, Sports Illustrated, Business Week, U. S. News, Popular Science, Popular Mechanics, This Week* and *Playboy,* as well as every automotive magazine. By month's end, virtually every publication of any significance had carried the Mustang message to hundreds of millions of people, both through paid advertisements and news stories.

No new car in history had ever received the publicity and attention that the media lavished on Ford's sporty small car, and much of the credit for this incredible PR job went to Lee Iacocca himself. "I am sure that no top executive in any big business corporation ever gave as much of his personal time, and as much time from other pressing work, to the introduction of a new product as Lee gave to this one," said Bob Hefty, the Ford public relations executive in charge of the Mustang campaign. "Whenever a writer or photographer came out here to work on a story about the car, he would drop whatever he was doing and spend a whole day, or sometimes two or three days, talking and answering questions. With a car like that, and a guy like him pushing it, how could we miss?"

As a direct result of this tremendously effective and well-coordinated effort, and simply because the car *was* so exciting, Mustang Mania swept the country almost overnight. "The Mustang is a jaunty, snub-tailed four-passenger cross between a sports car and a sedan," said *Newsweek* in its introductory cover article, "and Ford is spending more than $10 million to imbed it in the national consciousness like a gumdrop in a four-year-old's cheek."

Mustang interior featured bucket seats, full carpeting, deep-dish sport-type steering wheel. Sport console and "Rally Pac" gauges were options. Hal Sperlich, above right.

On the eve of the announcement day, a Mustang was used as the pace car for a Huntsville, Alabama stock car race. According to eyewitness reports, some 9000 people jumped the wall and surrounded the car to get a closer look. It was an hour later when authorities had finally restored order and could start the race. But this enthusiastic demonstration was just one small preview of what was to come.

When Ford dealers opened their doors on the morning of Friday, April 17th, their showrooms were literally swamped with people anxious to see—and buy—the new little car. The few Mustangs on hand were immediately sold out and orders were taken on the spot for 22,000 more, without a demonstration ride, even though many could not be filled for two months or more. The hysteria was reminiscent of that created some thirty-six years before when firemen in several cities had to hose down crowds clamoring to see the 1928 Ford Model A. That historic car had been the first completely revamped standard Ford in twenty years, but the Mustang was something different...a totally new car and concept, with a brand-new name and no history at all.

"I've never seen anything like it," enthused one dealer in Ferndale, Michigan. "People are in a trance when they come in. All they do is mutter, 'I gotta have that car.' " Some dealerships were so crowded that salesmen had trouble writing orders. One in Chicago had to lock his doors because he feared for the crowd's (and his own people's) safety. A Pittsburgh dealer had a Mustang on a wash rack and couldn't bring it down because of the throngs of people around it; and one in Detroit reported that his parking lot looked like a foreign car rally with so many sports car people coming in to see the new little Ford. Several dealers had corrals of live Mustangs in front of their showrooms, and one in Northern Michigan went so far as to pile horse droppings in front of his building with a sign, "Mustang was here!"

The dealers had promised Ford management to keep at least one Mustang in their windows until April 25th, but this proved hard to do. In Garland, Texas, the dealer found himself with fifteen townspeople bidding on his last Mustang in the window. He decided to sell to the highest bidder, who then insisted on sleeping all night in the car so that no one could buy it out from under him before his check cleared the bank. In all, an estimated four million people visited Ford showrooms during that first weekend of Mustang Madness, an all-time record.

Mustangs were on display in fifteen major airport terminals and more than seventy bank lobbies and shopping centers across the country. Two-hundred Holiday Inns also exhibited Mustangs in their lobbies or near their main entrances. The idea was to expose the car to as many people as possible in a short period of time. Ford Division executives made speeches in most large cities, and twenty-five lucky people in each audience received use of a Mustang for one week free

Pacing the 500 in '64. Mustang team receiving Industrial Design Institute Award, from the left, Woods, Najjar, Phaneuf, Halderman, Foster, Ash, Oros, Bordinat.

of charge. Mustangs were used as pace cars at auto races (including the 1964 Memorial Day Indianapolis 500) and to transport beauty queens in parades and ceremonies of all descriptions. Businesses and organizations all over America wanted Mustangs as contest prizes or to tie in with product promotion campaigns.

A California school teacher registered one of the few early complaints: Every time he left his new Mustang unguarded in public, it was quickly covered with the fingerprints of fondling admirers. "If I had known it would get all this much attention, I might not have bought it," he moaned. A cement truck driver in Seattle was so distracted by the Mustang on display at one dealership that he drove his truck right through the showroom window.

Among the many accolades heaped upon the first Mustang, including the prestigious Industrial Designers' Institute Award, perhaps the most cherished by Henry Ford II was the Tiffany Gold Medal Award, bestowed by the famed diamond merchant "For Excellence in American Design." Walter Hoving, Tiffany & Company chairman, presented the medal to Mr. Ford during the April 13th World's Fair press introduction ceremonies, and it marked the first time this prestigious honor had been awarded to an automobile.

Actually, according to then Mustang product planner Hal Sperlich, it had happened because Ford PR people had approached Tiffany, instead of the other way around. "Somebody said, 'You know, the car really ought to win an award; it ought to be an award-winning car,' but there wasn't anything suitable," Sperlich recalls. "So somebody was dispatched to see Walter Hoving, and Walter agreed...provided he could look the car over to make sure it was suitable. He came out and made some minor change in the grille or something, and the deal was struck."

The introductory ads were low-key, simple and stylish—what Iacocca called the "Mona Lisa" approach. Based on the earlier market surveys, where most people overestimated the car's value by $1000 or more, he was certain that Mustang's biggest selling point would be its price. "Never mind all that flowery talk you usually hand out," he had told the ad copywriters, "just put a big picture of the car up there so they can see how great it looks, and list the nice things they get with it—bucket seats, all-vinyl upholstery, wheel covers, floor shift. You might mention whitewall tires are $33.90 extra. Then in big numbers, let them see the price—$2368 f.o.b. Detroit. That's all you need to say."

"Presenting the unexpected...new Ford Mustang! $2368" trumpeted the national magazine ads to an estimated readership of sixty-eight million people that first weekend. The Tiffany Award was prominently shown and mentioned. "Mustang has the look, the fire, the flavor of the great European road cars. Yet it's as American as its name...and as practical as its price," read the copy. The standard equipment was listed and the car's versatility emphasized: "The basic Mustang is an eminently practical and economical car, yet, it was

Valter Hoving presenting Henry Ford II the Tiffany Award. Don Frey (left), Bob Tasca, the Tasca 505 and American Rodding's trophy for "America's Perfect Performance Car."

designed to be designed by you. You can make your Mustang into a luxury or high performance car by selecting from a large but reasonably priced group of options."

Hal Sperlich remembers being especially pleased by the ad campaign: "Probably one of the neatest things about the program was the simplicity of the advertising. So often when a new car comes out, the manufacturer feels he has to tell you everything...take you by the coat collars and tell you the thirty-nine virtues of his car. What we had in the ad was a white car in silhouette, its best view, with a girl in a gown and her man in a tux, and the price...very little else. Starkly simple. Such a beautiful, dynamic car for only this much money. I thought it was magnificent, a real work of art."

Soon the love letters started pouring in. Most people write to criticize a car, but that first summer brought some four thousand letters singing the Mustang's praises.

A Philadelphia mother wrote: "I'm madly in love with my new Mustang. For the sake of my brood, I've been dragging a nine-passenger station wagon around for the past fifteen years. For about fourteen years, I've been tired of this whole deal. My Mustang was my key to liberation. My sons refer to it as, 'Ma's mill with four on the floor and eight up front.' I've no idea what they're talking about but it sounds as good as the car looks."

From a forty-four-year-old Texas bachelor: "I traded my '62 Galaxy hardtop in on this pony, V-8, Rangoon Red with accent paint stripes, panel molding and air conditioning, and, man, this is the greatest! A widow with 7000 acres came sixty miles so I could take her riding in it. I thought the jig was up for me. Thank you, thank you, thank you!"

A Brooklyn man wrote to Lee Iacocca: "New York is no place to have a car. Pet owners urge their dogs on the wheels. Slum kids steal the radio aerials. Cops give parking tickets, and who knows someone who can fix them? Pigeons roost on the car, and worse. Streets are always torn up. Buses crush you, taxis bump you, and inside parking requires a second mortgage on the house. Gas costs thirty percent more than anyplace else. The insurance rates are incredible. The garment district is impassable, the Wall Street area impenetrable, going to New Jersey impossible. So as soon as I can raise the nut, I'm buying a Mustang."

The only complaints centered on availability. Henry Ford received a telegram in verse:

Henry Ford, I do declare
You have your Grandpa Henry's flair
He put a Ford in every home.
You put a Mustang there.
Congratulations.
The wait out here is somewhat sickly;
Could you fix me up more quickly?

Ford Mustang Hardtop with Vinyl-Covered Roof

A PRODUCT OF Ford MOTOR COMPANY

See the Mustang and ride Walt Disney's Magic Skyway at the Ford Motor Company's Wonder Rotunda, New York World's Fair.

Presenting the unexpected... new Ford Mustang!

$2368* f.o.b. Detroit

This is the car you never expected from Detroit. Mustang is so distinctively beautiful it received the Tiffany Award for Excellence in American Design . . . the first time an automobile has been honored with the Tiffany Gold Medal. Mustang has the look, the fire, the flavor of the great European road cars. Yet it's as American as its name . . . and as practical as its price—just $2,368 f.o.b. Detroit.

* That's the suggested retail price for the basic Mustang Hardtop. It does not include, of course, destination charges from Detroit, options, state and local taxes and fees, if any. Whitewalls are $33.90 extra and the vinyl roof covering is $75.80 extra.

It does include, however, at no extra cost, a padded instrument panel and full wheel covers, which cost extra on most other cars... as well as bucket seats; floor-mounted shift; wall-to-wall carpeting; vinyl upholstery; arm rests; cigarette lighter; room for four; sensibly sized trunk; sports steering wheel; courtesy lights; a 170-cu. in. Six . . . and more!

The basic Mustang is an eminently practical and economical car, yet, it was designed to be designed by you. You can make your Mustang into a luxury or high performance car by selecting from a large but reasonably priced group of options.

For added luxury choose such options as air conditioning, push-button radio, vinyl roof covering, 3-speed Cruise-O-Matic, power brakes, power steering—you name it.

Or, for sports car performance add the big 289-cu. in. V-8 engine (the same basic V-8 that powers the famous Cobra!), 4-speed stick shift (synchro in all forward speeds), and Rally Pac (tachometer and clock).

Ford Mustang Convertible

TRY TOTAL PERFORMANCE FOR A CHANGE!

FORD

Mustang · Falcon · Fairlane · Ford · Thunderbird

For an exciting, authentic scale model of the new Ford Mustang, send $1.00 to Ford Offer, Department 00, P.O. Box 35, Troy, Michigan. (Offer ends July 31, 1964)

Three young girls (ages five-and-a-half to ten-and-a-half) wrote saying they were saving their allowance money to buy their mother a yellow Mustang for Mother's Day, and asking, please, how much "would one of these pretty cars cost?" Later the mother wrote to say that she had sold her Falcon and bought a "pretty yellow Mustang."

A youthful sixty-one-year-old lady from Connecticut wrote: "Last Saturday I was taking my *mother* to dinner. We had to stop at a red light, and on the corner were six or eight children from twelve to sixteen. One hollered, 'Hey, look at the Mustang,' and another yelled, 'Yeah, and look at the old ladies driving it.' My mother is eighty-one, and she thought the children were rude, but I explained that the Mustang was a sports car and really, we shouldn't have one. But I have one and I'm proud, and I sure hope more people *yell* at me."

Such warm and witty letters from people saying how Mustangs had brightened their lives gave Iacocca and his people a cue for their subsequent ad campaign, which was destined to become an industry classic. Early TV spots had featured horses and more horses...even the U.S. Cavalry riding for Mustang. But these and the price-oriented print ads were replaced by a clever and amusing series of "Walter Mitty"-style pitches (after the fictional James Thurber character who dreams of being a jet pilot or a race driver), featuring drab housewife Sarah, bookworm Emily, chicken-hearted Felix and other such shy, retiring types who find new lives of romance and excitement with their Mustangs.

The best-remembered of these depicted the secret life of Henry Foster, a wimpy, soft-spoken antique dealer who is seen leaving his shop for lunch in derby hat, conservative dark suit and foppy pince-nez glasses. As Henry rounds the corner and approaches a bright red Mustang, the gossipy old lady in a nearby tea shop croaks: "Have you heard about Henry Foster? Something's happened to Henry." He throws away the derby and glasses, doffs his coat to reveal a racy red vest, and takes a sporty plaid tweed hat and racing goggles out of his lunch bag, then slips behind the wheel, smiling.

The next scene shows a very dashing Henry pulling up in his Mustang to a lovely young lady who has been waiting for him in a green meadow with a picnic lunch and a bottle of wine. "A Mustang's happened to Henry," purrs a sexy, seductive voice. He jumps out of the car, flings himself down on the grass beside her, laughs merrily and throws aside his hat...along with all his cares and inhibitions. "Something's Happened to Henry" was widely praised as one of the nicest automobile ads ever seen on TV, and it became almost as famous as the car.

While the low advertised price certainly brought a lot of people into Ford showrooms, fewer than ten percent of the first two million Mustangs actually were sold at anywhere near that base figure. Most buyers opted for the V-8 engine and a wide variety of luxury and/or performance extras, bringing the average retail delivered price closer to $3000 than $2400...and it was on these options that Ford made its biggest profits. The car was unique in that it could be virtually anything to anyone. It was economical, practical (yet youthful) transportation to legions of young working men and women, a macho tire-burner to performance enthusiasts and a mini-Thunderbird to luxury seekers. Amazingly, none of these three "faces" of Mustang seemed to clash with the others.

"That was the magic of this car," says Iacocca. "If you can turn everybody on, then you really have a success. Who could not like the style for its day? It stood out, yet it was everyman's car. It had mass appeal, and it gave birth to the 'do-it-yourself' car."

Traditionally, some automobiles are "men's cars" and some are "women's cars," but Mustang seemed to appeal equally to both. At

The Mustang's initial ad campaign was starkly simple, classy and very effective. Above: The Mustang's 164 hp 260-cubic-inch V-8 engine.

one point, there was a shortage of V-8 engines, and the J. Walter Thompson agency was instructed to build a whole ad campaign around six-cylinder Mustangs for young career women. "I think Thompson got a little carried away on that one," Iacocca chuckles. "He called it 'Six and the Single Girl.' But it sold the hell out of them to young girls, twenty-one or twenty-two, getting their first jobs and buying their first new cars."

Analyzing the Mustang's visual appeal, Petersen's *Complete Ford Book* compares it to the '55-'57 Thunderbird: "Fact one: the two-seater design is very popular, especially with the young. Fact two: even young car buyers often have a family to transport, thus making the two-seater car impractical. Conclusion: build a car that looks like a two-passenger sports model, but actually has a rear seat. Enter the 1964 Mustang, available as hardtop or convertible. In terms of basic styling, the Mustang was comparable to those early two-seat Thunderbirds, yet it had a back seat. The rooflines and silhouettes of the two cars were very similar..."

Car enthusiast magazine ("buff book") writers and editors had been invited to the Dearborn Proving Ground in January, and even though none of the prototypes available for testing had had the optional handling suspension or high-performance 289 V-8 engine, the resulting reports in May issues were almost universally complimentary. "A market which has been looking for a car has it now," began the *Car Life* story. "It is a sports car, a *gran turismo* car, an economy car, a personal car, a rally car, a sprint car, a race car, a suburban car, and even a luxury car."

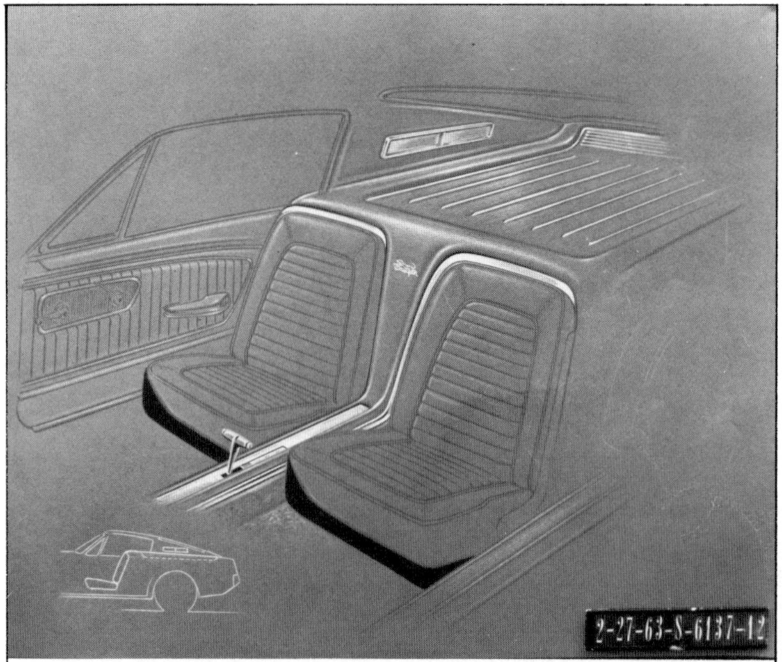

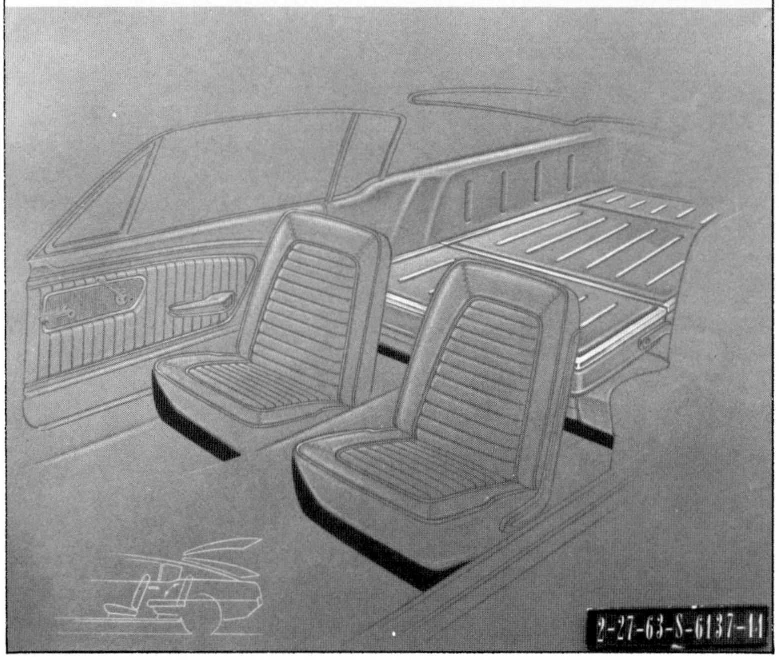

"The inherent balance is good, the center of gravity is low, and the stiff chassis is well able to handle the abuse," wrote hard-driving Jerry Titus in *Sports Car Graphic.* "Easily the best thing to come out of Dearborn since the 1932 V-8 Model B roadster," enthused *Car and Driver.* And even *Road & Track,* never a fan of Detroit engineering, conceded that "the Mustang is definitely a sports car, on par in most respects with such undisputed types as the MG-B, Triumph TR-4 or

Concept sketches and fender identification variations considered for 2+2.

Sunbeam Alpine."

Road & Track's Gene Booth added in his driving impression: "The Mustang seems to lift its nose and charge around the bends in easily controlled drifts, kept in hand as much by the throttle as by the steering wheel. Body lean, unlike the Falcon, is minimal and the underpinnings are well-damped to eliminate the spongy porpoising which is all too common with domestic cars."

"In concept," said *Car Life,* "the Mustang draws from the original Thunderbird and the Corvair Monza; in execution, it has ancestry in the Fairlane and Lincoln Continental; and in appearance, it reflects the Continental Mark II." Later in its report, the magazine concluded: "The car may well be, in fact, better than any domestically mass-produced automobile on the basis of handling and roadability and performance, per dollar invested."

All was not kudos, however. High on the complaint lists were Mustang's poor performing and fade-prone drum brakes; slow steering (even with the optional faster ratio); cramped seating position (the deep-dish wheel was too close to the chest, seat travel was inadequate for even medium-tall drivers, and some complained of a lack of foot space); cheap, Falcon-derived instrument panel; and too-soft leaf spring rear suspension. But only one publication, *Car and Driver,* found fault with Mustang's styling: "There is a non-functional air scoop along the body sides," griped the magazine's writer, "and a clumsy, protruding grille between the single headlamps."

Full road tests came later in the year and in general were no less enthusiastic. One exception was *Road & Track*, which tested standard-suspension Mustangs before the high-performance version became available. "The ride is wallowy, there's a tendency for the car

The 2+2 in clay, May 1963, an instant hit with management and produced virtually as shown save for Cougar identification. Note Avanti and Jaguar XK-E in background.

to float when being driven at touring speeds and the 'porpoise' factor is high on an undulating surface," the magazine complained in its August issue. The report concluded that Mustang presented "little difference (except in appearance) from the typical American sedan."

Even persnickety *Consumer Reports,* however, was impressed by Mustang's "almost complete absence of poor fit and sloppy workmanship in a car being built at a hell-for-leather pace." And when West Coast buff books were provided with the first production "HP" car (271 bhp 289 engine, heavy-duty four-speed transmission, handling suspension and 5.50/5.90x15 Firestone Super Sport Tires) their response was nothing short of ecstatic: "The car goes, and damned well...the stability is excellent and you can honk around most any corner at racing velocity well under control," said *Sports Car Graphic's* Jerry Titus. "The rear end stayed glued to the track no matter how hard we pushed it. Body lean was minimal under all conditions," reported *Motor Trend.* And *Car Life* bubbled: "The HP Mustang backs up its looks in spades. It promises, it delivers, and for good measure it does even more than one could reasonably expect...It's been some time since we enjoyed doing a road test so much."

As always, makers of various other products began to cash in on the Mustang magic. Young people's clothing stores were selling Mustang shirts and pants, sunglasses, boots, earrings, key chains, tie clips, cuff

Left: Grille textures and lamp shapes tried on the '65 2+2 GT clay models. Below: Mockup showing production 2+2's folding rear seat and cargo floor.

links and hats, and one clothing chain called its youth department the "Mustang Shop." Scale-model Mustangs were hot sellers, and some 93,000 small, pedal-operated children's Mustangs were snapped up by eager parents during the 1964 Christmas season.

The word "Mustang" quickly became part of the language. "Mustangers" were fun-loving people who drove Mustangs. A California apartment builder coined the term "Mustang Generation" to describe his young, single tenants—because there were so many Mustangs in his parking lots—and used it in promotional brochures. The *Wall Street Journal* then picked up the term and used it in a front page headline for a story on advertising for the twenty-to-thirty-four age group.

Mustang clubs sprang up like mushrooms in springtime. The National Council of Falcon Clubs, formed (with help from Ford) in 1963 after the Falcon Sprint had won its class in the Monte Carlo Rally, changed its name to National Council of Falcon-Mustang Clubs and later dropped the "Falcon" altogether. Ford Division formed a Ford Motorsports Association whose member clubs were principally Mustang organizations, and the J. Walter Thompson agency founded *Mustanger* magazine. These clubs, more than 400 strong at one time, sponsored thousands of gymkhanas, slaloms, autocrosses, rallies, hill climbs and other fun events for families and singles alike, and later they gathered in "Mustang Corrals" at road racing courses throughout the country to cheer their favorite Mustang racers on to victory.

The 2+2 Fastback debuted in the fall of '64 as did a sporty GT package with side stripes, and exhaust tips extending through lower rear pan.

Just six weeks after its introduction, Mustang had become the top-selling compact-size car and ranked seventh among all U.S.-market nameplates. Within four months, more than 100,000 Mustangs had been sold, and it was the fifth-ranked car on the charts. In its first twelve months on the market, the frisky Ford pony sold to the tune of 418,812 units out the door—a new all-time record for a first-year entry. That record had previously been held by Ford's own Falcon, and it was Iacocca's professed goal to do better with his Mustang. By April 17th, 1965, he had beaten Falcon's first year performance by exactly 1638 copies...not bad for a car that originally had been targeted for less than 100,000 units per year.

Successful Ford products in the past, including Falcon, often had "cannibalized" sales from other Ford cars, and it was widely predicted by outsiders that Mustang would do the same—hurting Falcon, Fairlane and maybe even Thunderbird to some degree. But reasonable estimates as the year progressed placed the number of Mustangs sold at the expense of other Ford marques at only about fifty percent—meaning the other half was coming out of competitors' hides.

Ford Motor Company's share of the total growing domestic market had shrunk from 28.5 percent in 1961 to 24.9 percent in 1963 in spite of Falcon's popularity in the compact market, and was as low as 23.9 percent when Mustang hit the market in April 1964. By the following September, the company, as a whole, was up to 27.1 percent and Ford Division had climbed from 20.0 percent to 22.5 percent of the U.S. new-car business. Some of this gain was due to increased appeal of other 1964 Ford products, but the major portion was attributed directly to Mustang sales and to the youthful new pony's showroom drawing power and the favorable image it lent Ford Motor Company's entire product line. Not everyone bought a Mustang, but many who came to see it drove away in some other Ford car.

Mustang's own share of the market, with just one model in two body styles available, rose from 1.9 percent in April to 5.8 percent in August and 5.6 percent in September 1964, when strike-caused shortages began to distort the picture. And there was no way of knowing how many more could have been sold if supply could have kept up with the fast-growing demand. One interesting study conducted in mid-September showed that nine percent of all Mustangs then being built could have been sold within the city limits of Dayton, Ohio!

Buyer research confirmed, as expected, that a majority of Mustang purchasers were between twenty and thirty-four years old, although the car's appeal was definitely not limited to young people...some

Above: Shelby '65 GT-350, the early prototype lacking hood scoop and large bumper air intake of production version. Below: Specially prepared Mustangs driven by Peter Procter and Peter Harper finished first and second in class in '64 Tour de France. Right: Bob Johnson (#33) and Tom Yeager in GT-350's at Mid-Ohio, 1965.

sixteen percent of its buyers were between the ages of forty-five and fifty-four. More than forty percent were in the $5000-to-$10,000 income bracket, suggesting that the low-price incentive was indeed strong; yet almost fifteen percent made $15,000 or more per year, which was good money in 1964. Nearly two-thirds were married, fifty-two percent had some college education and another thirty-eight percent were high-school graduates.

Fully fifty-three percent of Mustang trade-ins were non-Ford products, and seventy percent more Chevrolets were traded for Mustangs than for other Ford products. Additionally, Mustang attracted five times as many foreign-car trades as did the other Ford cars. Eighty-five percent of the Mustangs sold were equipped with white-sidewall tires, eighty percent had radios, seventy-one percent V-8 engines, fifty percent automatic transmissions and ten percent got the "Rally Pac" (tachometer and clock) option designed for fun driving rather than utility.

Certainly much of Mustang's early success was as much fortuitous timing as it was inspired planning. The Ford pony couldn't have been launched at a better time in the country's history. The nation was in a carefree and youthful mood in the spring of 1964. President Lyndon Johnson had just announced a cut in income taxes that would increase everyone's take-home pay, and 1964 and 1965 were both economic boom years as a result of that and other positive factors.

As Iacocca had foreseen three years earlier, the World War II babies were coming of age, going to work and enjoying their new-found purchasing power in a thriving economy. For the first time there were more Americans under twenty-five than over. There was pre-Vietnam tranquility and optimism on the nation's college campuses—no demonstrations or drug problems and little concern as yet over the environment and automotive emissions or safety. Mustang, with its sassy good looks and spirited performance, was exactly the right car for that large and impatient phalanx of buyers turned off by both the excesses of big cars and the dullness of most smaller ones.

"We were very fortunate in that we hit at exactly the right time," Iacocca explains. "After the Korean War, everything was on allocation, and things really didn't start moving again until the late Fifties. By 1964, it was a euphoric time; I mean, they were even cutting taxes. It was just dumb luck that we had the world's biggest showroom—the New York World's Fair—as a launching pad. It was the combination of the World's Fair launch, the fact that we did have a rather unique and different car, a realization that the youth market was bulging, and most of all an economy that was really being heated up by the government's cutting taxes and telling people to go out and spend some money. With those ingredients, it would have been hard not to succeed."

Among the fifty-or-so options that made the first Mustang nearly as much fun to order as it was to drive were: air conditioning ($283.20), four-speed manual ($188) or three-speed automatic ($189.60) transmission, power brakes ($43.20), power steering ($86.30), simulated knockoff racing ($18.20) or wire ($45.80) wheel covers, Rally Pac ($75.95), pushbutton radio with antenna ($58.50), rear seat speaker ($11.95) sports console ($51.50), vinyl-covered roof ($75.80), rocker panel moldings ($16.10) and special handling suspension ($38.60). Also on the list were several items taken for granted as standard equipment today: outside rear view mirror ($2.25), back-up lights ($10.70), padded sun visors ($5.70) and windshield washers ($13.50). For the serious rally driver there was even a compass and tachometer option, complete with diagram for do-it-yourself in-dash installation, for a "mere" $78.75; and the performance enthusiast could order factory exhaust cut-outs ($57) and a variety of other HP equipment.

But probably of greatest concern to most Mustang buyers was the choice of available engines. At first there were just two, the base (Falcon) 170-cubic-inch, 101 hp six and the two-barrel, 164 hp, 260-cubic-inch Fairlane V-8 ($116). Next came a four-barrel, 210 hp, 289-cubic-inch, regular gas V-8 ($181.70), and (three months after introduction) a high-performance, 271 hp 289. This tire-burner was essentially the same as the 289 used in Carroll Shelby's Cobra sports car, complete with 10.5:1 compression, solid lifters, beefed valved train and dual exhausts, and it sold for the princely sum of $435.80.

With all three plants on-stream and struggling to satisfy the huge market demand, there were few changes made for the '65 model year beginning in September (officially, the '64½ Mustangs which had debuted in April had been designated "first of the '65's"). The 170-cubic-inch six was replaced by a peppier 200 c.i.d., 120 hp unit as base engine, and the 260 V-8 was dropped in favor of a 200 hp, two-barrel 289. The passenger seat was made adjustable and an alternator, an improved battery and a theft resistant fuel filter cap were added.

Among several new items on the option list were front disc brakes ($56.77), a limited-slip differential ($41.60), styled steel wheels ($119.71) and an exciting GT equipment group to tie in with the GT-40 road racing cars which were carrying Ford's colors in international competition. At a fairly reasonable $165.03, this package was available with either of the four-barrel 289 engines and included dual exhausts extending through the lower rear body panel, the special handling suspension and front discs, grille-mounted fog lamps, a new five-gauge instrument cluster, "GT" identification and side stripes. Later in the year came a luxury Interior Decor Group ($107.08) and a full-width front bench seat with center armrest ($24.42).

By far the most important development, however, came on September 9th, 1964 when the super-sexy fastback 2 + 2 model was unveiled. As far back as February 1963 the idea of a fastback had been germinating in the minds of Gene Bordinat's Mustang styling group. A rear hatch version with a folding back seat and one with no rear seat at all were among the early paper proposals, and by early May a finished clay model was shown to management. Says product planner Dick Place, "Nobody outside of the styling center ever saw that car until the day it was shown to Mr. Iacocca...and he said, 'That's what I want. Go!' It was approved that day and we went."

"We had worked up such a head of steam on the first Mustang that we were already looking for variations on the theme," adds Bordinat. "Some people we surveyed thought fastbacks were great, and an

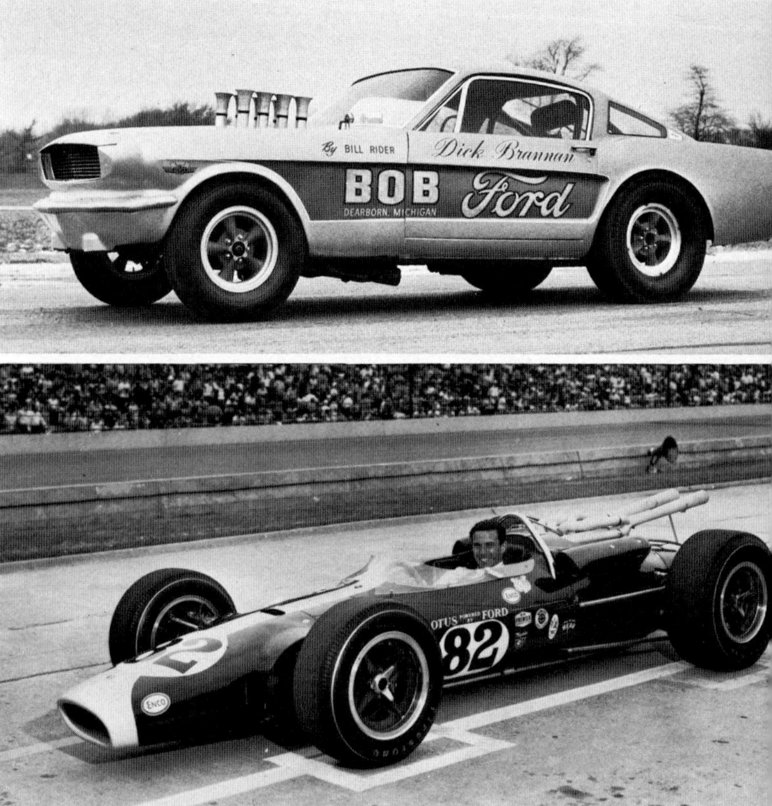

Drag racing during 1965-'66 was primarily dealer-sponsored, the altered wheelbase

equal number preferred notchbacks. So we did the fastback very shortly after approval on the Mustang program without anybody asking us to do it, and it was immediately a turn-on car for a lot of people. We showed it one afternoon and people sort of walked around it and oohed and ahhed. The decision to produce it was made as an emotional binge only...no prudent analysis or a damned thing."

The production 2 + 2 arriving in Ford showrooms September 25th had a fold-down rear seatback and a divider panel that swung out of the way to combine the interior cargo area and trunk into one long, carpeted compartment for transporting skiis and other long items inside the car. Functional air louvers in the rear "C" pillar provided a pleasing styling touch as well as efficient flow-through ventilation when opened from inside, and both headliner and sun visors were color-keyed to the interior trim. Needless to say, the 2+2 was an

uel-injected 427 GT-350 built by Rider and driven by Brannan. Jim Clark won Indy in 1965. Shelby's Cobra Daytona coupes brought World Manufacturer title to U.S.

instant hit and probably made a lot of earlier hardtop buyers wish they had waited.

Most everyone agreed that Mustang looked good, and equipped with the high-performance option it performed well enough, but it was still no match for Chevy's most powerful Corvette or Pontiac's 389-cubic-inch GTO. It seemed that something even more exciting than the GT 289 Mustang was needed to give a performance image boost and attract some of those hard-core horsepower and sports car buyers away from the competition. Ray Geddes, then overseeing many of Ford Division's high-performance programs, suggested bringing in the snakemaster, Carroll Shelby.

Shelby, then in the midst of his successful Cobra racing effort which was blowing off Corvettes at home as well as factory Ferraris abroad, was summoned to Dearborn for a meeting with Lee Iacocca. The Ford Division boss asked him what could be done to the Mustang to make it competitive in SCCA sports car competition. Shelby said it would be no problem working over the car and all they had to do was build a hundred like it to satisfy SCCA requirements for a "production" racer.

The first twelve racing Mustangs, essentially stripped-down 2+2's with much-improved and stiffened suspensions and well-tweaked 289 c.i.d. engines, were screwed together at Shelby's Venice, California shop by Christmas 1964. Just one week later—on January 1st, 1965—one-hundred Shelby-ized Mustangs were lined up in neat rows for SCCA officials to inspect. It was an amazing feat for the Shelby organization, the SCCA people were duly impressed, and the car was declared legal for racing in the upcoming 1965 season—as a B-Production sports car, against small-block Corvettes and E-Type

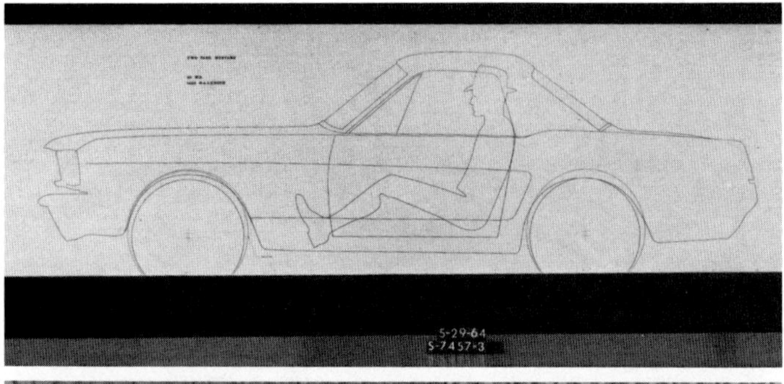

Still toying with two-seater concepts after four-place Mustang was introduced, this two-passenger coupe got only as far as clay model. Below: A new show car designed to preview the '65 2+2, this model was done with different front-end treatments on each side so stylists could evaluate both without having to build two different models.

Jaguars. What SCCA didn't know at the time, however, was that the last eighty-eight of those hundred cars had been built on the San Jose assembly line, with the Shelby crew merely adding details after they arrived at the shop.

Involved in the project in addition to Shelby and Geddes were engineer Chuck Cantwell, hired by Shelby as director of the performance Mustang program, and Sam Smith and Klaus Arning of Ford. It was Arning who had been responsible for computer-designing the suspensions of both the Ford GT-40 Le Mans car and Shelby's killer 427 Cobra racing roadsters and 289 Daytona coupes, and he applied a bit of the same computer magic to the Mustang suspension to make it a viable racing design. Ken Miles, Shelby's talented Cobra race-car and test driver, did most of the on-track development.

All that was needed now was a name as hairy-chested as the car. "We were all sitting around one day in one of the back rooms across the street from the Venice plant. We had three or four people from Ford and some of our people, and we were trying to come up with a name for the car," Shelby explained at the January 27th press introduction. "Some thought it should be called this and some that, and I finally asked (Shelby chief engineer) Phil Remington how far it was to the building across the street. Phil paced it off and found it to be about 350 feet. So I said, we'll call it the GT-350." The story may be true or it may be a Shelby put-on, but the name stuck even

though it had nothing to do with the car. The Ford people may have liked it because they thought the enthusiast public would associate it with 350 cubic inches or 350 horsepower, but Shelby said it wasn't that important anyway...if the car was good, the name wouldn't matter; if it was bad, the name wouldn't help.

Ford had optimistic ideas at first of producing some 200 GT-350's a month, but the overworked Shelby American people managed to crank out only twelve full-race units and 550 street versions during the '65 model year. In 1966, Shelby GT-350 production totaled three racers, 1433 street cars, 936 of the famous (mostly gold-on-black) Hertz rental units and six handmade prototype convertibles.

The stripped 2 + 2 bodies arrived at Shelby's plant, now relocated into surplus hangars at Los Angeles International Airport, minus hood, grille bars, side trim, wheel covers, rear seat and seat belts. Then the GT-350 treatment began. A fiberglass panel went on where the rear seat used to be, and the spare tire was mounted on it with a cover. A fiberglass hood with hold-down pins and a functional scoop was added, plus a small Mustang emblem over the stock honeycomb mesh grille. The deep-dish steering wheel was replaced with a wood-rimmed aluminum racing wheel which provided two inches more arm room. Seats were the best Mustang units available for comfort and side support, seat belts were three-inch-wide competition-type, and a tachometer and oil pressure gauge were added in a pod on the dash. Styled steel wheels (15x5.5 inches), huge racing stripes and smaller side stripes with "GT-350" lettering completed the visual package.

The racing version, which came to be called GT-350R, was further lightened by some 250 pounds with plastic side and rear windows, a deeply-contoured fiberglass bucket driver's seat, magnesium racing wheels, a fiberglass lower front pan with center cut-out for added air cooling and other modifications. The C-pillar vents were covered to improve aerodynamics, and shoulder belts, roll bar, fire extinguisher, thirty-four gallon fuel tank, and a full set of racing instruments were added.

Both street and competition GT-350's got the full Arning suspension treatment, which consisted of relocated front upper control arm pivot points, Koni adjustable racing shocks all around, anti-hop rear axle torque arms, one-inch front sway bar and quicker steering (19:1 and 3.25 turns lock-to-lock versus the factory optional 21:1 and 3.5 turns). Brakes were 11.3-inch discs in front with competition pads and 10-inch x 2.5-inch drums with metallic shoes in the rear, and the full-race cars also got brake cooling scoops at all four wheels. Goodyear 7.75x15 Blue Dot high-performance tires were standard equipment on both versions, while Shelby-designed aluminum wheels were optionally available in widths up to seven inches.

Under the hood was a 289-cubic-inch engine with its output increased from the normal 271 to a more fitting 306 hp via a high-rise aluminum manifold, Holley 715 cfm, center-float, four-barrel carburetor, tubular headers and a straight-through, glass-pack exhaust system terminating just forward of the rear wheels. A larger radiator and a 6.5-quart aluminum oil pan with internal baffles were added to improve engine cooling and lubrication, and the package was topped off with a pair of impressive-looking Shelby finned-aluminum rocker covers. Racing versions were built to order with ported and polished heads, higher compression, special camshafts, blueprinting and other modifications, some putting out close to the 350 horsepower the car's name implied. Borg-Warner T-10 four-speed transmissions were used with a limited-slip 3.89:1 rear axle in street cars and 3.70, 4.11 and 4.33 ratios additionally available for racers.

Press and enthusiast reaction to the GT-350 was predictably ecstatic. "This is what the high-performance Mustang should have been in the first place" was the consensus. It was fast, loud, stiff and genuinely exciting—in effect, an off-the-shelf road racer at a relatively affordable $4547. At last Ford had a viable muscle-car competitor, although it was available at first only through certain choice dealers who also carried Shelby's Cobra sports cars. And, to the delight of Ford Division racing people, it immediately dominated SCCA's B-Production class in the capable hands of Ken Miles, racer/writer Jerry Titus, Shelby engineer Chuck Cantwell, Bob Johnson, Mark Donohue and others, and went on to win National Championships in

The Bertone Mustang, created on commission by Automobile Quarterly.

External changes to '66 Mustang were few. Base models received revised wheel covers and side ornamentation, and large grille bars were dropped so emblem could "float."

1965, '66 and '67.

It was fortunate that the car was so good right out of the box, because race boss Jacque Passino and his group were certainly being kept busy on many other fronts. Mustangs had replaced Falcons in international performance rallying, had won the 1964 Tour de France contest over stiff competition and were doing well in other events worldwide. The Indy engine project was going full force, with Jim Clark's Ford-powered Lotus winning the famed 500 in 1965, Ford stock cars were dominating NASCAR competition, Shelby's Cobras were humbling Ferraris in international GT racing, and the fast but fragile GT-40's had been joined by a handful of awesome 7.0-liter Ford Mark I's in the company's quest of a win at Le Mans and the World Manufacturer's title. Although a fairly low-priority project, there was also limited factory participation (through performance-oriented dealers) in the fast-growing American sport of drag racing.

Back home in Dearborn, Ford stylists were already hard at work developing the next generation Mustangs for 1967, and in their spare time were still playing with Mustang-based two-seater concepts and the occasional show car to complement Mustang displays on the auto show circuit. One of the nicest independently-produced Mustang show cars, however, was designed and built by Carrozzeria Bertone of Turin, Italy, on commission from *Automobile Quarterly* magazine. This sleek beauty served to demonstrate what could happen when tasteful Italian styling was applied to the basic Mustang chassis and drivetrain—and it, too, became a fixture in the Ford Total Performance traveling road show both here and in Europe. Introduced at the April 1966 New York International Automobile Show, it easily took "Best of Show" honors and became the subject of a *Road & Track* feature story, among others.

On the other end of the car-enthusiast spectrum, *American Rodding* magazine awarded a special version of the 2 + 2 fastback Mustang its "Perfect Performance Car for 1965" title. Called the Tasca 505 Mustang, this car was twentieth in a series of personalized cars made to order for Bob Tasca, president of Tasca Ford in Providence, Rhode Island. Reportedly generating some 505 hp, the Tasca 505 Mustang's engine was stroked to 325 cubic inches and fed by dual four-barrel Holley carburetors on a high-rise manifold. It was capable of turning under-twelve-second quarter-miles at more than 120 mph. External modifications included a two-and-a-half-inch lengthening at the rear end, European-style rectangular headlamps and blue anodized wheels, while the interior was customized with Mustang-embossed leather seats, Persian rug carpeting and a Shelby American instrument cluster.

After seventeen record-breaking months as a 1965 model, Mustang

GT, 2+2 and luxury models had no rear fender "scoop" ornament as before. Taillamps on all versions were changed to three individual lenses, and GT had flip-open gas cap.

debuted in 1966 trim on September 16th, 1965. Understandably, the changes were few—chrome grille bars were gone and the running horse emblem now "floated" ahead of a fine horizontal bar grille, the side scoop ornament was revised to include three horizontal bars (similar to those on the original Ash/Oros Cougar clay model and the earliest full-size drawings), and the wheel covers and fuel filler cap were revised for more of a competition look, the GT's gas cap getting a real pop-open feature. Inside, the door, seat and instrument panel trim were revised, and the five-dial GT cluster became standard on all models. New options included a stereosonic tape system and deluxe retracting seat belts (with a thirty-second warning light). Also, the thirteen-inch wheels and tires formerly standard on six-cylinder models were replaced by fourteen-inchers.

Shelby's GT-350 was also little changed for 1966, but it did get functional side scoops for rear brake cooling, a lovely plexi-glass window replacing the C-pillar louvers, a quieter exhaust system that extended all the way rearward and a slightly softer suspension package. New options included automatic transmission, Detroit Locker rear axle, fold-down rear seat and even a Paxton supercharger said to increase the engine's output to more than 400 hp. Also, while all 1965 GT-350's were white with blue stripes, the '66 color selection increased to include white stripes on blue, red, black or green. Nineteen sixty-six was also the year of those famous Hertz "Rent-a-Racer" Shelbys.

At 11:02 a.m. on Wednesday, February 23rd, 1966—less than two years after the first production Mustang rolled off Ford's Dearborn assembly line—the millionth Mustang was completed. This happy event broke another Falcon record and was celebrated by a party at which Capt. Stanley Tucker, a St. John's, Newfoundland airplane pilot and owner of Mustang Number One was presented with Mustang Number 1,000,001 in exchange for his historic car. The one-million mark in sales was expected to be passed before Mustang's second birthday on April 17th.

Not only was the car immensely successful in its first two years on the market, it was also immensely profitable for the Ford Motor Company. With the average Mustang going out with nearly $400 in options, gross profits on the car totaled something like $1.1 billion over the two-year period. Lee Iacocca, Don Frey, Hal Sperlich and almost everyone associated with the program were quickly promoted. Mustang single-handedly had created a brand-new, highly profitable market segment; and Lincoln-Mercury Division was preparing its own pony car (wearing Joe Oros' Cougar name), Chevrolet was rushing its Chevy II-based Camaro into being, and other imitators were soon to follow.

5.

ENCORE

An interesting and often frustrating thing about the auto business, particularly in the days of two-year model change cycles, was that you had to go back and design a successor to a new model even before you knew how the public would react to the original. In the Mustang's case the April mid-year introduction helped, but little did the growing ranks of Mustangers know that almost as soon as the original had hit the streets, its hard-working creators were already toiling back in Dearborn on the second-generation Ford pony for 1967.

By early summer 1964 there were several '67 Mustang proposals on paper and in clay, and the designers, engineers and product planners were hustling from meeting room to styling studio and back, scratching their collective heads, biting their fingernails and furrowing their brows over Act Two. Obviously the car had been an instant hit, but what was its staying power? Would it be a fad and lose momentum in a year or two? Should its successor follow the same tracks, build on the same theme, or should it be bolder...or more conservative?

And what would the competition do? Chevrolet was in the habit of trying to one-up almost instantly anything Ford came up with that looked promising. What would Chevy's "Mustang" look like? How would it perform? And how soon would it be brought to market? Chrysler already had its own Plymouth Barracuda, but it was little more than a quickly-concocted glassback Valiant. What would the second-generation Barracuda be like? Ford had discovered and exploited a brand-new market niche; but the need for such a product had seemed so obvious to Iacocca and his group. Could the others be far behind with serious competition?

"At that point in time we kept wondering when we were going to see some competition, and we were continually amazed that we didn't hear of anything going on," recalls Tom Feaheny, who was chief engineer on the '67 Mustang. "It was a long time before we knew the Camaro was coming, and we were quite amazed that it seemed to take so long."

Introduced September 30th, 1966—the fastback Mustang for '67.

Over at Chevrolet, meanwhile, the young bucks who wanted a fast answer to Mustang were experiencing the same disappointment and frustration that had plagued Iacocca during the early stages of his pet program: They couldn't sell it to upper management. GM brass was taking a conservative wait-and-see attitude. They had just gone through an expensive redesign and development effort on the second-generation Corvair for '65, a beautiful creation that insiders were already calling the "poor man's Corvette." Chevrolet already had five separate car lines (big Chevy, Chevelle, Chevy II, Corvair and Corvette) to wrestle with, and the last thing needed, management people felt, was a sixth. Surely the good-looking, sporty, sophisticated, fully-independent suspension, turbocharged Corvair could deal effectively with Ford's new sporty small car. Or could it?

By August, however, when Mustang production hit 100,000—fully a month before the public debut of the new Corvair—management's resolve dissolved. Chevrolet would have just two years to come up with a competitive Chevy II-based ponycar.

In October a group of young GM engineers, fresh out of college, assembled to hear a stirring presentation by styling vice-president Bill Mitchell. After the talk, they were invited to ask questions. "When will GM have an answer to the Mustang?" one inevitably queried.

"We *have* an answer to the Mustang," Mitchell shot back. "It's called Corvair." So secret was the fledgling Camaro project at that time that GM management wouldn't even drop a hint to its own young engineers.

"It was a long ways down the road," says Feaheny, "before we were aware that they were coming after us. The party line at GM was that the Corvair *was* their answer to the Mustang, and we were kind of believing it. Of course they didn't want their dealer body thinking that it wasn't." Perhaps it could have been, except for one major problem: It was a six-cylinder car, and even a turbocharged six-cylinder couldn't match the power, the torque, even the sound or the image of Ford's Mustang V-8. The '65 Corvair was pretty, it was sophisticated, it handled beautifully, and it may have been a poor man's Porsche... but not a poor man's Corvette, or any man's (or woman's) Mustang.

"At the time the '67 was planned, we really didn't have any idea that the original was such a winner," remembers Ross Humphries, who had taken over as chief Mustang product planner under Hal Sperlich. "Things did look awfully rosy, but we didn't know how long it was going to last.

"Hal's feeling was that in the past when we had brought out a new car that was a winner, we had kind of sat back and rested on our laurels and didn't do enough to upgrade the car and perpetuate it, to keep the momentum going. And soon our friends across town would come back and do us one better. Hal's philosophy on the '67 Mustang was

1967
1967

A variety of front treatments were tried early in the '67 program.

to one-up the original in every respect...model availability, options, handling, performance, braking, comfort, quietness...even appearance where we could without making a major change."

Says chief engineer Feaheny: "It was an opportunity to do a lot of refinement work. The first Mustang had surprised a lot of people, including Ford people, with its success. At the time it was developed, there were misgivings within the company as to whether it was even a worthwhile project. Frankly, the amount of engineering effort in that car was not as great as it could have been. It did not get the full-blown effort it really deserved, but was a success in spite of that. By mid-'64 we had a car that was a sensation in the marketplace, but we were getting criticized for some of its weaker aspects. We really wanted to do the job right the second time around."

There were four major thrusts to the '67 engineering program. First was the general refinement and development effort, concentrating especially on ride and handling. Second was adaptation of '66 model Falcon and Fairlane chassis componentry (with coil springs above the upper cross members in front), which was considerably improved over the '64-'65 Falcon pieces used in the first Mustang. Third was to bulge, stretch and strengthen the car enough to accommodate Ford's big-block 390-cubic-inch V-8 engine and the associated heavier-duty hardware it would need throughout. Pontiac's GTO had touched off the muscle-car wars, and Mustang would need more power and torque than even its lively high-performance 289 could deliver to remain competitive.

All this was pretty well cut and dried. The engineers and product planners knew where they were going and set out with clear directions on how to get there. Not so over at styling, where design executive Gail Halderman's group was struggling with different concepts under the general directive to "change it but don't change it."

"At the time we were doing some of this we really didn't know how successful the original was going to be," says he, echoing Ross Humphries' comments. "We knew by the time it was finally approved, but not when we were starting the project. We did several proposed designs because at first we were just not sure where the car should go.

"Back in those days," Halderman continues, "Iacocca appeared daily. The Mustang was his baby, and he watched it very carefully. We really didn't do anything on that car that he wasn't fully aware of and part of."

By September 1964 three clay models had been completed, two hardtops and one fastback. One hardtop retained the original Mustang's formal, angular roofline and proportions, while the other was more rounded and "soft" in contour. The fastback featured a bold rear-window louver treatment, but its sleek shape was more sexy and less "hairy" than the original. Several front, side and rear treatments were tried on these models, most of them attractive and appealing, but none seemed to achieve the desired effect. They might have been nice-looking small sporty cars, but they were not Mustangs.

Light car design executive Don Kopka, in an October 1966 presentation to a Society of Automotive Engineers group, described some of the gyrations the '67 project went through before arriving at an acceptable solution:

> Our mission was to refine and improve the breed without losing any of the Mustang's personality and without any sheet metal changes that would destroy the strong identity established by the million-and-a-half Mustangs that were expected to be on the road before the 1967 model first saw the light of day. Some of the things we tried were a little crazy and a little extreme. Part of our business always seems to involve reaching way out and then backing up by degrees until the happiest solution is found.
>
> In one of our early exercises, we tried double hop-up fender forms. It was an interesting theme, but it seemed to chop up the car and destroy the classic Mustang proportions...
>
> We tried an extremely simple design with straight-through lines. No hop-up, no bodyside sculpturing. Once we finished the model, it just didn't look like a Mustang. It was attractive enough, but it looked more like a small sedan than a sports car.
>
> In our first crack at the 2+2 model for 1967, we continued to pursue the semi-fastback style of the 1965 fastback Mustang; but it was softer, with more flowing forms. The louvered backlight might be considered a bit much, but this model had many very interesting aspects.
>
> However, under the influence of competition cars such as the Ford GT, we decided that a full fastback would be more suggestive of performance...The louvered vent gates in the C-pillar were dropped in favor of open grillework.
>
> The most significant element of one model was a character line running the full length of the body. We discovered that it detracted from the strong feeling of the rear wheel opening by interfering with the hop-up configuration of the rear quarter panel.
>
> We tried large single taillights and a convex form in the lower back panel. But people know the Mustang by its three individual taillights, so we got off this theme without delay.
>
> Another model retained the straight-through character line and introduced a new sculptured look leading to the

Proposed designs ranged from the gently curved to the sharply angular.

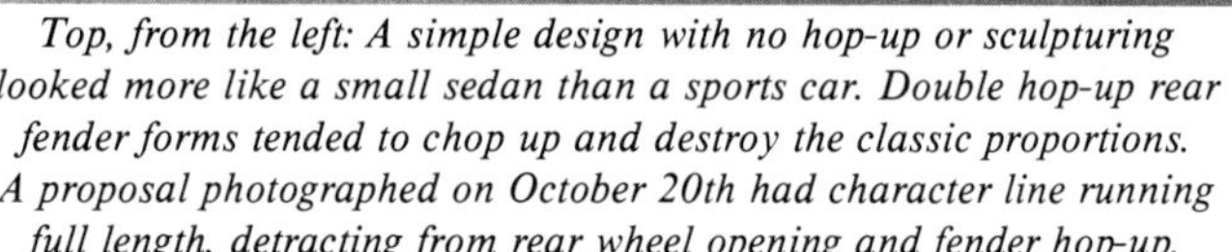

Top, from the left: A simple design with no hop-up or sculpturing looked more like a small sedan than a sports car. Double hop-up rear fender forms tended to chop up and destroy the classic proportions. A proposal photographed on October 20th had character line running full length, detracting from rear wheel opening and fender hop-up.

Center, from the left: Photographed in November and close to final shape except for straight-through character line and Ford GT-style side sculpture. In December, the front was nearly finished, with designers still looking at different sculpturing and character lines. The final design, same profile as original but deeper sculpturing.

Below, from the left: First crack at '67 fastback had soft, flowing forms and louvered backlight. Under influence of Ford GT race cars, second 2+2 design had full fastback, aggressive side sculpture, competition-style fuel filler cap. The '67 fastback GT as it was finally to be, same look but broader-shouldered than in 1965-1966.

> scoop. But it was a case of too many design elements conflicting in the rear quarter area.
>
> By the time the front-end theme was just about baked in, we still were evaluating alternate side details, including a different way of ending the character line in the quarter panel. All the while, we wanted to preserve the one-third/two-thirds proportions characteristic of the Mustang silhouette.
>
> The result of all that effort is the approved 1967 model. We think it is obviously Mustang, yet a definite improvement of the breed. The profile retains the same classic proportions, but the sculpturing leading to the air scoop ahead of the rear wheels has a more built-in appearance. The rear quarter panel flares out more boldly to encase the scoop.
>
> The new Mustang is broader and more solid looking than its predecessors, with a wider stance and more form to the bodysides. The familiar running horse emblem is framed in an enlarged grille opening, and on GT models auxiliary driving lights are mounted on the horizontal bar that extends from each side of the frame.

What the designers had done of course was come right back to the original style. It was a bit larger, a bit hairier, a bit "softer" (more rounded) and a bit fuller in the fenders to accommodate the added wheel and tire widths for '67-'68—but it had the same mouthy grille and swept-back headlamp theme, except for the longer fastback line the same roof and window treatments, and the same basic side scoop and rear end appearance. Nobody could mistake it for anything else. It was indeed "changed but not changed," because as Iacocca had seen more and more Mustangs on the road, as dealer cash registers had kept ringing up more and more sales, as Mustang mania had sunk deeper and deeper into the country's collective youthful consciousness, it had become increasingly apparent that the car was *right*. It would have been downright foolish to mess too much with such a good thing.

"We really took a number of cracks at it," says Halderman, "but the way it turned out was to take the theme that had been established and make more of it. For '67 the theme revolved around more performance, so we made it a little stronger in appearance all over. The side scallop got deeper, for instance, and the grille and rear panel were enlarged. But we were very adamant about not changing the side fender/quarter panel profile...that rear hop-up look."

Tom Feaheny's engineers, meanwhile, were busy on the ride and handling program, in addition to many other improvements under the new skin. "There was an awful lot of time and effort spent on the '67

Mustang," he relates, "not in dramatic things, but mostly in taking advantage of a better package that had become available in '66 to do a lot of refinement work in keeping with the car's image and character.

"The '67 was tightened up quite a bit, both in base form and with the handling package, and a lot of development went into it. There had been evolutionary changes to the original, of course, but '67 was the first year we had a chance to take another look at the whole package. The direction we had was to make it a little firmer with less roll, but still with a good ride.

"I think we've always felt that the ultimate engineering goal in the chassis area is to have a car that's comfortable, that won't jar your teeth loose, but also will handle safely. The Mustang, being a low, sporty type of car, was a delight to work on. The image was there to let us go a little firmer than you would for the average soft, spongy, full-size American car and to give it a lot better handling...but not to the point of a teeth-jarring ride.

"Given the more primitive hardware of the day, I think the '67 Mustang was a really fine-handling car...more than just cornering ability, but a feeling of real security for the driver...the ability to maneuver the car with confidence, knowing where it's going to go."

Asked whether his group had benefited directly from any of the hardware or geometry changes that had been incorporated into the Shelby cars, Feaheny replies that none of the Shelby hardware found its way back into the production car, "but we did benefit from the interchange of ideas back and forth. We didn't specifically pick up what Carroll had done...in our view he'd gone too far for a road machine...but the direction of the work he'd done and the results he had achieved did influence the development of our car. We did make some changes that were intermediate between where we had been and where he had gone.

"We were influenced by the Shelby development, but we were critical of it from the standpoint of a street machine because of the harsh ride and because it wasn't forgiving enough. He had modified the suspension geometry, for instance, to change the toe curve, but he had done it in a very extreme fashion that we thought compromised ride...and while it made the handling superb for a race driver, we were concerned because it changed the handling to the point where it was no longer forgiving.

"In developing handling packages on a production car, we always want to insure that it is not too easy for the amateur driver to get into trouble. Some modified cars are fine for a professional who keeps both hands on the wheel and pays attention, but if you make a mistake and get a wheel off the pavement, you'd better know what you're doing.

"We want to get a car that's forgiving for the inattentive driver as much as possible so that if he runs into a pothole or gets a tire off the

Above: Still experimenting with the fastback design in January 1965.

road or has to make a sudden maneuver, he doesn't all of a sudden have more than he can handle. We're reluctant to go into handling suspensions that require the kind of attention to driving that some of the racing versions do in order to get the last tenth of a second in lap time."

Another major project, of course, was designing around the larger, heavier 390-cubic-inch engine. Besides the need to strengthen everything top-to-bottom, bumper-to-bumper to take the big block's added weight and low-end torque, there was a tremendous weight distribution problem to be dealt with.

"We did have trouble trying to make that package handle because it was so nose-heavy," says Feaheny. "I think all of us would have preferred to stay with the 289 engine rather than going to a 390, but it turned out to be a very acceptable package and handled quite well, although it did have some light-rear-end characteristics. We ended up with a very large stabilizer bar on the front to control the roll, and then made adjustments at the rear to keep the thing in balance.

"In the end, we felt objectively, in fact, that the 390 Mustang was a lot better than some of the other muscle cars of that day with great big engines up front and bad weight distribution, which were really quite bad for handling. The first 390 Mustangs had lots of torque at the low end and would go down the quarter-mile in a hurry, yet you could take them around a corner and not be embarrassed at all."

Over in the product planning department, Ross Humphries' group, among other things, was reacting to some of the few customer complaints about the original car. "Not enough rear seat room was a basic problem with that sort of package," says he. "I recall that we tried to improve the back seat knee room in the '67, and we shoved the back seat rearward to at least be able to reflect a minimum of improvement in legroom. Front seat travel was another thing...we had a fix out in the field for long-legged people with the original car, and we tried to do a better job the second time around. Also, I was indirectly involved with a disc brake development program to help the people who wanted to go racing."

As a result of all this work and much, much more, the '67 Mustang that appeared in dealer showrooms Friday, September 30th, 1966 was a far better car than the original. Nearly every system, from suspension to brakes to steering to climate control had been thoroughly redesigned and improved. The styling was hairier, yet still distinctively Mustang; ride, handling and driving characteristics were better; there was a wider selection of engines and drivetrain components and several important new options, including speed control, a Tilt-Away steering wheel (borrowed from Thunderbird) that not only adjusted for angle but also swept up and away when the door was opened, AM/FM stereo radio and AM with stereo tape, front power disc brakes (standard with the GT equipment group), fully-integrated air conditioning and an interior decor group that included simulated woodgrain on the instrument panel and a sexy overhead console with individual map lights.

Wheelbase remained the same at 108 inches, but track was increased two inches to 58 inches front and rear. Overall height was up a half-inch to add a little interior headroom, width was up 2.7 inches to accommodate the larger wheels and tires, overall length had grown by two inches, trunk and interior dimensions were slightly increased and the base six-cylinder hardtop's weight was up some 140 pounds compared to the original's 2562 pounds. Mustang was

Below: The GT with quad exhausts and textured appliqué on rear body panel. The convertible with wide-oval "sports" tires on styled steel wheels. Inside the '67.

still a bargain, however, at less than a dollar a pound: $2461.46 base.

In addition to the larger grille opening, revised side "scoops" and other styling changes already mentioned, the '67 with exterior decor equipment featured a special hood with twin indentations housing engine compartment vents and turn signals visible from the cockpit, GT models got quad exhaust tips, and fastbacks sported a cleaner twelve-louver roof vent design. The rear panel was now concave (Ford called it "performance oriented") with a "knock-off-hub" fuel filler cap and could be decorated with flat black paint or a choice of grey or body-color textured appliqués with various optional appearance packages.

Wide-oval "sports" tires were available on V-8-equipped cars and standard with the 390 engine. Seats and interior trim also were redesigned, and the new instrument panel featured speedometer/odometer and alternator/oil pressure gauges (or optional tachometer) in two large, round dials, plus three smaller dials for fuel and temperature gauges and the optional clock, all under a sun-shading "twin eyebrow"-design padded panel. The optional center console now swept upward to merge with the dashboard, and an available convenience panel added reminder lights for door ajar, parking brake, low fuel and seat belts.

Engine choices were the 200-cubic-inch six, a 200 hp "Challenger" 289 V-8, a 225 hp "Challenger Special" 289, the 271 hp "Cobra" 289 and the 320 hp "Thunderbird Special" 390 V-8. Transmissions were a fully-synchronized three-speed floor shift, a four-speed close ratio manual, and the new "Select-shift Cruise-O-Matic" that allowed manual shift control for the first time with a Ford automatic. In '67 only, cars equipped with this transmission and the GT appearance package were called "GT-A" for "GT-Automatic."

New polyethylene-filled ball-joint sockets helped reduce steering effort and increase precision, and the turning circle diameter was reduced from 42 to 37.1 feet. The new linkage also permitted a reduction in ratio from 27:1 to 25.3:1 with manual steering and from 21.4:1 to 20.3:1 on power steering-equipped cars. New-design window and door seals reduced interior wind noise, and a new window regulator improved side window stability and reduced the cranking effort. Other new-for-'67 features included an optional all-glass, double-folding convertible rear window, reversible keys and a keyless locking system, and foot-operated windshield washers (now standard).

A long list of new safety features also became standard equipment on the '67 model, some in response to government edicts and some on the company's own initiative. Included were a dual hydraulic braking system (one master cylinder for the front brakes, another for the rears) plus a brake trouble warning light; padded armrests, windshield

you agree with Carroll Shelby
t good driving is a fine art? Then
se all new 1967 Shelby GT cars
custom-crafted for you. By
orporating his competi-
n-proved design and
ineering features in
Mustang, Carroll
lby has created two
que road performers
carry the *lowest* price
s of *any* true GT cars.
he GT 500 features a brand-new
ra LeMans dual 4-barrel engine,
eloped from the V-8 that
ered the 1966 LeMans winners.
350 power comes from the high
ormance Cobra 289 with free-
athing Shelby induction and
aust. All-synchro four-speed box
or heavy-duty Cruise-O-Matic are optional on both cars.

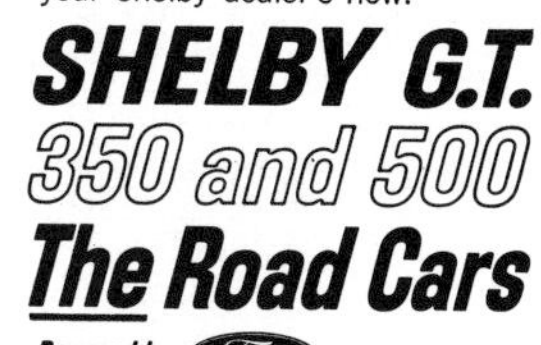

These goodies make your Shelby GT one of the *safest* cars you can drive: Massive disc front and air-cooled drum rear brakes. Shelby-modified suspension for 30% less cornering roll. Crisp 16-to-1 power steering*. LeMans-proved wide tread nylon super-safety tires. Integral roll bar*, double shoulder harness*, quick-release seat belts and eye level brake and turn indicator lights.

Naturally, you'll find true GT features. Unique Shelby styling. Luxury interior with bucket seats, complete instrumentation, wood-rim steering wheel, folding rear seat*.

You should expect a lot from a car built by America's first F.I.A. World's Champion. You'll get all you expect when you drive a Shelby GT 350 or GT 500. One is waiting at your Shelby dealer's now.

SHELBY G.T.
350 and 500
The Road Cars

Powered by Ford

Shelby American, Inc., 6501 West Imperial Highway, Los Angeles, Calif. 90009. Builders of the Cobra, Manufacturers of Cobra high performance parts and kits.

*optional at extra cost

eft, from the top: Mach II, running prototype for proposed Shelby Cobra replacement. Allegro II. Autolite-I, the Bonneville Salt Flats car. Super Mustang dragster.

pillars, sun visors and instrument panel; a lane-change feature in the turn signal switch; door locks that could not be overridden by the inside handles; breakaway day/night mirror and remote control outside mirror; seat-belt reminder light and pushbutton buckle releases; four-way emergency flashers; thick laminate safety glass windshield; backup lights; tire safety rims; corrosion-resistant brake lines; and front seat anchors for the optional shoulder harnesses.

Nineteen sixty-seven also was an interesting year for the Shelby Mustang, because it marked the beginning of a more active Ford Division involvement with the car—and for that reason some purists insist that post-'66 Shelbys were not really Shelbys at all. Both front and rear body sections were replaced with racy fiberglass units designed by Ford's Chuck McHose in conjunction with Pete Brock and others from the Shelby organization. In front, the hood scoop was enlarged and the grille opening enclosed by a formidably deep cowling. Twin high-beam headlamps were mounted in the grille's center—except in states where the law required wider spacing. The rear was distinguished by a very aerodynamic-looking formed-in spoiler and huge horizontal Cougar-style taillamps, while impressive functional scoops replaced both the production fastback roof's ventilation louvers and the fake fender ducts, the latter for rear brake cooling. The first hundred or so '67's even had a gimmicky brake/turn signal light behind these side scoops.

Underneath, the '67 Shelbys got larger Goodyear wide-tread tires and computer-designed suspension refinements, but lost the traction bars, limited-slip differential and Koni shocks, which were replaced by less expensive Gabriel adjustables. A padded, racing-type interior rollbar protected the occupants and was fitted with attachments for inertia-reel shoulder harnesses.

By the car's third birthday, April 17th, 1967, the others (especially Camaro) had gained in strength, but Mustang still led Camaro, Firebird, Barracuda and Cougar combined in total sales. Nearly 1.5 million Mustangs had been built and sold by that date, and there was no indication that its popularity was waning. "The Mustang has been the Cinderella car of the industry since the day we introduced it," said Don Frey, who had succeeded Iacocca as Ford Division general manager. "Sales on the car exceeded our expectations from the start, and I'm happy to say the demand shows no sign of slackening." Through March, Mustang had maintained 5.2 percent of the total new-car market compared to 2.1 percent for Chevy's Camaro and about 4.0 percent for the other ponycars combined. Retail value of the 1,434,969 Mustangs sold through the end of March was almost $5 *billion*, and the average option load had climbed from $358 in early 1964 to more than $500 per car in 1967.

Just one day after the third birthday celebration, *Car and Driver* announced that the '67 390 Mustang GT had been selected as outstanding car in its class in the magazine's annual reader's poll. "This is a most significant and deserving recognition for the Mustang GT," said *C/D* editor Steve Smith. It was the third consecutive year that Mustang had won a *Car and Driver* readers' poll award.

To show the world that Ford was still thinking on the subject of two-seater sports cars, an exotic mid-engine prototype called "Mach II" was unveiled at the winter 1967 Chicago auto show. Styled personally by design chief Gene Bordinat and produced by Roy Lunn's Special Vehicles group (of mid-engine Mustang I and Ford GT race car fame) in conjunction with Kar Kraft (Ford's outside racing shop), the Mach II was built on a modified Mustang underbody and used standard Mustang components wherever feasible, including bumpers, front suspension, front and rear brakes and high-performance 289 engine. Not a show car, it was an actual engineering prototype ordered by Don Frey to examine the possibility of producing such a vehicle to replace Shelby's two-seat Cobra—but it never got beyond the consideration stage.

On the other hand, a stylish, ninety-nine-inch-wheelbase, front-engine roadster which took to the show circuit beginning in mid-September was strictly show. Named "Allegro II," it was called by Ford a "second generation version of the original Allegro," the fastback coupe that had started life in 1961 as the clay model "Avventura," which had helped lead to the original Mustang.

Mustang production in model year '67 totalled 472,121 units, well over half that of the full-size Ford and twice the number of intermediate Fairlanes built. The general industry sales slowdown had affected Mustang to a lesser degree than most other cars, and the total sold since mid-'64 had continued to climb to more than 1.6 million.

As expected, Mustang was little changed for '68. The additional required safety features (collapsible steering column; side marker lights; redesigned interior door handles, window cranks, control knobs and coat hoods; padded console and front seatbacks, locking seatbacks with release levers) and Phase One emissions controls were added, exterior and interior trim and detailing were revised, engine and option choices were expanded, and the front suspension was further refined for improved ride and handling.

In the styling department, a concentric chrome ring was added just inside the grille opening, the horizontal grille bars were eliminated from GT models, GT stripes became a tapered affair following the bodyside contour lines, the side scoop was simplified, the side emblem got script lettering, the popular sculptured hood with built-in vents and turn signals became standard on all models, and the fuel-filler cap was changed to a new-design twist-off type. Inside, a new padded, color-keyed steering wheel, redesigned bucket seats, new trim patterns and a wider color choice were the major revisions. Finally, a new convertible top boot was stretchable, color-keyed and had hidden fasteners.

Engine choices now ranged from the standard 115 hp, 200-cubic-inch six to a new 390–horse, 427-cubic-inch V-8 with lightweight pistons and super-duty crankshaft and connecting rods (which, unfortunately, was available with automatic transmission only). Between these extremes were a mild 195 hp 289 V-8, a new 230 hp 302 V-8 and the very strong 325 hp 390. Emission controls were called "Improved Combustion System" (IMCO) on automatic-equipped cars and "Thermactor Emission Control System" with manual transmissions. Two 289-cubic-inch engines were dropped for '68, including the high-performance 271 hp version.

Among the new options were a rear window defogger, a collapsible

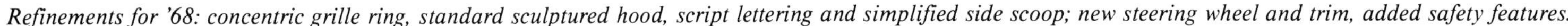

Refinements for '68: concentric grille ring, standard sculptured hood, script lettering and simplified side scoop; new steering wheel and trim, added safety features.

1968

Above: Early 1968 GT-350's and 500's nearing completion on A.O. Smith Company assembly line in Ionia, Michigan. Below: The hood scoop was moved forward, center lights replaced by outboard-mounted fog lamps and a convertible was added for the 1968 Shelby line.

spare tire to improve luggage capacity and a "Sports Trim Group" that included a two-tone hood (body color and flat black), woodgrain instrument panel appliqué, wheel opening moldings, vinyl seat inserts (except on the convertible), and styled steel wheels and wide oval tires on V-8 equipped cars. In addition, the optional power front disc brakes were improved, and both they and Michelin radial tires (introduced in limited quantities in mid-'67) became available with any V-8 engine. "The radial tires didn't get a whole lot of notoriety," chief engineer Tom Feaheny points out, "but that was the first step in what became a total revolution in tires for the American industry. It was one hell of a development."

Nineteen sixty-eight marked the beginning of the end for the once-mighty Shelby Mustangs. Production was moved from the West Coast Shelby factory to an A.O. Smith Company facility at Livonia, Michigan. Ford Division wanted more control over the cars, and Shelby himself was increasingly busy with racing and other projects. Styling changes were minimal—longer hood scoop, revised taillamps, Lucas fog lamps replacing the center-mounted high beams—but the GT-350's gutsy, high-revving 289 engine was replaced with a 250 hp 302, the new emission controls hurt performance of both models, and their weights and prices were up from '67. A sexy convertible version with a built-in, padded rollbar added new interest, however, and people still liked the image and appearance enough to buy a record 4450 '68 Shelbys.

In November, Ford added an economy fastback "Mustang E" model with an extra-large torque converter automatic and super-low 2.33:1 rear axle coupled to a new 155 hp, 250-cubic-inch six. Near the other end of the size spectrum, a 280 hp, two-barrel carb 390 V-8 joined the lineup a few days later. There was also an interesting Shelby-esque appearance package developed for the hardtop, complete with fog lamps, exposed turn-screw hood latches, side stripes and scoop, rear spoiler and Cougar/Shelby-style taillamps. Design studio photos show this car with "GT/SC" identification for "GT/Sport Coupe," but the package ultimately was promoted and sold in California-only as the "GT/CS" California Special.

Most exciting for performance enthusiasts was the mid-year introduction of Ford's 428 Cobra-Jet engine, which came with a vacuum-actuated ram-air hood scoop, flat-black center-hood section and GT-style side striping. Rated horsepower of the Cobra Jet was 335 at 5400 rpm, while torque was a pavement-ripping 440 lb/ft at 3400 rpm. The 10.6:1 compression ratio 428 made use of Ford's high-performance 427 cylinder heads, valve springs and dampers, "header-type" exhaust manifolds, a 735 CFM Holley four-barrel carburetor and oversize intake and exhaust ports.

Available with either automatic or four-speed manual transmission

Left: Mustang became a bona fide muscle car with addition of the Cobra Jet package with functional ram-air hood scoop in 1968½. Above: The Shelby-esque styling package became the GT/CS (for California Special) in production and was marketed on West Coast only. Below: Capable of sub-twelve-second quarter-miles as modified and driven by "Dyno" Don Nicholson and others, Cobra Jet Mustangs were soon moved from SS/F to the faster SS/E in NHRA drag racing. The Shelby with Cobra Jet was GT-500 KR, for "King of the Road."

Above: David Pearson (#15 Cougar) was fast qualifier, Jerry Titus (#17 Mustang) the winner of the June 1967 Trans-Am at Mid-Ohio. Below: Jim Adams gets fuel and advice from Shelby mechanic Cantwell during race. Page opposite: '68 Trans-Am trophy and, from the left, Jerry Titus, SCCA's John Bishop, Carroll Shelby, Jacque Passino.

driving through a standard 3.50:1 or optional limited-slip 3.91 or 4.30:1 rear axle, the Cobra Jet also came with Goodyear Polyglas wide-oval tires and its left rear shock absorber moved behind the axle to reduce wheel hop on acceleration. All three Mustang body styles could be Cobra Jet-equipped for $420.96 over the 289 V-8, and they were covered by Ford's then-current five-year, 50,000-mile warranty.

Shelbys with this new 428 were called "GT-500 KR" for "King of the Road" and were quicker than the "ordinary" GT-500's in spite of their twenty-horsepower lower rating on paper. Seems Ford had underrated the Cobra Jet in hopes of gaining a classification advantage in NHRA drag racing competition. It worked. The Cobra Jet Mustang, capable of sub-twelve-second quarter miles in drag-race trim, was initially placed in the SS/F class—but later moved to the tougher SS/E category.

The first Mustang ever seen in road racing competition, early in 1964, was a 1964½ hardtop on the tight, twisty Waterford Hills course near Detroit. To say it was less than impressive would be charitable. The small V-8 pulled it smartly down Waterford's only real straightaway, but its braking and handling were simply awful—and it was embarrassingly beaten after a close twenty-five-lap contest by, of all things, a well-modified VW Beetle. The driver was Bill Clawson, a Ford engineer doing a bit of development testing on his

own, who would go on to help significantly in whipping Ford's new sporty car into a respectable road-racing machine for himself and others to campaign in SCCA's A-Sedan amateur classification.

But while the amateurs were soon carving a reputation for Mustang in SCCA trophy racing, Shelby and Jacque Passino were pressing for a professional series as a showplace for their cars' talents, one as meaningful to sporty-car people as NASCAR was to the family-sedan crowd. With competing ponycars forthcoming from GM, Chrysler and even gutsy little AMC, SCCA was not long in sensing the potential of such a series, and the Trans-American Sedan Championship was born at Sebring, Florida on March 25th, 1966.

While this first event was taken by Jochen Rindt in an Alfa Romeo GTA, the early lead was disputed by Bob Tullius in a Dodge Dart, Charlie Rainville and Scott Harvey in Barracudas (all factory-supported) and none other than A.J. Foyt in a privately-entered Mustang. Although Foyt's Mustang broke after thirty-two laps, and the other competitive American cars were slowed by tire wear and other troubles, the race was a hit and the Trans-Am series was on its way. Six more 1966 meetings produced four wins for Mustang and a manufacturers' title for Ford.

The following year saw the likes of Dan Gurney, Peter Revson and David Pearson combining for four victories in factory Mercury Cougars, Mark Donohue taking three in a Roger Penske-prepared Camaro and magazine editor Jerry Titus winning four in the Ford-backed Mustang. After a season-long battle, Ford squeaked by Mercury for its second series championship by a mere two points. Among the many other name drivers who turned up in the 1967 Trans-Am were Parnelli Jones, Lee Roy Yarborough, Cale Yarborough, Milt Minter, Bob Bondurant, George Follmer, Jerry Grant and Peter Gregg. In just its second season, SCCA's Trans-Am had become one of the most important, and probably *the* most exciting, professional series in road racing.

Ford launched the '68 season with a Jerry Titus/Ronny Bucknum win at the Daytona 24-Hour, armed with a new twin-four-barrel, tunnel-port 302 V-8 producing some 400 horsepower—fifteen percent more than the previous year's race-prepared 289. Built to the stringent SCCA Trans-Am rules (305-cubic-inch maximum engine displacement, solid rear axle, eight-inch wheel width and 2800-pound minimum weight) by Carroll Shelby, and driven by Titus, Bucknum, Horst Kwech and Allan Moffat, the two team Mustang entries nevertheless managed only three wins to the ten of Donohue's Camaro, and the Ford people were frustrated in their attempt at a third straight series victory. But they, and everyone else, would be back loaded for the proverbial bear in 1969.

6.

MUSCLECAR MADNESS

Boss 429 for 1969: inspiration by Knudsen, perspiration by Lunn.

When the fall of 1965 rolled around in Dearborn, Michigan, incredibly, it was already time to start thinking about the '69 model Mustang, which would debut just three years later. While the chassis engineers were still putting final touches on the '67 handling package, the advanced design people were busy turning out the first clay model of the '69 program.

This model was obviously based on the existing '65 car, and did not yet show the longer, lower, wider lines of the coming production '67; but it did indicate some interesting new thinking in the headlamp and side scoop areas. Photographed in October, the car was softer and more rounded than the original '65 and had hidden headlamps, with the designers trying different styles of headlamp doors, fender profiles and scoops on each side.

By January 1966, there was a totally different Mustang concept on view in the Ford advanced studio. This one had a much longer and lower nose, no side scoop or sculpturing at all and a front fender line that swept up into the roof just aft of the door. It was an interesting and fairly attractive design but was in no way related to the Mustang look and image that was becoming so well established, and it was soon discarded.

Several more ideas followed in the next few months, some along traditional Mustang lines and others pursuing the ultra-long hood, hidden headlamp and slab-sided approach. One model that was photographed in June and July looked like it could have come from the Studebaker styling studios instead of Ford's. It had the basic Mustang roof and rear quarter profile, plus the '67 model's enlarged grille, but its wraparound front corner lights, protruding fender louvers, highly peaked front fenders and two-toned side sculpturing were strictly "Buck Rogers." Around back, the traditional three-element taillamps were retained, but they were integrated into the chrome bumper (like those of a later Oldsmobile Cutlass design).

At about the same time, full-size renderings were being done in the studio to explore some other new and different Mustang ideas. One was a sloped-roof, high-backed fastback that could almost have been a two-door wagon; another an open, targa-topped beauty with a low, deeply sculpted crease from front bumper to rear. Both were clean, attractive designs, and while the targa never got beyond the paper stage, the sleek wagon idea later was translated into a fiberglass model. Also, significantly, the fastback/wagon's dominant side-view feature, a large scoop high on the rear quarter, provided the idea for a similar design on the production '69 SportsRoof model.

Several more clays were done and redone during this period, and other features of the eventual '69 Mustang began to come into focus. There was a very soft, rounded concept with rectangular exhaust tips, a small hop-up at the trunk lip and strange, five-element horse-collar-shaped taillamps. Another had vertical rectangular headlamps, large air scoops between the grille and corner lamps and an aggressive side scoop looking like an air outlet just behind the door. A third had downward-sloping rear fenders and a protruding rectangular grille opening suspended between the hood and the bumper—and a roof and window shape close to what ultimately arrived on the production '69.

Another series of drawings was done in an attempt to get some Thunderbird influence into the car, and the rear views showed larger, more squared-off deck shapes (for increased trunk room), all dominated by various interpretations of the three-element vertical taillamp design. After this investigation came another round of clay models with rear-facing side scoops and/or sculpturing, plus high, boxy rear ends...but the T-Bird influence idea (happily) was scrapped and the '69 frontal design soon returned to about where the '67-'68 model was in terms of size and shape. Hidden headlamps also seemed to be back in favor, possibly influenced by the optional headlamp covers on Chevy's '67 Camaro, which debuted at about this time.

A stubby, sexy-looking 2+2 fastback was done in October with finned hood "bumps," high rear-quarter air scoops, high taillamps and no quarter windows at all. "We went through a period where we were chopping about six inches off the back," says then Mustang design chief Gail Halderman. "But then we went to two inches and finally back to where we had started, because we still had to package a spare tire, fuel tank and some luggage room back there. But roofline-wise and scoop-wise, that one almost looked like what went out two years later." Further developments of that design retained the hood bumps, high scoops and hidden headlamps but were not quite so chopped-looking and explored some different roof and window shapes, finally coming around by February to the SportsRoof profile that was to be approved for production.

1969
BOSS
429

Above: With varying ideas each side, the first '69 clay model was clearly based on '65 car. Below: Comparison of modified '67 (left) and radical new concept for '69. The proposal from January 1966.

Perhaps the most stunning Mustang model done during this period was a beautiful two-door wagon with an elegantly aerodynamic roof kick-up and taillamps arched high over the rear glass. "That one was pretty well liked," Halderman laments. "I think we could have sold it." The Mustang wagon was done in fiberglass, with a low, "exit"-type scoop on one side and a high intake scoop on the other—but, sadly, it never was approved for production. It may not have been much in the practicality department, but Mustangs never have been bought for practicality. Chances are it would have sold well on sheer looks alone, and would be a highly desirable collector's piece today.

By early in 1967 the '69 Mustang design and most details were fairly well set. The hidden headlamps, which had endured through much of the decision-making period, were finally abandoned in favor of a quad light arrangement with two inside and two outside of the grille opening. The general shape, as it turned out, was little altered from '68, the major changes being more rounded quarter-window and roof shapes and the addition of a built-in tail spoiler on the fastback, now called "SportsRoof." Parking lamps were tucked neatly into the lower intake area below the bumper, the six separate taillamp lenses were set out a bit from the rear panel surface, and the 2+2's sail panel louvers were replaced by a round crest and swing-out quarter windows. Coupes and convertibles got an air outlet-style trim piece ahead of their rear wheels, while the SportsRoof got the snazzy (but non-functional) high air scoops.

Howard Freers, chief engineer on the '69 Mustang project, remembers that his engineering program did not involve any major changes in the vehicle. "It was a polishing, a honing, of the '68 car," he relates, "a facelift rather than a major re-do. The basic package wasn't changed. Except for honing, the ride, steering effort, cornering ability, crosswind stability, things like that, were all fundamentally equal to the '68 Mustang. The major program objective was to make sure that the optional V-8 was better than the one in '68."

That new engine, of course, was the mighty 428 (a derivative of the 390) which ultimately made it into some production Mustangs late in the '68 model year. There were two versions in '69, both sharing identical specifications and power ratings on paper: the 428 V-8 and the 428 Cobra Jet Ram-Air V-8. But there were some major differences in capabilities and construction. The latter, in addition to its obvious Ram-Air "shaker" hood scoop, had a 735 c.f.m. 4-bbl. (vs. 600 c.f.m. on the "regular" 428) and some of the toughest internal parts available. It was a thinly disguised drag racing engine, and its advertised power and torque outputs were grossly understated—no doubt to hoodwink car classification people in the drag race sanctioning bodies, and perhaps some insurance people as well.

Late in 1966, Ford had displayed a chopped and lowered Mustang-based show car called "Mach I." A two-seater fastback coupe with huge air intake scoops ahead of the rear wheels, built-in "ducktail" rear spoiler and twin racing-style flip-open fuel caps in the roof, it looked like a cross between a production 2+2 and a GT-40 race car—and it provided a clever preview of the coming '69 car (and performance-oriented Mach I name) fully two years in advance. For '68 the Mach I was slightly facelifted and shipped around the show circuit again, just in case anyone had missed the hint.

These were happy, crazy, performance-mad years...before the emissions and safety people had gained much of a toe-hold, before insurance premiums had raged out of control and before any serious thought of a fuel-supply problem. Fast cars were still affordable and gas was downright cheap. The factories were racing each other on every front, and everyone was trying to out-drag, out-corner and out-macho everyone else. Performance department budgets were loose as a race engine's piston clearances, and a development engineer's job in those days had its lighter moments.

Matt Donner, leader of the ride and handling group under Howard Freers, recalls a few of the better anecdotes from the '69-'70 development program. It seems there was a particularly nasty, narrow, winding road near Covington, Kentucky, that was a favorite of the group, but every so often one of the engineers would make a mistake and stuff an expensive prototype into a ditch, or worse. No one was ever hurt as a result of these off-road excursions, but the damaged vehicle would have to be towed to a cooperative Ford dealer in Cincinnati for quick, overnight repairs before the test trip could recommence the following morning. When this happened to trip leader Tom Walsh for the third time in a row, the story goes, after one of his cars had taken an unplanned detour through a farmer's fence, down a hill and between a pair of small trees that were not quite as far apart as the car was wide, the Cincinnati dealership became known among the Ford people as "Walsh's Garage."

Then there was the time when Donner and executive engineer Jack Prendergast, driving the lead and number two cars through a small town in West Virginia, were arrested for speeding (at about 20 mph) through a school zone they didn't know existed. They were escorted to the town hall, where a scruffy-looking judge fined them heavily before letting them go. Afterwards, they went back to look for the sign they had missed and finally found it...hand-printed on an eighteen-inch-square piece of cardboard, nailed to a tree.

Donner also describes a photo taken of Freers' boss at the time, Tom Feaheny, while he was riding as a passenger around the Dearborn handling course in a 428 Mustang. The car was negotiating an especially fast turn, and Feaheny was sitting very erect, with a too-small helmet balanced on his head and a look of sheer terror in his

Above: A "196X" clay model from June-July begged the question: Is it Mustang, Studebaker or Olds? Below: Full-size concept drawings from mid-summer of 1966 indicate the fastback/wagon and Targa ideas.

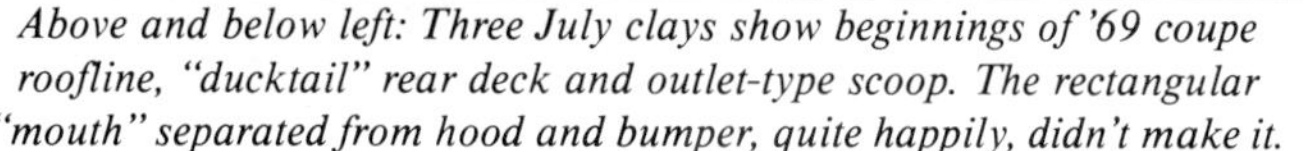

Above and below left: Three July clays show beginnings of '69 coupe roofline, "ducktail" rear deck and outlet-type scoop. The rectangular "mouth" separated from hood and bumper, quite happily, didn't make it.

Across the top: August renderings under instructions to get T-Bird influence and larger trunk into Mustang. Below: Unfinished September clay with reversed sculpturing and scoop and Avanti look to the rear.

eyes. "Tom looked as if he were in the final stages of a preparation procedure for bailing out," Donner laughs.

And who could forget the day at Ford's Kingman, Arizona desert test facility when development supervisor Dave Doman, freshly returned from an assignment at Ford Australia, was demonstrating his method of keeping cool between some quarter-mile acceleration tests. Doman had learned in Australia that the air was cooler near the ground and was squatting down when someone noticed a desert scorpion trying to grab onto a low-hanging portion of his anatomy. "It wasn't a timed run," Donner reports, "but it was said that Dave turned in a better time down the dragstrip than the Mustang did that day."

It was February 6th, 1968, when Henry Ford II shocked the automotive world by hiring Semon E.(Bunkie) Knudsen away from General Motors to become Ford Motor Company president. Knudsen, like Lee Iacocca, was a hard-charging, dynamic, ambitious leader who had just lost out to Ed Cole as GM president, and he arrived at Ford amid a tornado of press and industry attention and full of big ideas on how to attack his former employer in the marketplace. Perhaps fortunately, it was too late in the '69 development program to make any major changes, but the grooves under Knudsen's office chair hadn't grown very deep before he had mobilized his Mustang forces to create *the* killer street car for a mid-year debut.

The coming striped and scooped Mach I SportsRoof, with standard 351 and optional 428 V-8 engines, was certainly quick and racy-looking enough to satisfy the bulk of high-performance Mustang buyers, but it was no match in agility or spirit for Chevy's super-hot Trans-Am race series-inspired, small-block Camaro Z-28. Knudsen

This attractive but large-looking model came from the September 9th clay. Auxiliary lights took the place of headlamps, which are hidden in grille area. Three-element taillamps are retained in boxy rear deck.

A severely chopped musclecar model with high rear fender scoops, rectangular grille opening, hidden headlamps, high taillamps and finned hood extrusions was done in October. Rear roof shape and scoops were close to what would be the production '69 SportsRoof.

wanted a street Mustang that would be the closest thing possible, within the confines of mass production and limited cost, to the Trans-Am road racing cars; a street Mustang to blow away the high-revving, hard-cornering Z-28...and he wanted it fast.

He put Larry Shinoda, a talented designer of performance-image cars whom he had hired away from the GM studios, in charge of the appearance package, and set Howard Freers' chassis development engineers to work on the handling program. Freers doesn't recall any direct Knudsen involvement in the '69 Mustang engineering program, but he does vividly remember being directed to create "*absolutely* the best-handling street car available on the American market...bar none! Matt Donner was given a free hand, with F60 tires, very wide-rim wheels, stiff suspension, big sway bars, the whole shot, to make that car as good-handling as it could possibly be on that chassis.

"We even discussed calling it 'Trans-Am,' after the race series, in some of our meetings," he continues. "But Pontiac snapped that one up before anybody could do anything about it." The name ultimately chosen for Ford's Z-28-killer was "Boss 302," after its super-beefed 302-cubic-inch V-8 engine, a derivative of the actual small-block Ford racing engine...and in keeping with the role intended for it in the street-rod pecking order.

So fast was the Boss 302 during its development on the Dearborn handling course that Matt Donner insisted on using full road racing driver safety equipment: SCCA-approved helmet, fireproof driving suit and underwear. "It was the first time he'd ever done any work where he wanted that sort of equipment," says Freers, "and we bought it for him. I'm sure the Boss 302 was the fastest thing that ever went around that Dearborn track!"

Although Knudsen spent most of his time running the company and much of the rest leaving his mark on the Thunderbird (the "Bunkie Beak" or "Knudsen Nose," which had become a Pontiac trademark when he was general manager there) and the Lincoln luxury cars, chief Mustang product planner Joe Gilmore recalls considerable Knudsen involvement in the "Boss" programs. "There was a lot of attention given to the Mustang at that time," says he, "because Knudsen was so excited about those kinds of cars. Shinoda was doing all kinds of special versions of it, and I think it helped the Mustang by creating a lot of additional public interest, especially the bright colors...shocking blue, orange, white and yellow. It was the time of miniskirts and all that, and special colors were everywhere...although none of those ever sold very well on the car."

One major problem that the Boss 302 program created came as a result of adding the big, hard F60 tires. "That F60 tire was a beast," Freers relates, "and when we put it into our rough-road durability cycle it literally tore up the front end of the car. The upper control arm mounts bolted through the front suspension tower structure, and that tire was so rough it was breaking the towers. As a result of including that tire in the program we had to go back at the last minute and put some rather sizable reinforcements into the vehicle...across the board, because you can't schedule structural changes for just a certain amount of the cars being built. The cost and difficulty of doing that bothered me quite a bit, but we had to do it."

When the '69 Mustang was unveiled on August 28th, 1968, only two "exciting new additions to the breed" were present for early muster: Mach I and a luxury hardtop version called "Grandé." The new theme for 1969 was the "The Going Thing," and the new Mustang was touted as "longer, lower, wider and more comfortable than ever before" by Ford Division general manager John Naughton.

In addition to its standard 250 hp 351-cubic-inch engine and optional 428, Mach I featured "GT handling suspension," high-back bucket seats, "racing-type" exposed hood locking pins, simulated teakwood-grained console and instrument panel, color-keyed dual "racing" mirrors and special ornamentation and striping. Grandé, on the other hand, had simulated teakwood throughout its interior, plus "hopsack cloth" and vinyl seats, wire wheel covers, a narrow exterior paint stripe, softened rear suspension and fifty-five extra pounds of sound insulating material. Clearly Ford was gunning to expand both the high-performance and luxury-oriented fringe elements of its Mustang customer body.

The traditional vent windows had been lost to the cost-cutters' hatchet, supposedly for enhanced appearance and increased visibility (two better reasons are less weight and wind noise, but no reference is made to either), and improved weather stripping lessened wind noise inside the cabin. The convertible's rear quarter windows were slightly larger than before, and (like the hardtop's) rolled down, while the SportsRoof's new quarter windows were a swing-out design. A four-pod cluster was part of the redesigned instrument panel, and interior roominess was increased a bit in most directions—except front seat legroom, the dimension most in need of improvement. Access to the rear seat area was improved by moving the center pillar four inches rearward and increasing the door length, although the rear seats still were of little use to anyone exceeding midget proportions. Finally, the "emergency" brake became foot-operated, released by a pull-lever below the instrument panel, and the standard heating and ventilation system was redesigned for increased air flow.

Engine choices ranged from the standard 200-cubic-inch six, through a 250 six, a mild 302 V-8, two 351 V-8's, a 390, the basic 428 and the Cobra Jet Ram-Air 428, the latter coming with staggered rear shocks to help control rear axle hop and wind-up during hard acceleration. New options included a deluxe three-spoke steering wheel (with an obnoxious rim-blow horn switch), power ventilation for force-fed air flow even at rest, intermittent windshield wipers and a Traction-Lok limited slip differential.

Production of the Shelby cars was moved to the Southfield, Michigan Ford plant as they became basically customized production Mustangs with fiberglass front and rear end caps. Their flattened nose and full-width grille were so liked by Knudsen that he directed Bordinat's advanced design group to incorporate much of their look into the '71 Mustang, thus the GT-350 and GT-500 provided a preview two years in advance of the '71 front end design. They were virtually covered with scoops—five NACA-type ducts in the hood alone plus functional brake scoops in the front fenders and upper rear quarter—and the side stripes were enlarged and moved up to mid-

Later that month, a car similar to that on the page opposite but somewhat less chopped and with two different side scoop and window treatments.

Above: A beautiful wagon with taillamps wrapping over rear window, this fiberglass model had complete interior, two side treatments. Below: Except for the hidden headlamps, hood bulges and horizontal taillamps, these early '67 models are very close to '69 SportsRoof.

flank, running front headlamp to rear bumper.

The new Shelby interiors were extra plush, with high-back bucket seats, wood-grained dash, leather-like vinyl steering wheel on a tilt-adjustable column, and full instrumentation in the console. The GT-350's 302 engine was dropped in favor of a four-barrel, 290 hp 351 Windsor unit with finned aluminum valve covers and a chrome dipstick, driving through a choice of wide- or close-ratio four-speeds, while the 428-cubic-inch GT-500 remained unchanged mechanically for 1969.

With the road-racing-image Boss 302 Mustang still under development for mid-year introduction, Knudsen dispatched a task force of four drivers and three specially prepared Mach I's to the Bonneville Salt Flats in search of some high-speed records to establish that model as the straight-line performance king. Lead driver and project coordinator was Mickey Thompson, Knudsen's favorite hot-rodder during his Pontiac days, and he was ably helped behind the wheel by Ray Brock, Bot Ottum and then drag-racer Danny Ongais. Hampered by Utah's cantankerous September weather, the group nevertheless managed to score some 295 United States Auto Club (USAC) closed-car speed and endurance records, averaging over 157 mph on one twenty-four-hour long-distance run.

This achievement was amply displayed in Mach I advertising and in special high-performance Ford "Buyer's Digest" catalogues featuring the company's speed-oriented models and available hop-up equipment. "Ever since 1903," proclaimed the catalogue's introduction, "when Henry Ford built Old 999 and won his first race, Ford has been building high-performance machines. And proving them by winning...at Bonneville, Pomona, Indianapolis, Riverside and Le

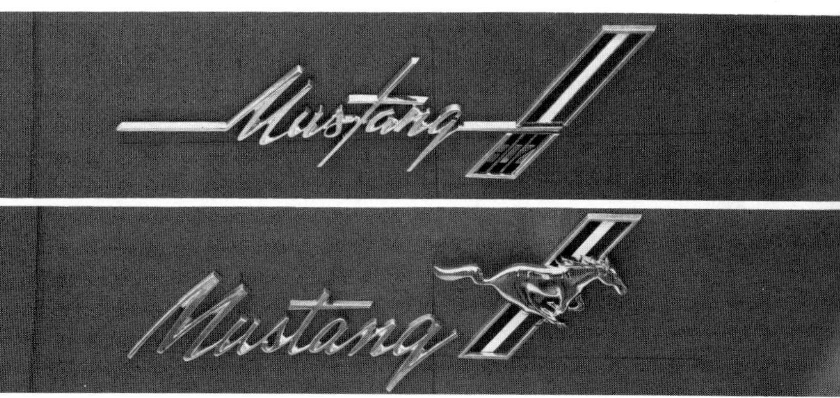

Mans. But there's more to Ford performance than a worldwide winning streak. The same Ford engineers who stretch their minds to win on the tracks are involved in designing performance cars and parts you can buy."

Of course, the long lapses in Ford's competition and performance interest, including the AMA-ban years just prior to Lee Iacocca's Ford Division takeover and "total performance" revival, were conveniently forgotten. And lest anyone think the company was promoting irresponsible street racing, the catalogue closed with an admonition: "Speed belongs on the track or the strip, not on the street. Your Ford dealer urges you to drive safely." Thus was the growing army of safety fanatics in Washington (hopefully) mollified while Ford was spending millions to build and race the fastest production-based cars in U.S. industry history.

But, as Eric Dahlquist pointed out in an August 1968 *Motor Trend* article, since Ford's return to serious racing it had won countless stock car races and two Trans-Am road racing titles, its engines had displaced the ageless Offy as "hot ticket" at Indy, and its endurance cars had challenged and triumphed at Le Mans, Daytona, Sebring and elsewhere. "Total Performance" was working well on the track, yet not so well on the street. In 1966, Ford and Mercury together had captured a paltry seven percent of the 600,000-unit high-performance new-car market, and 1967 wasn't a whole lot better. Why? Not enough raw power.

"Ford's undoing," wrote Dahlquist, "was in the streets, those great public racing courses at the end of every American driveway. The answer, of course, was the 428 Cobra Jet package that finally reached the streets in mid-year '68, much of the credit for which must go to ex-

Above and below: Front end concept of June 9th showing first use of quad headlamps; February 22nd design was close to production '69 except for grille: March 11th idea was probably under consideration for 1970. Center: Three attempts at new-for-'69 script emblems.

Left and right: Production '69 Mustangs and Cougars rolling down Dearborn assembly lines. Across the top: Four large drawings of the proposed 1968

GM vice-president Bunkie Knudsen...When Mr. Knudsen came from GM, he brought along a strong belief in the value of performance." Knudsen had given the green light to racing boss Jacque Passino, and Passino had wasted little time in getting the 428's awesome power into the cars.

"There are lots of people around here that give the kids too little credit," said Passino at the time. "They can't see offering them a lot of horsepower that they can't get to the ground right away. I don't subscribe to this. I think if we give the kids the power, they'll buy the tires and clip the springs and do whatever else they have to to get traction. But, first they need the power."

Hard on the heels of the pavement-rippling 428 Cobra Jet Mach I came a very special project headed up by Roy Lunn of Mustang I mid-engine sports car and GT-40 race car fame. Lunn was working with Kar Kraft, Ford's racing right arm, on the Trans-Am cars and other high-performance projects when he was directed (at Knudsen's bidding) to figure a way to wedge the massive 429 high-performance engine into the Mustang.

"It was in the days just after Knudsen came on board," Lunn explains. "He was a real stock-car enthusiast, and so stock-car racing was being given a big thrust again. To remain competitive, we had to get that 429 hemi-head engine qualified, and the requirement was that you had to build a minimum of 500 in production vehicles. The question was which vehicle would be suitable, and the 429 Mustang ultimately came about as being a logical choice."

Kar Kraft managed to accommodate the 429 by slightly altering the '69 Mustang suspension, enlarging the engine compartment and opening up the front fenders for tire clearance. Amazingly, the front tread was increased by only 0.8 inches to 59.3 inches. Even after these modifications, it must have taken the world's biggest shoehorn to stuff that monster in; and it was no joy to service even with its spark plugs right on top of the heads.

Under-rated (as usual) at 375 hp, the street/race 429 featured aluminum heads with canted valves, enlarged ports and "crescent-shaped" (hemispherical) combustion chambers, plus a forged steel crankshaft, forged connecting rods with half-inch bolts, forged "pop-

version of the Mach I. Center: The Mach I which toured U.S. automobile shows in 1968 featured glassed-in headlamps and large GT-40-like side scoops.

up" pistons and rocker arms, four-bolt main bearing caps, high-rise aluminum intake manifold, and "dry decking" in place of normal gaskets. The idea was to combine high horsepower and low-end torque with high-rpm durability, and just in case all that wasn't enough for any boy racers with extra cash burning holes in their pockets, there was lots more available at Ford dealer "Performance Corners" to make it go even faster.

Lowered an inch in front, the "Boss 429" was decked out with a standard front spoiler and huge ram-air hood scoop, F60-15 Goodyear Polyglas tires on seven-inch-wide chrome rims and a "competition" suspension consisting of super-stiff springs, staggered rear shocks and large front and rear sway bars. And, in spite of that enormous hunk of iron over the front wheels, claimed weight distribution was 56 percent front, 44 percent rear.

A heavy-duty four-speed and 3.91 to one locking rear axle had the job of putting all that power to the drive wheels, power steering and manual disc brakes were mandatory options, and such luxuries as automatic transmission and air conditioning were strictly not available. Other goodies making up this factory-to-you drag racer included special cast aluminum rocker covers, Holley 735 c.f.m. four-barrel carburetor, high-capacity engine oil cooler, 65-amp alternator, 85 amp-hour trunk-mounted battery and even a power steering oil cooler.

A late-November press release promised the "429 Mustang" in December, even though the project hadn't gotten under way until late summer. As it was, Lunn and his troops (under plant manager Fran Hernandez) did well to get the first one off their special Brighton, Michigan mini-assembly line by January 15th, 1969. Once under way, the line rate slowly climbed to the target of ten cars per day until a total of 852 had been built for the '69 model year. Production shut down in July but then resumed in August, and 505 '70-model Boss 429's were built through December 1970.

In spite of its impressive specifications, the monster 429 was never quite as quick in street Mustangs as the Cobra Jet Ram Air 428. "There was no incentive to make the package a complete racing car as delivered," says Lunn. "It was really just a hairy, crazy road machine for people who liked that sort of thing...and a means of keeping competitive in stock-car racing." Unless a buyer went the extra mile to thoroughly modify both engine and vehicle for serious competition, it remained a very complicated, very expensive cast-iron status symbol in a car too small, light and unsophisticated for its real potential. But what collector's items those 1357 Boss 429's are today!

Another Roy Lunn project, but one that did not reach production, was an interesting "Low Investment Driveline" (LID) two-seat, mid-engine Mustang that was investigated as a very special mid-'71 variant to counter the expected '72 mid-engine Corvette. The idea was to mount the 429 engine and transmission facing rearward, with a special 180-degree gearset and driveshaft transferring power back to a conventional rear axle, thereby saving the considerable cost of designing, tooling and developing a transaxle. One prototype was constructed using a 1969 Mustang fastback, but (like the mid-ship Corvette) Lunn's LID concept never went much farther than that.

In February 1969, *Car Life* magazine tested a luxury Mustang Grandé, equipped with the new-for-'69 small-block 351 V-8, and the write-up was music to the product planners' ears. "When the designers put the comfort in, they didn't take Mustang's traditional nimbleness out," said the article, adding that "the 351 is a good solid engine for daily driving: responsive at low rpm, quiet and strong for its weight. A better engine for a Grandé-class car would be hard to find."

The following month *Car Life* worked out a 428 Mach I, calling it the "best Mustang yet and quickest ever." There were criticisms, of course...near-useless trunk (gone was the original 2+2's handy folding rear seat) and strong understeer combined with unresponsive steering at the cornering limit—but the article overflowed with printed praise:

> It's here. The Mustang Mach I, equipped for the enthusiast, is:
>
> The quickest standard passenger car through the quarter-mile we've ever tested (sports cars and hot rods excluded).
>
> A superb road car, stable at speed, tenacious on corners with surplus power and brakes for any road situation.
>
> Pleasant just being driven around. The potential is barely tapped on a trip to the store, but the driver doesn't suffer reminders of the price he paid for qualities he isn't using...
>
> The greatness shows up best on a winding mountain road. By choosing the optimum combination of suspension geometry, shock absorber valving and spring rates, Ford engineers have exempted the Mach I from the laws of momentum and inertia, up to unspeakable speeds.
>
> ...the Mach I growls through turns, eating up bumps in the road and camber changes, while the big engine catapults it

Mustang for '69. Above: the new luxury model Grande hardtop. Below: "E" economy version of SportsRoof. Bottom: Mach I with 428 Cobra Jet package. Left: The Shelby version, merely a SportsRoof with add-on front and rear fiberglass sections, scoops, stripes and multi-ducted hood, which turned out to be preview of '71 front-end look because Ford president Knudsen liked it.

from turn to turn, and the big brakes haul it down to cornering speed, time after time.

Only on a real road-racing course did the Mach I's limitations as a cornering machine become apparent, but it more than made up for that small failure in *Car Life*'s acceleration tests: 5.5 seconds zero-to-sixty and 13.90 seconds through the quarter-mile at 103.32 mph. Top speed at 6000 rpm in fourth gear was reported as 121 mph. The front shock absorbers had passed away from hard cornering by the time the magazine's editors had completed their spirited testing, but they had died a valiant death. "Mustangs can be great," proclaimed the page one sub-head. "All it takes is a big engine, big tires and careful planning."

By late March the killer small-block Boss 302 was ready for business. If Lunn's Boss 429 was the factory drag racer, Matt Donner's Boss 302 was your basic factory road racer. The Shinoda visual treatment included elimination of the SportsRoof's simulated side scoop, a C-shaped stripe with "boss 302" lettering, functional front spoiler and black-out hood, rear deck and back panel; plus (optionally) a set of wild black louvers on the rear window and an adjustable stand-up airfoil over the tail. Just to make sure that no one could mistake it for anything more run-of-the-mill, the only available colors were eye-assaulting bright yellow, Calypso coral, Wimbledon white and Acapulco blue.

But it was the Donner group's chassis refinements under the gussied-up body and the hot 302 under the blacked-out hood that really made this car stand out from the crowd—and set it door-to-door with Chevy's 302 Z-28 in the small-block musclecar market competition. Weight distribution was a respectable 56/44 front-to-rear (a claim that is much more believable with this car than with the Boss 429), suspension was heavy-duty all around and featured the staggered shock arrangement now common to performance Mustangs, and the steering was tightened to a 16 to one ratio and 3.74 turns lock-to-lock to give extra-quick response. Both front and rear treads were increased to 59.5 inches and wheel openings were slightly widened to accommodate the F60-15 fiberglass-belted tires on seven-inch-wide magnum styled steel or optional chromed "magnum 500" steel wheels. Floating-caliper power front disc brakes with ventilated cast-iron discs were required equipment with the package.

The 302-cubic-inch H.O. (high output) engine came in both racing and street versions, the latter putting out a rated 290 horsepower at 5800 rpm and 290 foot pounds of torque at 4300 rpm...the former close to 450 usable horsepower. New canted-valve cylinder heads breathed through a high-rise intake manifold and (for the street) a 780 c.f.m. Holley four-barrel carburetor. The canted valves formed a wedge-shaped, triangular combustion chamber and allowed more

Center: Three specially modified Mach I's set 295 USAC speed and endurance records in September '68; note low profile of cars and absence of side scoops. Above and right: Highly modified 429 canted-valve engines were "dressed" at Kar Kraft in Brighton and then shoehorned into Mustang engine compartments. Roy Lunn (left) and Fran Hernandez smile with the first one finished.

efficient flow in and out of the cylinders, more pushrod clearance for the inlet ports and increased space for extra-large valves...2.33-inch intakes and 1.71-inch exhausts. Valve lifters were solid to accommodate a quicker cam and very precise valve timing.

Internal beefing for this high-rpm screamer was similar to that of the H.O. 429, with oversize forged four-bolt main bearing caps, forged connecting rods, caps and bolts and forged, extruded aluminum pistons. Every Boss 302's forged steel crankshaft was electronically balanced, both statically and dynamically, in the engine while running under its own power. Chrome or cast-aluminum rocker covers, a high-capacity dual-point ignition system, four-speed manual transmission (with ratios specially spaced to match the 302's output curve), and a 3.50 to one rear axle completed the package. Optional locker rear axles were available in 3.50, 3.91 and 4.30 ratios.

The racing 302 H.O. got special machining for dry-decking instead of gaskets, a special intake manifold with individual runners, two four-

the two rival cars turned identical 14.85-second quarter-miles, but the Mustang's 96.15-mph trap speed was slower than the Camaro's by nearly five miles per hour. "The Boss had much more power off the line, and with its bigger tires it had more traction," the article explained. "It is faster to (a given) speed through the gears." The Z-28's 101-mph trap speed, however, indicated that it turned out more sheer horsepower in street form. The Boss 302 Mustang's zero-to-sixty time was reported by *Car Life* as 6.9 seconds.

"Inside," the magazine added, "the Boss is standard Mustang fastback. Good bucket seats in front, the infamous sculptured and fabric-covered park bench in back. The fastback Mustang is closer to a two-place car than any other four-place car on the market."

While Ford stock cars, drag cars (Danny Ongais' Mickey Thompson 427 Mustang "funny car," for one), endurance cars, and Ford-powered Indy cars were now winning with regularity, the factory Trans-Am forces had dropped their championship title to rival Chevrolet. Knudsen wanted the Trans-Am back in Ford's trophy case, and special vehicles manager Jacque Passino was instructed to go out and get it. Two separate teams were dispatched to do the job, one headed by Carroll Shelby and the other under ace stock-car-builder Bud Moore. In their enhanced arsenals was the revised 302 racing engine, which Passino said produced "more power in all ranges" than the previous year's tunnelport version. The Ford drivers weren't too shabby either...Peter Revson and Dan Gurney in the Shelby cars and Parnelli Jones and George Follmer in the Moore machines.

The season started on a high note with Jones taking the opener and Sam Posey (subbing for Revson, who was at Indianapolis) winning the second. Chevy-driver Ron Bucknum took the third series contest, but then Jones and Follmer came back with one each for Ford...making the score Mustang four, Camaro one. The next seven, however, went to Chevrolet (one by Bucknum and six by Mark Donohue in the Penske car), giving Camaro its second straight season crown and Mustang its second straight loss.

Also competing semi-seriously in '69 were Pontiac (Firebirds) and American Motors (Javelins); and these two and every other domestic maker seemed to decide simultaneously at year's end that winning the Trans-Am would sell a lot of ponycars...which set the stage for a most entertaining factory battle the following season.

The 1970 models that debuted on September 3rd, 1969, as expected, were little-changed from the '69's. The grille opening was widened, the outside set of headlamps replaced by three small, simulated scoops on the fender leading edges, and the Mustang emblem moved front and center in the new horizontal-bar grille. Knudsen had hated the non-functional side scoops and had them duly

Mustangs for '70. Top: Ready for introduction, a convertible prototype.

scrubbed from all body styles and the rear quarter panels slightly altered for a cleaner look. Around back, the tri-element taillamps were recessed into the rear panel. Grandé for '70 came with a standard "three-quarter Landau-style" vinyl roof, black rear panel and black aluminum rocker panel moldings, Boss 302 got modified striping and trim, and Mach I featured Shinoda-inspired grooved aluminum rocker moldings, rectangular grille-mounted auxiliary lamps and a honeycomb back panel insert under a spoiler stripe and die cast "Mach I" lettering.

Fiberglass-belted bias-ply tires became standard on all 1970 Mustangs, as did the '69 Mach I's high-back bucket seats, and four-speed cars benefited from a smooth, new Hurst shifter and linkage design. Other changes included redesigned semi-oval steering wheels (both two- and three-spoke) to enhance instrument visibility and ease driver entry and exit, externally adjustable headlamps and a tamper resistant (non-reversing) odometer. New options were a Convenience Group (with automatic seatback releases) and quick-ratio manual steering gear for performance-oriented buyers, while safety additions included reflective side marker lamps that flashed with the turn signals, three-point lap/shoulder belts for outside front occupants, and a new (required) transmission/steering/ignition lock to deter potential thieves. Performance models got a redesigned in-line dual exhaust system and high-performance rear axle, and the Boss 302's rear window louvers and adjustable rear spoiler became available on all SportsRoof Mustangs.

The engine lineup for '70 was little changed except for a brand- new big-block 351 cubic-inch four-barrel V-8 with large ports and canted valves similar to those in the 429. Also the 302 and small-block 351 got a revised front accessory drive, and the base 200-cubic-inch six benefited from addition of the 250 six's cylinder head for improved efficiency.

It's not clear when production of 1969 Shelbys ended and the '70's began, because the last 600 to 800 were merely given minor striping and front spoiler changes and designated 1970 models. It *is* known, however, that the last Shelby Mustang was completed in November 1969, and that total production of the '69-'70 breed was 1085 GT-350 fastbacks, 194 GT-350 convertibles, 1536 GT-500 fastbacks and 335 GT-500 convertibles: 3150 in all. Total for the five-year span of Shelby race-cars-turned-street-cruisers was 10,825, every one a personal statement and a collector's item worth treasuring.

There was a proposal in September to replace both the Shelby and the Boss 429 with a new 1970½ model using the 429 engine and modified Shelby front-end fiberglass bodywork. Known internally as the "Composite Mustang," this car was to be cheaper to build than a GT-500, with a more distinctive appearance than the Boss 429 and better performance than the 428 Mach I. Two prototypes were constructed featuring the Shelby front ends (with hood and fender scoops filled-in to "get away from the Shelby look," according to Fran Hernandez) and rich-looking Mercury Cougar instrument panels, the name "Quarter Horse" was chosen, and several series of tests were run by Kar Kraft, but the car was not approved for production.

On Thursday, September 11th, 1969, just eight days after the 1970 models were introduced, Henry Ford fired Bunkie Knudsen as suddenly and mysteriously as he had hired him a year-and-a-half before. It was said that Knudsen had moved too fast, alienated too

Above and below: The Grandé with scoops which didn't make it, and the sans-scoop, partial-vinyl-roof version which did. Left: Boss 302. Right: Mach I 428.

many Ford people, stepped on too many toes. Certainly he was strong-willed and had intended to run the company his own way or not at all. Certainly he had his own strong ideas about styling, which hadn't always endeared him to Gene Bordinat and his folks at Ford Design. Some executives had resigned during his brief reign as president, and others (including Lee Iacocca, then executive vice-president, North American Automotive Operations) had threatened to do so. Iacocca, too, was a strong-willed executive, and Knudsen had clashed with him on several occasions.

So Knudsen, who had created the Boss machines, altered the '70 models and virtually dictated design of the coming '71-'73 cars, was out; and Iacocca, who had created the Mustang in the first place, was destined to ascend to that vacant Ford president's chair in little more than a year.

In spite of such executive-office politics, Mustang promotional activities continued as planned. One of these was a late October announcement that American Raceways Inc. had chosen the Ford ponycar to pace racing events at all five of its tracks (Michigan International Speedway, Atlanta International Raceway, Riverside International Raceway, Texas International Speedway and Eastern International Speedway) in 1970. "Mustang was chosen...because of its highly commendable position as America's number one compact sports sedan; its obvious influence on the performance market in the country; and its most important role in the growth of the popular Trans-American Sedan Series inaugurated in 1966," said ARI president Larry LoPatin on the occasion.

Having enjoyed more success than the Shelby effort in 1969, Bud Moore's team was selected to mount a massive factory assault on the 1970 Trans-Am title. Parnelli Jones and George Follmer remained as Moore's drivers, a veritable arsenal of cars and engines were readied, and the budget was reported to be nearly unlimited. "I was a little disappointed with last year's results—only three victories and four second-place finishes in twelve starts," said Moore in an April Ford press release. "But that's behind us and we learned enough in 1969 to make us real contenders for the championship this year."

One major engine improvement was a new "Cross-Boss" intake manifold, described as "a kind of torque box manifold designed to provide maximum mid-range power." Interestingly, Ford down-played the effort as "an independent two-car entry," apparently still smarting from accusations of having "bought" Le Mans and the World Manufacturers' Championship with its enormous GT racing budget

The season was close and competitive, with factory teams from Ford, Chevrolet, Pontiac, Plymouth, Dodge and American Motors, but the Ford forces prevailed on the strength of five wins by Jones and

Jones and Follmer posing and racing to '70 Trans-Am series title for Mustang.

Proposed 1970½ "Quarter Horse" featured modified Shelby GT-500 front fenders, hood and grille, with scoops filled in to eliminate Shelby look.

one by Follmer. The AM Javelin effort, ably led by ex-Chevy racers Penske and Donohue, got rolling late in the year and managed a trio of victories and a respectable second-place season finish.

Providing an interesting postscript to what was probably the best, and last, year of serious multi-marque factory road racing competition in America, *Road & Track* published a test of George Follmer's Bud Moore racing Mustang in the January 1971 issue. Zero-to-sixty time was 5.5 seconds, the same as a good 428 Mach I street car and not bad for a 302-cubic-inch machine not designed or geared for standing starts. The quarter mile was turned in 12.9 seconds at 110 mph, and top speed was reported as 151 mph at 7500 rpm in fourth gear. High-speed handling was stiff and touchy, but very precise in the hands of a skilled driver. "The suspension has been honed to a fine edge...," said the magazine. "We don't know how one would build a better Trans-Am car."

The next year would see the Mustang get bigger and heavier and the thrilling Trans-Am series get smaller and less significant. Everyone else had already dropped their Trans-Am-legal, high-performance, under-305-c.i.d. engines, and Ford followed suit with the end of its 1970-model production. With the government climbing high on their collective backs and their engineers hard-pressed to meet snowballing safety, emissions and damageability requirements, the manufacturers suddenly found themselves with more important things on which to spend their time and money than pursuing an elusive and expensive road racing title, the worth of which was undocumentable in terms of sales. Only the AM people wanted that title badly enough to keep their weak-selling Javelin in the Trans-Am wars for '71, and they would win it handily.

It was the end of an era, not only for American racing but for the American automobile itself, and things would never be the same.

7.

PUTTING ON WEIGHT

The horsepower race that had been going on since the automobile was invented was just about over by the time the 1971 Mustangs were introduced on August 20th, 1970. The Federal government's mushrooming mountain of safety and emissions and damageability requirements, over-reactions to legitimate concerns, combined with skyrocketing insurance rates, had caused a massive rethinking of priorities in Detroit. Motor City was a fortress besieged by regulatory Huns. The drawbridge was up and the moat loaded with crocodiles.

There would be no more factory racing for Ford...and, indeed, few more cars suitable to be raced. As the country and the industry struggled to recover from a mild recession, the Federal testing and the certifications and the paperwork necessary to appease the ravenous bureaucratic beast effectively ruled out, at least for the moment, any further thought of automotive excitement, performance or fun. It was the beginning of a new Dark Age for the American automobile, and in August of 1970, everyone in Detroit knew it.

But they hadn't seen it coming in the spring of 1967, when the 1971 car designs were first being carved into clay. They knew then that the Mustang would have to get bigger, fatter and heavier to accommodate the ever-growing engines and horsepower figures needed to keep the competition at bay in an ultra-performance-minded marketplace. Already, 320 hp 390-cubic-inch monster motors were being stuffed into a body/chassis never intended for more than a high-output 289, and within a year it would be the mighty 428. Pontiac's GTO had created the musclecar market almost simultaneously with the first Mustang's introduction in 1964, and by 1967 the movement was gathering speed like a rail dragster.

So the '71 Mustang would have to be bigger...longer wheelbase, wider treads, beefier chassis, suspension, driveline, and brakes, and larger wheel openings to take the bigger tires. At the same time it would have to be quieter, roomier, more comfortable, softer and more luxurious to satisfy the other end of the market. Of the so-called "three faces of Mustang," the profits were clearly generated by the luxury face as much as the macho face, and the expectations of small luxo-car buyers also were increasing every year.

Among the problems: "trying to make the car all things to all people."

"You run into the problem on a continuing basis of trying to make the car all things to all people," explains design chief Gene Bordinat, "and I think that over time the greatest fights we had with the Mustang were to keep the compromise package. The product planner's idea of how to increase the sales volume of a car is to make it accommodate more people and to add more creature comforts. But the minute you begin to fool with compromises in that sort of package, guess what? You end up with a two-door sedan.

"And then they wouldn't understand why it didn't look quite the same, and you have to explain that you can't have it both ways. An automobile is something that has four wheels, essentially near the corners, and you go from there. If you want a hot-looking car, you make certain compromises. If you want a conventional car, or a comfortable car to carry six people, you end up with a sedan. You can't make 'em serve both masters."

Right off the bat, the first clays looked monstrous next to the 1967-1968 cars. And were they ugly! One had a huge chrome bumper enclosing the grille and wrapping halfway around the recessed headlamps, and a convoluted, sickle-shaped side sculpture and scoop on one of its sides. Another had a mouth like a Grouper and a high sculpture/scoop that wrapped up into the roof. Both had huge, massive C-pillars and rear quarters; but both had interesting tunneled rear windows, one had decent-looking three-section taillamps, and the other (on one of its sides) had a cleanly sculptured character line extending from above the headlamp to just behind the door. There was some promise in these elements and they were to be carried on into later, better concepts.

By late September a third, much slimmer and more attractive model was completed. This one featured twin center-mounted grille lamps, front fender air scoops, fender-mounted bullet mirrors, a racing-style fuel filler high in the C-pillar, horizontally-slotted taillamps and twin rectangular exhaust tips centered below the rear bumper. It was still *big*, but it had some nice features and at least looked more like a sporty car than a sedan. And its straight-line side crease, tunneled rear window and basic body shape were close to the hardtop version of what would be produced three years later.

Several more interpretations were done on all three of these early models, some good and some not so good. There were slim full-width grilles with hidden headlamps, one of which floated under the hood sheet metal, exposed quad headlamp treatments, all sorts of horizontal

1965
1966
1967
1968
1969
1970
1971
1972
1973

Compared to the '68 Mustang in the background, the first '71 clay models (above and below) were fat and ugly. Page opposite: The June version (at the top), however, had roof profile, tunneled rear window and character line similar to what would be approved for production. Three months later the same model had much cleaner front and rear designs. Then, in November, hidden headlamps were tried.

and vertical slotted taillamp ideas, different styles of scoops, fenders, side sculpturing and window shapes, but none that seemed to offer The Answer.

By mid-January, 1968, two of the earlier hardtops had been redone and slimmed considerably, but both pursued the awkward floating grille theme, one with twin recessed headlamps and one with quads. The latter had "flying buttresses" flowing almost to the rear deck edge, giving it a fastback look from the front and sides, plus a four-slot air scoop arrangement in the rear fender's sharply sloped leading edge. But a third car, a long, low fastback with front fender scoops, deeply recessed grille and headlamps and a high, neatly sculpted rear quarter scoop on one side, was the real eye-catcher. On its left side was that clean, single character line ending just behind the door, and its taillamps were high in the ducktailed rear end.

It was this model, photographed in fiberglass on January 18th, that Semon E. (Bunkie) Knudsen would approve almost as soon as he had seen it shortly after taking over as Ford president in February. "He approved that '71 right in the studio," recalls Mustang chief designer Gail Halderman. "We asked if he didn't want to take it outside and look it over, and he said, 'No, I like it right here.' We said, 'Well, there are a couple more being done, wouldn't you prefer to wait and see how they turn out?' He said, 'No, I like this one.' We had never had approvals like that before."

Nevertheless, a whole series of full-size renderings was done in April to explore some alternative ideas, all showing the Knudsen influence. "He had a couple of ground rules that they must have used at GM," Halderman explains. "For one, the front fender height over the wheel had to be higher than the beltline at the door. He'd walk along and kind of visually measure each car." This produced sort of a cinched-waist, "Coke-bottle" look that resulted in the desired swoopy profile. None of these ideas, however, went any farther than the paper study.

By June both fastback and hardtop designs were fairly well set except for details. The favored fastback model had shed its rear quarter scoop but retained the front fender inlets and a mild scoop just behind the rear quarter window. Both of these, too, were destined to be scrubbed by Knudsen before reaching production. "The quarter window scoop went away eventually," says Halderman, "and the front fender inlets got filled in at the eleventh hour. He didn't understand them. He said if they aren't going to be functional, take them out."

In October there was a Ford-designed replacement for the Shelby Cobra, based (curiously) on the hardtop body instead of the fastback. "This was done when Ford Division decided it was not going to go with Shelby any more, they were going to do it all themselves. So we looked at a lot of ways to do it, mostly by replacing the front and rear sections as in '69-'70," Halderman explains. This one had a fairly good-looking rear section with slim horizontal taillamps and a fixed spoiler over the rear deck, but the front seemed a bit ungainly with its faired-in lights, low, angled mouth and ducted and finned hood. Perhaps fortunately, it was never approved for production.

Grille, hood and taillamp details remained undecided until the last minute, with various combinations being tried and rejected. There were plain grilles, sectioned grilles, some with horizontal or vertical bars, or both, and some with auxiliary lights of various shapes and sizes, not to mention several different styles of hood scoops and taillamps. But the final frontal solutions were a simple, single horizontal bar design with a corraled horse in the center for the base car, and a blacked-out honeycomb mesh with small horse and "tribar" and horizontal rectangular grille lamps for the Mach I and Boss. The latter two also would share a raised-center hood with two large semi-NACA-style air scoops. Around back were flattened and rounded triangular taillamps, divided into the traditional three sections, with a honeycombed back panel between them on the Mach I and black-out treatment on the Boss.

Meanwhile, it was up to then Mustang chief engineer Howard Freers to get the handling of this larger, heavier Mustang properly sorted and to make engine and driveline decisions in the face of all the legislation that would be in effect when the '71 hit the streets. "The 351 replaced the Boss 302 in '71 because it was a much cheaper engine to build," Freers relates. "That Boss 302 was a beautiful little engine, but *very* expensive. Also there were to be three different versions of the big 429 V-8 to replace the 428's...429 CJ (Cobra Jet), 429 CJ-RA (Ram Air) and 429 Super Cobra Jet.

"It took a tread change (from 58.5 inches to 61.5 inches front and 60.0 inches rear) to get those monsters in there, because the 429 with its canted-valve heads was a much wider engine than the 428, and that's why the car got wider. Also the wheelbase went up an inch to 109 inches, but most of the difference otherwise was sheet metal." Because of the bigger, heavier optional engines up front and the overall added bulk needed to carry them, the chassis people had to work hard to improve the handling, but the wider tread gave them an opportunity to do the job. "It was a major program objective, and I think we did it...on the base model as well as the big-engine jobs," comments Howard Freers.

The on-road test trips this time around proved to be much tamer than they had with the '69-'70 program, but there was one incident that provided an unplanned test of one newly required safety item. "On one of the '71 Mustang/Cougar trips, someone ran a red light and broadsided one of our $150,000 prototypes," Freers relates. "Un-

fortunate though the incident was, it did give us an actual test of the new side guard door beam in addition to all the lab testing done by body engineering. And it worked very well."

Ford was now in the habit of sending show cars around the country to preview upcoming production models, and true to form unveiled a sleek little beauty called Mustang Milano in February of 1970. Similar in shape to the coming '71 SportsRoof, the Milano was a two-seater with a slightly pointed nose divided into two rectangular grille openings, concealed headlamps, a multi-ducted Shelby-style hood and trick taillamps that glowed different colors to show whether the driver was coasting, accelerating or braking...amber, green and red, respectively. Done up in eye-straining "Ultra Violet" and with a set of luggage under the electrically-operated rear hatch made from the same light purple leather as the seats, 1970 auto show-goers could hardly miss it.

"Mustang invented the ponycar market in 1964 and has led it every year since," said Ford Division general manager John Naughton at the '71 Mustang introduction. "In 1971 it could be the most dramatic new car on the American road." Fact was, Mustang sales had tailed off every year since peaking in 1966, and for the 1970 model year the disappointing tally was but 170,003. It was thus with eager but uncertain hearts that the Ford executives introduced this much larger Mustang to a public beset with government-lowered automotive expectations and sky-high car insurance rates for anything even smelling of fun or performance.

Like it or not, it was the most changed Mustang in the car's seven-year history. The flat-topped SportsRoof certainly was dramatic, if not exactly svelte, and the Mach I and Boss 351 still retained much of their former macho. No question they were roomier, more comfortable, and more luxuriously appointed than before, as intended. But were they still "pony" cars, or just sexy sedans? The horsepower race, government regulations, Bunkie Knudsen and the quest for luxury had changed their character tremendously since that first tumultuous introduction in April 1964.

Some within the company weren't too pleased, especially those who had conceived and developed the original. "If we hadn't gone nuts and put the big Boss 429 engine in, the car never would have grown in size," said Lee Iacocca years later. "That was what triggered it out of the small-car world...performance, performance, performance!" "It was Bunkie's Mustang, the one that looked like it hit the wall," sniped Hal Sperlich.

In addition to its new look, over two inches more length and width and nearly 600 pounds more weight, the '71 Mustang did have a long list of new features and options. Windshield wipers were concealed and door handles flush to the body. Inside, the large speedometer, (optional) tach and a smaller central fuel gauge were recessed into a mildly curved panel in easy view of the driver. The available gauge package (oil, alternator and temperature), radio, heater/AC controls and (optional) clock were just to the right in a vertical center panel. The high-back bucket seats were a new design with molded foam cushions, the inner door handles were pull-type and the arm rests were extra-long for comfort and convenience. A new mini-console, standard in all models, housed the gear lever and a large ashtray.

Base engine became the 250-cubic-inch six, and six optional V-8's still provided a wide choice of performance potential. A two-barrel 302 was standard fare in the emasculated base Mach I; but either a two-barrel or a four-barrel 351 could be ordered to give it some semblance of its former reputation, or a 370 hp 429 (with or without Ram Air induction) with a 3.90 or 4.11 rear axle could put it right back into the street and strip competition league. Unique to the Boss 351 was a new high-performance, canted-valve 351 HO (Cleveland) engine rated at 330 horsepower.

Staggered rear shocks were standard on all models with 351-or-larger engines, and both base and heavy duty suspensions were slightly revised for better ride and handling. The new-design steering gear was constant-ratio with the standard suspension but variable-ratio with the stiffer "competition" chassis option. Also upgraded for '71 were the window regulators, ventilation and air conditioning, and the convertible's top mechanism. Finally, the Mach I pioneered a new resilient urethane body-colored front bumper (supposedly doubling as a spoiler), while the Boss 351 retained its racy aerodynamic chin

Page opposite: New front-end theme renderings were compared and the two most promising (the "A" versions) were put into clay. Both dual- and quad-headlamp styles were tried, the latter with unusual rear quarter louvers, short rear deck and fastback-like roofline. Above: A late-January coupe model revealed a clean nose, high tail. Below: The slope-roof coupe with vertical rear fender louver and another nose design was under consideration in March of 1968.

Above: The car that impressed Knudsen; minus high taillamps, scoops and extreme tunneled grille, this is essentially the '71 fastback that debuted in fall of '70. Below: Full-size alternative drawings showing Knudsen-influenced high front fenders, low curved beltlines.

spoiler. New options included power windows, electric rear window defroster, an exterior protection group and an ill-advised vinyl roof covering the SportsRoof.

Side guard door beams were the only major safety addition, but there was also a significant list of new emissions equipment to comply with '71 Federal standards. Ford dubbed its air injection system "IMCO" ("Improved Combustion"), and it was used on all except the Boss 351 and high-performance 429's with the "Drag-Pack" option, which used thermal reactors instead to control excess hydrocarbons and carbon monoxide. A new evaporative emission control system also was required equipment, and California cars that year were first to get the troublesome exhaust gas recirculation (EGR) for Oxides of Nitrogen (NOx) control.

On September 5th, 1970, Ford announced that the optionally available five-year, 50,000-mile engine/drivetrain warranty would no longer be offered. Instead, warranties on all components of all Ford cars would revert back to the traditional twelve-month, 12,000-mile terms. This was a competitive money-saving move, since GM and Chrysler were also dropping their extended warranties and calling a halt to what had been an industry "warranty war." Thus Ford's previous standard warranty of twelve months and unlimited mileage also became a thing of the past. Ford car prices at the same time were raised a flat five percent across the board, then later (October 10th) adjusted again to reflect equipment changes and the competitive position of various models. So the '71 Mustang was by now not only a foot longer, half-a-foot wider and 626 pounds heavier than the '65 version, it was also some twenty-two percent more expensive at $2888 base.

Not quite ready in August, the Boss 351 was publicly displayed for the first time at the November 21st-29th Detroit auto show. Fully instrumented inside and crouched on F60-15 white-letter tires on seven-inch-wide sport wheels, the race-bred Boss 302's replacement

Both the fastback and hardtop taking shape in mid-June. Ford designed

was claimed to deliver better handling, more power, more torque and more "tractability" than its predecessor, "resulting in the best all-around performer in Ford production-car history." The new Boss offered eleven different paint options, including four wild "grabber" colors...lime, blue, yellow and green metallic. In addition to the beefed springs and sway bars, a standard 3.91:1 Traction-Lok rear axle, quick 15.7:1 steering, four-speed transmission and Hurst linkage with a T-handle shifter were part of the Boss 351 package.

Shortly after the start of production, the third 429 V-8 referred to by Howard Freers came on-stream. Called the 429-4V (four-barrel) CJ with Drag pack, or just 429-4V SCJ (Super Cobra Jet), it was rated at 375 horsepower at 5600 rpm (versus 370 at 5400 for the regular CJ) and 450 ft/lb of torque at 3400 rpm, with or without Ram Air. There was also a last-minute change in the 351-4V's compression ratio from 11.0 to 10.7:1, leaving it with 285 advertised horsepower at 5400 rpm versus the 11.7:1 compression 351-4V HO's 330 hp at the same engine speed. Both 351's were credited with a torque output of 370 ft/lb, but the HO produced it 600 rpm higher in its rev range: 4000 versus 3400 rpm.

One problem with the new SportsRoof styling was seeing out of its nearly horizontal rear window. As *Car Life* put it in a September 1970 wrap-up of the '71 models: "The fastback or SportsRoof is actually a flat back. The roof angle is only fourteen degrees. The rear window would make a good skylight. A glance in the rearview mirror provides an excellent view of the interior with a small band of road visible near the top of the mirror. But the new roof looks good and has probably eliminated two questionable options: the rear window slats and the spoiler."

While some may not have appreciated those elements of the Larry Shinoda performance look, Ford product planners were busy applying other high-horsepower styling "cues" to low-performance models. While previous performance cars had had to "earn" their stripes, so to speak, the new practice at Ford in trying to boost sagging sales was to throw stripes, scoops and black-out trim all over ordinary, lower-priced cars to make them "sporty." The first example was the so-called standard "Mach I" with its base, underpowered, low-compression 302 V-8. The next came in April 1971 when Ford unveiled a "sporty" version of the standard Mustang hardtop, complete with Ram Air-style twin-scoop hood, blacked-out grille with auxiliary lights, color-keyed urethane front bumper and (worst of all) the Boss 351's side stripe package...all for only $97 over base price. This may have sold a few cheap hardtops, but it was also one more nail in the *real* high-performance Mustang's coffin.

The next step came in May when a new low-compression "mid-range-performance" 351 engine was released. Designed to run on 91-octane unleaded gas, and producing a rated 280 hp at 5800 rpm, this new "351 CJ" was essentially a hydraulic-lifter 351 HO with its compression ratio drastically lowered to 8.6:1. Available in all Mustang models except the Boss 351, it came standard with a non-locking 3.50:1 rear axle and required either automatic or four-speed manual transmission and the staggered-rear-shock "competition" suspension.

Mustang entered model-year 1972 virtually unchanged externally from '71, but nearly all performance-car pretenses were gone along with the various 429 c.i.d. powerplants. There were five models available—standard and Grandé hardtops, standard and Mach I SportsRoofs and the convertible—and only five engines—250-cubic-inch six (base on all but Mach I), 302-2V V-8, 351 -2V V-8, 351-4V V-8, and a new "351-4V HO," all running on low-octane regular fuel. No output figures were published, but Ford did make a point of mentioning that its '72-model emissions equipment reduced unburned hydrocarbons by more than eighty-five percent and carbon monoxide by almost sixty percent. Four-speed transmission was standard with the HO engine, the regular four-barrel 351 offered a choice of four-

...ts own '71 Cobra coupe after deciding to part company with Shelby. Mean but awkward, it never made it to production. Note '69 Shelby in background.*

speed or automatic, and the others came with three-speed manual standard and automatic optional.

The only significant visual change was a new, optional Exterior Decor Group for base models that included the Mach I-style grille and auxiliary lamps. A seat-belt reminder system was incorporated in accordance with Federal safety requirements, and outboard rear seat-belt retractors were added (for the same reason) to cars built after December 1st, 1971. There was also a new-design optional AM/FM stereo radio, a revised optional protection group (bodyside moldings and bumper guards front and rear) and upgraded interior materials in the convertible.

"Mustang still leads its field, and we don't expect any change in its market position next year," said Ford Division general manager John Naughton at the August 17th new-car introduction. "In 1972 Mustang retains many of the features that have combined to make it America's most successful sporty compact with more than 2.5 million Mustangs on the road." The sad fact was, however, that Mustang's sales had dropped to a new low of 139,942 for model year 1971. Chevy's Camaro had beaten it by over 1000 units for the calendar year, and there was no indication that demand for the larger, heavier Ford ponycar was going to grow any stronger in 1972. Mustang, and the world around it, were simply too much changed since the original had created such a sensation nearly eight years before.

It was clear during late 1971 and early '72 that internal battles over performance cars and engines were raging between Ford's upper management and accountants on one side and the engineers and product planners on the other. Early '72-model literature indicated that the Boss 351 would remain in the lineup for '72, but it had been scrubbed by introduction time. Then the de-smogged 351 HO (like the previous year's "351 CJ") did not become available until mid-'72; and it remained a limited-production item for a few months until it, too, was dropped after only 1000 or so had been built, according to engine development engineer John Bowers. This "semi-performance" engine retained the Boss 351's solid lifters and most of the good heavy-duty parts, so all it really lacked were higher-compression pistons and a racier camshaft. The factory was definitely out of racing, but at least a few people at Ford recognized in 1972 that some of its customers weren't.

"Obviously there had been a battle over the 351 HO," said *Car and Driver* after testing the first '72 example late in 1971. "The accountants can't justify this kind of car anymore and they've let everybody know it. The Mustang market is soft to begin with, performance runs against the strictly-functional grain of many buyers nowadays, and there is a kind of overriding fear that mud-slinging consumer advocates might hold up a new performance car as proof

Above and page opposite: Alternative rear and various front-end designs considered for '71-'73 Mustangs. The right ones seem to have been chosen. Below: "Milano, a sleek, two-passenger grand touring car...similar to those seen cruising the countryside near Milan, Italy," said the press release. First displayed early in 1970 and a preview of '71 fastback theme, the taillamps of this Mustang show car glowed green, amber or red, to indicate whether the driver was accelerating, coasting or stopping.

that the engineering department isn't spending every minute of its waking time on anti-smog and safety devices...

"In terms of straight-line power the muscles have atrophied in the past twelve months. John Bowers knows that better than anybody, and it makes him talk about 'potential' rather than what the 351 does right out of the box. Emissions come first these days, power second."

Under the revised, much more honest and realistic system of rating engines only by SAE net horsepower, the 351 HO was credited by Ford engineers with 275 hp at 6000 rpm...not too shabby by 1972-model standards. *Car and Driver* measured some respectable performance figures with it: zero-to-sixty mph in 6.6 seconds; 15.1 seconds at 95.6 mph in the quarter-mile; 120 mph top speed. For the short time it lasted, this final Ford high-performance engine could be ordered in any of the various Mustang models, and it came in a package with the four-speed transmission, F60-15 tires on seven-inch-wide wheels, "competition" suspension, disc brakes and heavy-duty radiator and battery.

In mid-December of 1971, Detroit got an unexpected favor from Washington: The Federal excise tax on passenger cars and light trucks was lifted in hopes of boosting sagging sales, and with them the nation's economy. Ford Motor Company sales vice-president M.S. McLaughlin said that removal of the excise tax "more than offsets price increases put into effect by Ford during Phase II of the Administration's wage-price program. Some of the new suggested (list) prices are even lower than those prevailing for comparable models a year ago." This, plus a reduction in the Mustang dealer discount (the percentage below list at which the dealer buys a vehicle) from twenty-one to seventeen percent, left the '72 base six-cylinder hardtop at a fairly reasonable $2697.66, nearly $150 less than before the tax cut and only about $60 more than the '69 model.

Another heavy blow to what remained of the macho Mustang's ego came in late February when it was grouped with limp-wristed Pintos

Production Mustangs for 1972. Above: Mach I and the hardtop, which was basically unchanged from 1971. Below: The convertible, with Mach I-like Exterior Decor option. Right: The red, white and blue "Sprint"-decorated hardtop, with Popular Hot Rodding editor Lee Kelley (in blazer) and Ford vice-president and Division general manager John Naughton, on the occasion of the magazine's honoring Mustang as Car of the Decade, March 6th, 1972. Page opposite: Mustangs for '73. Mach I, with the newly-optional forged aluminum wheels; the redesigned front end and Mach I stripes were the only major appearance changes. The Grandé hardtop. The convertible (with two-tone hood option), this the last convertible from Ford Division.

now body-colored urethane, protruded further forward and connected to impact-absorbing devices in the front body structure to meet '73-model Federal bumper requirements.

The 250-cubic-inch six-cylinder engine remained standard except in Mach I, which retained its base 302 V-8. The 351-2V and 351-4V optional V-8's were available in all models, the former requiring automatic transmission (because of emissions certification) and only the latter offering the optional manual four-speed. All came with exhaust gas recirculation (EGR) to reduce NOx emissions to Federal requirement levels. "This new system routes a portion of the exhaust gas back to the intake system beneath the carburetor to dilute the incoming fuel/air charge and reduce combustion temperatures," explained Ross Taylor, who was then Ford Engine and Foundry Division chief engineer.

"Peak NOx concentrations occur near ideal air/fuel ratios and best combustion efficiency," Taylor continued, "and increase with engine

load as the combustion temperature rises. A richer fuel mixture reduces NOx but increases emissions of hydrocarbons. A leaner mixture and a retarded spark reduce NOx somewhat but create driveability problems. Because of these factors, and to achieve the degree of NOx control required, the EGR system was developed." Ford had difficulty certifying some of its '73 engine/drivetrain combinations for emissions compliance in time for the fall introduction, and driveability did suffer a bit with some of these early EGR systems; but the law was The Law. Actually, the engine people did well to accomplish what they did in the little time they had.

Other technical changes for '73 included standard power front disc brakes on convertibles and 351 V-8 equipped cars; larger and better front drum brakes for other models (due to a Federal brake performance standard); improved (and slightly longer) front shock absorbers for better rebound control and road feel; and an upgraded optional electric rear window defroster. New options were forged aluminum wheels, steel-belted radial tires, a two-tone hood (with non-functional twin scoops and twist-type hood locks) and a leather-wrapped steering wheel.

Mustang in its last year before a complete redesign and re-sizing, was the only Ford Division car line still with a convertible version, and it continued to offer the widest selection of models in the "small specialty" class. It did still have some sex appeal, and it could at least be dressed to *look* like a performance car. "In spite of many challenges," understated John Naughton at the '73-model introduction, "Mustang remains the sales leader in its segment of the market. We feel the 1973 Mustang furthers the image of excitement and individual appeal that made it a success from its beginning."

Car sales in 1973 continued their strong post-recession rebound and ended the year by setting an all-time record, despite the crippling Arab oil embargo and fuel shortage that began in the fall. Ironically, the "big" Mustang that had become so primarily to accommodate Ford's massive, thundering 429 engines had lost those engines after just one year on the market—and its sales had continued to decline. With the ponycar market seemingly on the rocks even as pre-embargo new-car sales in general boomed, Chrysler and American Motors decided to drop their Barracuda, Challenger and Javelin after the '74 model year, and GM came within a hair of canning its Camaro and Firebird.

But not long after the fattened '71 Mustang had hit the streets, Ford designers and engineers were already at work on a smaller, lighter replacement that they hoped could recapture the original's youthful image and appeal.

8.

THE LITTLE JEWEL

"Ford Listens Better" was the company line, and in this case it certainly did listen to the depressing sound of steadily falling Mustang sales. The old "happy" letters from satisfied Mustangers were being replaced by complaints that the car was outgrowing its market.

"I would like to see Ford Motor Company take the Mustang back to the original size," wrote a St. Louis owner. "Economy with style is what I'm interested in. It always seems when you people have a good thing, you over-improve on it." "You are making a good American sports car into a luxury bus," groused a man from Connecticut; "...too quiet, soft and big," griped an Iowa College student.

As early as 1968, a Ford stockholder and '65 Mustang owner named Anna Muccioli stood up at the annual spring stockholders' meeting and complained to Henry Ford II himself: "Why can't you just leave a sports car small?" she asked. "I mean you keep blowing them up and starting another little one, blow that one up and start another one. I mean why don't you just leave them?"

Her remarks drew a round of applause from the other stockholders and an honest reply from Ford, who said he agreed. "Hopefully," he added, "we will keep in mind what you say here and, hopefully, we will have a product that will be satisfactory to you."

Lee Iacocca, now company president, had watched with growing concern as his popular little car had ballooned in size and weight during the late 1960's, while small cars from Europe and Japan were growing in appeal. In November 1969, he voiced his concern to the company's top management at a conference in Greenbrier, West Virginia. Out of that meeting came top-priority plans to build a new sporty small car for the 1974 model year, based on the '70 compact Maverick shell. A second program, code-named "Arizona," was to investigate an upmarket variation on the upcoming '71 Pinto subcompact for 1975.

A coachbuilding assist from Italy, a new idea, a satisfied Iacocca.

Nat Adamson, advanced product planning manager, was given responsibility for the Arizona car, and several conceptual clays and some exploratory packaging studies were undertaken by Advanced Design. "Many of these were two-seaters or two-seaters with a bench," says Adamson while some were merely sportier or more luxurious Pintos with different front ends and other detail changes.

Initially, "Arizona" was intended to be a new and separate nameplate, while the Maverick-based program (dubbed "Ohio") was supposed to provide the desired smaller Mustang. This 103-inch wheelbase car took up most of the advanced planning group's time throughout 1970 and into 1971, while the Arizona remained a lower-priority job. "The compact Maverick then seemed like a very small car to us," said Adamson later, "especially when we compared it to that year's much bigger and longer Mustang. And the Maverick was selling very well at the time."

But Lincoln-Mercury Division's German-built Capri, introduced in the United States in April 1970, had surprised Ford management with its overwhelming acceptance. The first 18,000 Capris were snapped up almost as soon as they had hit the beach, a long waiting list of youthful buyers had developed, and by that winter the four-cylinder, sporty subcompact Capri was well on its way to sales of nearly 170,000 in its first two years on American soil. It was becoming clear that, even as Ford's Pinto, Chevy's Vega and American Motors' Gremlin were beginning to counter the wave of economy import popularity, an important new small-car market was emerging. This feeling was reinforced by the equally instant success being enjoyed by Datsun's 240-Z, Toyota's Celica and other small sports and sporty cars.

To help gauge public reaction to various future small car concepts, a research clinic was conducted at the Long Beach Convention Center. Some 200 participants were shown a tiny Honda 600, a variation of the ultra-basic "Fiera" vehicle that Ford was designing for developing countries, a trio of the sporty Arizona concept models in metal and fiberglass, an Opel GT, a Datsun 240-Z, a Porsche 914, a Triumph GT6 Plus, a Spitfire, an MGB GT, a conventional Pinto, a Vega, a Camaro, a Plymouth Duster and a Toyota Corona.

Results of this survey showed that people were not interested in the Honda or Fiera, at least for the early 1970's, but were very much interested in sporty subcompacts. The conclusion was that Ford could be successful with a new subcompact-size car that was more stylish and exciting than the basic Pinto. Thus encouraged, Adamson and his group stepped up their design and package investigations and began looking at powerplant possibilities for the Arizona car.

Ghia

August through November contest among Advanced, Interior, Ford and Lincoln-Mercury studios produced 150 concepts on paper, fifty in clay, some far-out, some practical. The sleek fastback "Ancona" in background (page opposite, center above photo) was first driveable Ghia prototype, produced in fifty-three days.

but (as in the early 1960's) people were becoming more conscious of fuel consumption and economy of operation. And a growing number of them were willing to pay a little more for something more sporty, better built, better looking, better equipped, more luxurious, and more exciting than the basic economy subcompact. Just as ten years before, there was a brand-new market opportunity emerging that no American manufacturer had yet addressed. The question no longer was whether to make the Mustang smaller; it was how much smaller?

So Adamson's proposal to produce the Arizona car was not only approved but accelerated. It was decided to forget the Maverick-based Mustang, move the Arizona program up to '74, and develop it into the next-generation Mustang. The next day, much to his delight, Adamson was promoted to light car planning manager and given this new Mustang project as one of his key responsibilities. Production was scheduled to begin in July 1973...just two years away.

At this time Bordinat and DeLaRossa were still trying to design the car around that long and bulky, old "straight-six" engine. "Finally," Bordinat recalls, "Don put his studio to work on a clay model showing how large the Mustang would have to be to accommodate that big I-6 engine. He got me to call Lee over for a look at it. Don became, shall we say, very forthright and told Lee that if we really wanted to make a smaller car we had better start with a smaller engine because this one with this engine in it was getting bigger even before it was designed. Lee agreed with us, and that was the end of the I-6. The next thing we heard was that the choice of engines would be a new small 2.3-liter four-cylinder and a larger-displacement version of the German Capri V-6, so we were able to get down to making the rest of the car smaller, too."

Once again Iacocca was taking a very personal interest in the design of an all-new Mustang. "He was planning an entirely new kind of domestic car for a different kind of customer," said Hal Sperlich, "so naturally he wanted it to look different from the other cars on the market, different from the Mustangs of 1971, 1972 and 1973, different from the Pinto and different from the Capri, too." What he was looking for was a certain exterior elegance that would give the impression of fine workmanship and quality throughout. The early, Pinto-based Arizona designs did not possess this elusive quality, but the Italian Ghia prototype and a second Ghia model, a clean "pagoda"-roofed notchback, did.

There was considerable debate about whether the new car should be a fastback or a notchback. It was agreed that the convertible model would be dropped since increasing popularity of air conditioning, sunroofs, and stereo sound systems were hurting convertible sales, and the ragtop was also under fire as a safety hazard. But, although notchback and fastback Mustang sales had been running neck-and-neck ever since their prices had been equalized, management seemed determined to go with one or the other for '74 rather than continuing both body styles. One obvious reason was to save the added cost of designing, tooling and producing two different bodies; another was to achieve maximum impact with the introduction of a single model.

"That says to the audience, 'This is it!' " says Bordinat. "You don't want two different cars up there sharing the spotlight and saying to the customers, 'which one do you like better?' So we didn't want two models, not if we could avoid it. But the crazy feeling in the market reaction to comparisons of the fastback and the notchback was making it very difficult for us. If the people were leaning seventy-to-thirty one way or the other, we would have gotten a clue to which way to turn. But the market was polarized like crazy, split right down the middle, fifty-fifty. We were afraid to make a decision so we kept putting it off and putting it off."

Bordinat also was strongly opposed to making any sort of compromise between the two extremes. "The industry has tried that with various cars in the past," said he, "cars that were neither out-and-out notchbacks nor fastbacks but somewhere in between. They were nice cars but they got lost in the landscape."

To hasten creation of an acceptable design and help solve this fastback versus notchback dilemma, Iacocca had Bordinat stage a design competition among four of his studios similar to the one which had produced the very successful original Mustang design back in 1962. "Lee thinks that pitting our guys against each other breeds our best stuff," Bordinat quipped later. "I've tried to disagree with him, but every time we do it, we get an exceptionally good car." Actually this sort of friendly competition was becoming increasingly common at Ford Design, according to design executive Fritz Mayhew, who was involved in the '74 Mustang contest. "Such a contest is typical of our system," says he, "because it's a very competitive system."

The competition ran for three months, beginning in August 1971; and designers from the Ford, Lincoln-Mercury, Advanced and Interior Studios came up with 150 sketches and put as many as fifty of those ideas into clay before their final candidates were selected. All were designed around a set of "hard points"--such as headroom, reach distances, seating positions, lines of visibility and steering column and wheel positions--which had been determined by the packaging engineers. "The enthusiasm of the troops was tremendous," said Lincoln-Mercury design director Al Mueller. "You could tell it was a labor of love, not just a job. Some designers would come in on their own time to work."

The four studios were free to do whatever concepts they fancied within the boundaries of good taste and reasonable cost...fastbacks, notchbacks or compromise solutions...and while some were far-out,

Above: DeLaRossa's formal notchback "Anaheim," the car that was admired by Iacocca and others, bombed in Southern California, proved a hit in San Francisco with the result that a notchback was put back into the 1974 Mustang program. Below: The striking fastback from Al Mueller's Lincoln-Mercury Studio, the winner hands-down of the design competition; with high, oval grille at headlamp level added to lend original Mustang character; and executives Stu Frey, Jack Eby and Harold MacDonald looking over proposed Mach I version. A coatless Al Mueller working on front fender and belt lines with a full-size tape drawing and an assist from Ford chief car product planner Jim Cappalongo. Right: A short wheelbase tape drawing was cut out and compared to clay model, to ascertain what the car would look like as a two-seater.

others were practical, and most contributed something useful toward answering the overall question of how the mid-Seventies Mustang should look. And even while the competition was still going on, promising candidates were shipped to California for research clinic evaluation and then back to Dearborn for further development.

A San Diego clinic in September polled 542 small-car prospects (142 of whom were Mustang owners), but the results were split among preferences for compacts, sporty compacts and sporty subcompacts. Most agreed, however, in favoring high-nosed hoodlines and fastback roof styles. A week later, the planners staged another clinic in Anaheim, California, the results of which clearly pointed to the sportier of two fastbacks on display and to the oval-type Mustang grille with exposed headlamps. The one notchback model, created by DeLaRossa's Advanced Studio and heavily influenced by the notchback Ghia prototype, bombed so badly in this study that it came to be called the "Anaheim" car.

Back in Dearborn, a clinic was held in late November to compare five of the best '74 Mustang models, including (as a benchmark) the ill-fated Anaheim notchback. Again, the notchback's appeal was only about half that of the fastbacks; but, significantly, those who did praise its "foreign, classic lines" were mostly in the over-twenty-five age group. A few days later it was time for final judging and selection by Iacocca, Bordinat and product development vice-president Harold MacDonald. Al Mueller's Lincoln-Mercury Studio had put all its bets on a striking fastback model, in shiny persimmon paint, that somehow managed to look longer, lower and more substantial than anyone thought such a small car could. The Ford and Interior Studios also were betting on their best fastbacks, but DeLaRossa was sticking with his European-look Anaheim notchback in spite of its poor showing in West Coast clinics. Iacocca and some other executives had been favorably impressed by the notchback car's clean good looks, and as he viewed it on this crisp November morning he remarked to Bordinat that it still looked good to him.

But Mueller's sexy, persimmon-colored fastback emerged the hands-down winner. "Mr. Iacocca's procedure at these showings usually is the same," recalled Mueller later. "He walks around the cars a few times and listens to the comments of others. Then he says exactly what he thinks—either pro or con. He really flipped over our fastback. His cigar must have rolled around three times. We had won."

But Iacocca also felt that the Mueller design was a bit too radical. He wanted the low, "V"-shaped beltline to come up a bit, and he wanted a more Mustang-like front and other cues to remind people of the original car. The designers were quick to comply with a high, wide, mouthy grille opening and centered horse emblem, plus an interpretation of the old side scoop idea that had long since been dropped from the production car. "It's interesting," comments Fritz Mayhew, "that the side scoop re-appeared at all, since most designers were convinced at that point in time that it should go away. But Iacocca wanted to go back to the original cues."

The approved model then went to the Design Center's Feasibility Studio where mass-production experts would determine whether there would be any significant difficulties in tooling or assembly. Simultaneously, work began in the Ford and Interior Studios to come up with a suitable interior to match the classy exterior appearance. Only about thirty percent of the design work had been done up to that point, and now it was up to the Ford Studio to direct completion of the remaining seventy percent in the nineteen months left before production start-up in July 1973. This short time period between styling approval and production was still another way in which the '74 Mustang program resembled the original's some ten years before.

So the new-generation Mustang was finally on its way, and the fastback versus notchback problem was solved. Or was it? DeLaRossa had stuck with his notchback concept because he had been so captivated by the smoothly integrated front-to-back proportions of that second Ghia model, proportions that made it seem to be moving while at rest...proportions much like those of the original Mustang—long, flowing hood and short, chopped rear deck. You can't get that effect without a notchback roof, he had told himself.

"The Ghia model, despite its caved-in pagoda roof, really pulled us up short," DeLaRossa remembered later. "We had been thinking of the sporty small car of the future in terms of the then sporty car of 1971, a fastback or semi-fastback. But if we wanted to design a modern second generation of Mustangs, why not recapture some of the flavor of the famous original model of 1965? That was a notchback. The fastback Mustangs were offshoots that came in later. So we got to work on a notchback with that fully integrated front and rear end."

The result was the spunky Anaheim notchback which had met rejection in California, in Dearborn and ultimately in the final judging. But it was still stuck in Iacocca's mind like corn in a farmboy's teeth. In February 1972, three months after the competition supposedly had been decided, the product planners and researchers decided to conduct another West Coast clinic, this time in San Francisco, to gauge the public's potential demand for the sporty

Howard Freers shows Harold MacDonald a portion of the innovative isolated subframe of the Mustang II. "Shake, rattle and roll" machines inside and the Proving Ground outside were used for tests. Page opposite: Charles Keresztes fashions the new emblem; when Lee Iacocca spotted his "group" version he insisted horses be limited to "twenty-one per car." Meanwhile designer Jim Arnold folded his arms and listened to Dave Ash talk about the interior seating.

subcompact and see where they thought such a car would be priced. A few days before the test models were to be shipped, Iacocca surprised everyone by telephoning to order the Anaheim notchback dug out of mothballs and sent off along with the others.

"I'll never forget the day I went out there," relates product planner Nat Adamson. "It had been a long day, it was snowing in Detroit and raining in San Francisco, and when I got off the plane Chuck Morgan came running up and asked me to come over to the clinic instead of going to my hotel. There seemed to be some sort of problem. DeLaRossa's notchback was doing very well, and it was not supposed to." Adamson had been worrying that the new Mustang's volume potential might be seriously hurt by limiting it to a single body style, and the notchback's surprising popularity in San Francisco confirmed his feeling that going fastback-only would be a mistake.

Iacocca heartily agreed, and suddenly the notchback was thrown back into the program just sixteen months before start of production. It was too late, and would have been too expensive, to tool up for two different lower bodies, so the Ford designers were faced with the difficult problem of grafting a notchback roof onto the fastback body and making common doors work with both. "It seems we go through that with every Mustang program," shrugs design executive Jack Telnack. "We always start with the fastback...gotta be a fastback... then we find out the surveys still say fifty-fifty and we have to add the notchback."

The San Francisco survey, besides showing what Iacocca and others had suspected all along...that tastes were different there than in Southern California...also produced encouragement for the small Mustang concept as a whole. Participants priced the notchback at an estimated $3840 and the fastback at $3810, both more than $800 over the '74 Mustang's projected base price; and the responses indicated a potential 400,000-unit market for such a car.

At last, in the spring of 1972, basic plans for the new sporty subcompact were in place and its exterior design approved. There were details remaining to be worked out—extra engine cooling intakes were added below the bumper; the taillamps were redesigned and dropped to a lower, less vulnerable position just above the bumper, which also provided a lower lift-over height for cargo loading through the rear hatch—but the wheelbase had been set at 96.2 inches, the two-body-style approach had been finalized, and the new 2.3-liter overhead cam, four-cylinder engine was already well along in development. Four major objectives were set for the final product: high perceived value for the money, sensible size, engineering excellence and high style.

"All the 1974 Mustang will have to be is one thing," said Iacocca during the planning stage. "It will have to be a little jewel." What he

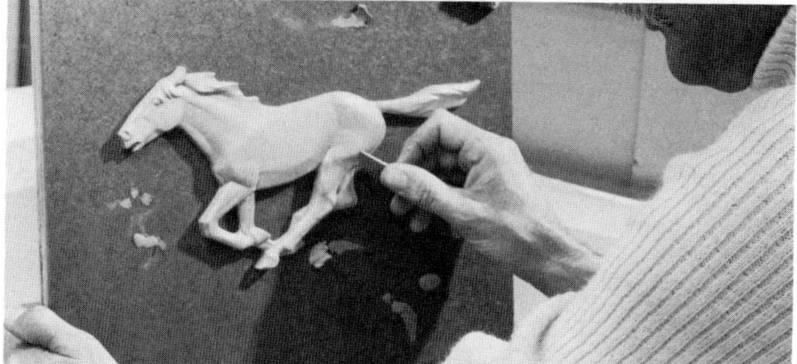

meant was that it would have to stand above all other four-cylinder small cars, domestic and foreign, in quality, fit and finish, and in what engineers call "NVH"—noise, vibration and harshness. What people really wanted, he reasoned, was a truly *fine* small car that radiated excellence inside and out, with the ride and quiet of a much larger car.

Suspension solutions to accomplish this at first were too costly for the projected sub-$3000 base price. But then program engineers Bob Negstad and Jim Kennedy, under Mustang development engineer Paul Nyquist, came up with a unique solution that came to be regarded as the single most important component of the Mustang II chassis—a U-shaped, isolated subframe to which the front suspension and engine were mounted. This innovation (known internally as the "toilet seat") had the effect of soaking up most road shock and powertrain vibrations before they reached the seats and steering wheel, producing an uncommon level of NVH isolation in a small, unit-body car.

Another problem, the annoying shakes and "moans" that four-cylinder engines tend to transmit through the body at certain rpm's, was effectively solved by going to a larger diameter driveshaft and increasing the bolt-circle diameter where the transmission bolts up to the engine. This involved retooling both engine block rear faces and transmission housings, at a cost in the millions, but Nyquist was able to demonstrate the idea's worth on test fixtures and sell it to management.

More rubber insulation was used throughout the car's structure than in many larger cars, and on the floor was a new type of material that was laid during assembly and then melted and flowed to form a

tight, soundproof bond from high heat in the paint-baking oven. Another important engineering feature was precise rack-and-pinion steering, with an optional power assist—at a time when power rack-and-pinion steering was available only on a handful of European luxury cars.

Extensive proving ground and laboratory development testing was conducted with pre-production cars, including hundreds of passes over a rough-road course to determine precisely how much and what kind of rubber material worked best between the isolated subframe and the body. "You have to juggle various weights of rubber to determine how many pounds per square inch of shock pressure it can absorb effectively without wearing thin or hardening," Nyquist explains. "If it's too soft, the weight of the load on the suspension system flattens it so you get worse impacts than if it's too hard. The only way to test these alternatives is to put one of them in the car and drive it on the test track. Then change the components and drive the car again and compare that test with the previous tests, over and over and over, and then go to Arizona and try it in hot weather, which may give you an entirely different effect. Then to Minnesota and try it in the cold, because you started these tests in May and now it's getting to be late in November. Meanwhile, you are running other tests on forty-nine different other problems in the same car."

There is also a tremendous amount of indoor testing to be done, on various components as well as the car as a whole. For instance, the

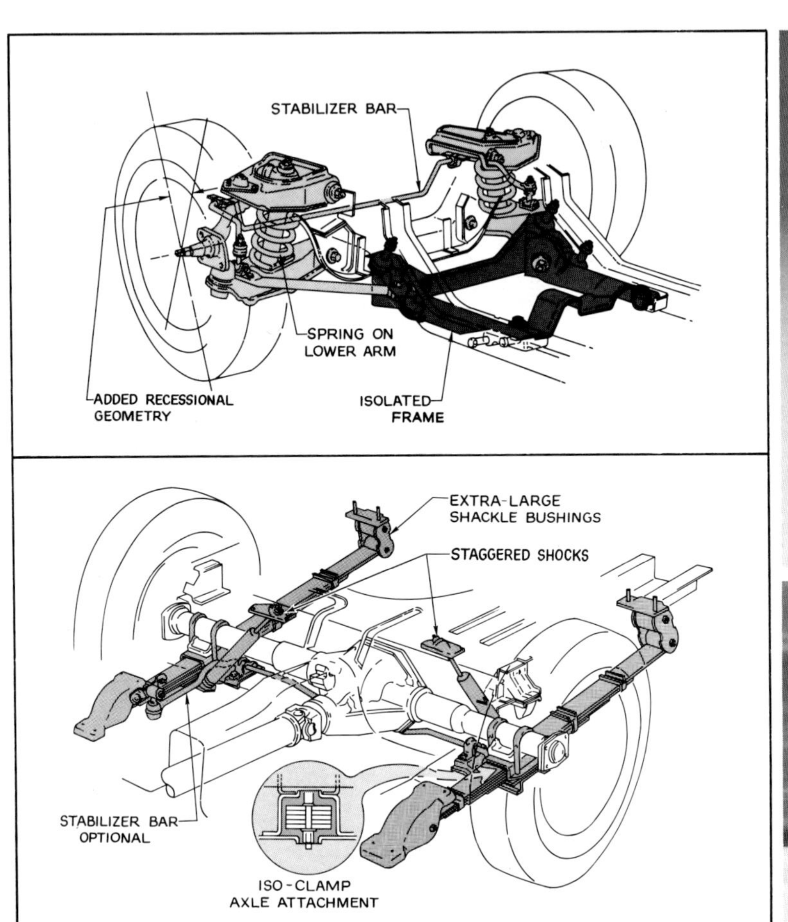

Mustang II spent a lot of time on Ford's "shake, rattle, and roll" machines, which can be programmed to duplicate a fast trip down any sort of rough road or even during shipment on a railroad car. The operator starts the car, "drives" it up to speed, then gets out and sits down beside it to monitor his instruments and listen for any rattles, creaks or groans as the test "trip" is made.

Five major areas of development were stressed to make the new Mustang better than the much larger 1973 version—ride, NVH, handling, damage protection and reliability. Improved ride was accomplished by redesigning both front and rear suspensions with lower spring rates and better isolation, moving the front springs down to the lower control arms and staggering the rear shocks. Better NVH control came as a result of the isolated subframe, new transmission bolt pattern, fifty percent more chassis insulation and other features such as increased compliance in both front and rear suspensions to allow the wheels to move rearward when hitting a bump.

Handling features included the revised suspension designs, rack-and-pinion steering, a standard front stabilizer bar and both "rally" and "competition" suspension options. For damageability protection (in accordance with government five-mph impact standards) both front and rear bumper systems were a new design incorporating shock absorbers filled with Poly Gel, a thick, jelly-like substance, to provide up to two inches of damage-free bumper contraction.

Base engine was an all-new, metric, 2.3-liter, overhead-cam four-cylinder offering performance comparable to the old 200-cubic-inch six in a 1965 Mustang. "We decided to make the 2.3 a metric engine for interchangeability with the 2.0 in other Ford products," explains E.A. Hardy, who was manager of four-cylinder engine engineering. "The trend toward going to metric measure in the U.S. also might have had a bearing on our decision." This was the first all-metric engine built in the U.S. and the first domestic Ford four-cylinder in modern times. It had service-free hydraulic valve-lash adjusters (unique for an overhead cam four-cylinder) and was designed and developed with its major emissions componentry built in rather than added on. The optional German-built 2.8-liter V-6 was basically similar to the engine already in the Capri and other European Ford products, except that the displacement increase required a new engine block. Available transmissions were an all-new four-speed manual standard and a three-speed automatic optional.

A near-incredible amount of time, trouble and special attention went into giving the car the superior fit and finish that Iacocca demanded for his "little jewel." Says chief car engineer Stu Frey, "Lee made it very clear to me personally that he would expect the car to show the same high quality in attention to details as a Mercedes-Benz, or higher if possible." Frey spent two weeks in Europe

Page opposite: Mustang II's suspension, overhead cam engine; Peter Revson driving a '74 Mach I on a rainy day in May 1973. Above: The Sportiva II show car. Below: DeLaRossa with the "Ancona," the Ghia "pagoda-roof" notchback, the "Anaheim," the production '74 Mustang Ghia they inspired. Stockholder Anna Muccioli is given a personal preview by Henry Ford II of Mustang II. She liked it.

Below: Mustang II fastback and Ghia for 1974. Above right: John Dinkle testing first 302 V-8 Mach I for Road & Track *magazine. Page opposite: 1975 Mustang notchback with new "opera" window, compared to 1957 Thunderbird. Above: Crushing dullness of 1975 model year typified by Mustang II fuel economy test photograph.*

studying methods of design execution used there, and decided upon returning to "take every cotton-picking part in the car, every single bit of trim and molding and every nut and screw and bolt, and make a clay model of it...so we could study it in three dimensions and decide how it could look better, or in the case of nuts and screws, how it could be hidden. There was no mystery to it; it was just a matter of making the parts so that they would fit into each other as neatly as possible."

This was accomplished by copying Mercedes' technique of using concealed butt sleeve joints, instead of the traditional American overlap joints, to connect pieces of trim and molding wherever possible, by shaving manufacturing tolerances to the bare minimum and by designing the interior piece by piece before adding its structural elements. Visible screws inside the car were either eliminated or carefully hidden, a completely new high-luster aluminum alloy that would not turn "milky" with age was developed, and even the "flash" lines between sections of the plastic bumper covering were eliminated by careful hand buffing during assembly.

"It costs much more money to do a fine job on such details than it does to do it the other way," said design chief Bordinat later. "On this car they didn't wait until the last minute to open up the purse strings, which Lee has done in the past to turn an acceptable car into a really good car. This new Mustang was planned as a top quality job right from the very start. I am not a very enthusiastic fellow, but I think this is the most finely finished automobile that any American manufacturer has ever made."

To go with the Mustang's new size and image, it seemed appropriate to come up with an updated running horse emblem. This

job was given to Charles Keresztes, a Hungarian-born Ford interior designer who also happened to be an accomplished horseman and animal sculptor. After studying paintings of American Mustang horses in Frederic Remington's *Great Pictures of the Old West*, Keresztes made some preliminary sketches and then sculpted a clay figure of a fast-running, high-spirited Mustang that was an instant hit with everyone at Ford.

But designers will be designers, and there was disagreement about how many horses should be put on the sides of various models, which way the front and rear emblems should face, whether the "II" should be a Roman or an Arabic numeral, where it should go in relation to the horse, and other such details. Keresztes also had done a beautiful sculpture showing four frolicking horses, and when Iacocca spotted this one day, he stopped short, took his cigar from his mouth and eyed the designers coldly. "I want you guys to know," he said, "that from now on you're limited to no more than twenty-one horses per car."

That was the end of the four-horse emblem idea, and each car ultimately got one per side (facing forward), one front and one rear, both running toward the passenger's side...so the one in the grille was still going clockwise, as seen from the outside of a race track. "The guys who told us in 1964 that the horse runs the wrong way will be telling us that all over again," said Iacocca; but the designers preferred it that way and argued that the Mustang is a wild horse, not a race-track horse, and can run any way it wants.

The development progressed without any major traumas through the summer and fall of 1972, and then on December 8th it was time for Iacocca to drive the car for his first time. Together with Bordinat, he tested an automatic notchback and a four-speed hatchback, both equipped with the optional V-6 engine, power steering and brakes, and air conditioning. He stepped into the notchback, stroked its wood-grained instrument panel and plush carpeting, buckled the new inertia-reel lap and shoulder belt, noted the headroom inside and winked at Bordinat in the passenger seat next to him.

He started the engine, revved it and listened intently, put the transmission into drive and motored smartly away. He drove it both fast and slowly, flinging it around the test-track's curves and headlong down the straights. He was duly impressed by the little Mustang's performance, stability, road holding and ride, qualities that made it feel like a much larger vehicle. He remarked to Bordinat that maybe the isolated subframe had been worth its cost after all.

The test was repeated in the four-speed car, and both men agreed that it seemed even more nimble and responsive with the manual transmission. Finally satisfied, he drove back into the test track garage and switched off the key. He sat there for a moment in silence, chewing on his cigar. Then he looked at Bordinat. "We've got a smash," he said with obvious delight.

Seven months remained before start of production on July 30th and only nine before public introduction in September, and there were still some minor wrinkles to be dealt with. "Putting the isolated sub-frame into the car and getting it smoothed out by Job One was tight time-wise," remembers group vice-president, product development Harold MacDonald. "But we didn't have any job-stopper problems. We struggled with the cost more than anything, plus the notchback versus fastback decision." Stu Frey recalls some discussion over whether the car should have a frame around its door glass or not (sedan or hardtop), which was resolved in favor of the hardtop design, and points out that there was difficulty getting some of the trim and other small parts in time because of the late styling approval. "But there were no last-minute tragedies, no deathbed scenes," he adds.

To get an informed outside opinion on the car's performance and handling, the engineers invited race driver Peter Revson to the Dearborn track in May 1973. He drove a four-speed "Mach I" fastback equipped with the Rallye package, and seemed impressed in spite of the rainy conditions that day. "The car performs well without sacrificing any comfort," said Revson after the brief test. "The power rack-and-pinion steering is sensitive and doesn't wander. It's not a Trans-Am car of course. But then again those things drive like coal cars, and I'm sure you guys aren't trying to build coal cars."

Naturally, the hard-working public relations people were busy planning a strategy for launching the Mustang II as elaborate as the engineers' development program. They saw a number of advantages that would ease their task of promoting the new little Mustang: still-exciting name and mystique; a "generation" had been named for it; it was the latest American import fighter, a truly fine, small, sporty car; high perceived value at a modest price; nimble, good-handling, unusually quiet; contemporary design with interesting dimensions and two body styles to appeal to a broad range of tastes. Disadvantages, on the other hand, were an increasingly crowded small-car marketplace; depending on conditions, a price possibly higher than that of the larger 1973 car; design that might not be perceived as *different* enough for an all-new entry (the fastback roofline's resemblance to Pinto's was especially bothersome); a shorter car with less rear legroom than the 1965 Mustang, but heavier and slightly slower.

Plans were made to capitalize on the name and re-establish the "Mustang Generation"; promote the car as an import fighter; emphasize the "jewel-like" quality and reasonable price; stress the practical new dimensions, handling and quietness; play up the contemporary design and two-body-style availability; and fortify Ford's role as an innovator of timely and important new products. Information and "sneak" photo material were made available to the media through a carefully controlled program to create advance expectations. Key TV, radio and magazine representatives were invited to Dearborn for advance confidential briefings and showings. It had been recommended that Ford Design build a Mustang II-based show car for display throughout 1973 at race tracks and car shows—as had been done with the original "Mustang II" show car back in 1963-'64—and the targa-top Sportiva II was created.

Interestingly, the new name was itself a public relations idea. Says one internal publication: "The suggestion put in writing on August 7th, 1972, by North American Operations Public Relations that the new car be called Mustang II has high merit. As the tenth Mustang, the new car is subject to being accepted as just another model year if it is called simply the 1974 Mustang. On the other hand, a name like Mustang II in itself would serve to communicate the idea of a new generation of Mustangs, and would spark interest on the part of the press and the public."

The company was at once confident and nervous about launching this new, smaller Mustang. Demographic studies showed clearly that the postwar baby boom was moving through America's economy like prey through a snake's body, and in 1974 that bulge would be solidly in the middle of the affluent, upwardly-mobile twenty-four-to-thirty-five age group. These were the same young people who had been captivated so completely by the original Mustang ten years before, and it was absolutely crucial to have a product that would appeal to them in the fast-changing environment of the mid-1970's.

Mustang was still dominating the ponycar market, but that market had slipped from a high of 10.6 percent of U.S. new-car sales in 1967 to a mere three percent by 1973. At the same time, imported sports and sporty cars had enjoyed a 300 percent increase in sales in seven years, numbering a significant 311,000 units in 1972. While there was no direct domestic competition for these popular sporty imports, the closest thing to them was Chevrolet's Vega GT, 75,000 units of which had been sold in 1972.

Thus Ford was once again gambling on entering a brand-new market segment for U.S. manufacturers and, as in 1964, a lot was riding on the outcome. "In 1974, we tried to start all over, if you will, recognizing the trend toward lighter-weight, more fuel-efficient cars," says Harold MacDonald. "It was quite an important step within the company at that time, recapturing the smaller car. We expected that that was the way to go, but we weren't sure. It was a dramatic change philosophically."

And once again Lee Iacocca was betting his reputation and a few hundred million company dollars on his faith in market research and his own intuition. He had hit the target dead center in 1964...but then his predecessors had been equally confident in launching the ill-fated 1958 Edsel. "It's a whole new ball game," said he shortly before Mustang II's introduction. "In a game like this, it costs you a mint just for the kick-off, so all of us had better be right." Another Ford executive commented, "It's the kind of drama, if you will, that is very seldom seen in modern American business. Maybe in the old days—the old Henry Ford did things like that, although he could afford to take such chances—but you don't see much of it today." Henry Ford II's pre-introduction comment? "We've done our homework. We believe the final grades will bear this out."

Below: 1976 "Stallion" blackout trim package shared with Pinto and Maverick produced yawns, but Cobra II conjured images of original Shelby Mustang excitement. Above: Exciting too, and seen here at Daytona, was "Kemp Cobra" built by IMSA GT road racer Charlie Kemp.

When Mustang II finally was introduced to the daily press on August 28th, 1973, it wasn't much of a surprise. In accordance with the well-planned interest-building PR campaign, Iacocca himself had announced that the new car was on its way as early as April, and a series of "controlled leaks" since then had managed to reveal most details and dimensions. Plenty of photos also had been published throughout the spring and summer, so by late August you would have had to be in outer space somewhere to not know what "Son of Mustang" was going to look like.

The formal notchback, with a roof shape similar to 1965-'66 Mustangs, was featured and emphasized partly because Ford wanted to stress its mini-luxury theme rather than the fastback's more sporting character—but mainly because the latter's roofline bore some resemblance to Pinto's, and the last thing the company wanted was to have press reports start talking about Mustang II's lowly Pinto heritage. Actually, the car was much less Pinto-based than the original had been Falcon-based (only part of the rear floor pan and some drivetrain and chassis components were shared with Pinto), but Ford officials rightfully feared that identification of their "little jewel" with the econobox Pinto could put off a lot of prospective buyers. Plans for a base two-seater fastback were scrubbed at the last minute; and the "Ghia" name was used (instead of "Grandé") for the luxury notchback.

Iacocca confidently predicted that Mustang II would "turn the small-car market on its ear," just as the original had in the mid-1960's, and that Ford would sell all it could build. Production had begun on schedule in Dearborn, and plans were laid to add a second plant in San Jose, California in February if demand was as strong as anticipated. Newsmen at the August introduction were told that Mustang II would deliver about 20 mpg, would cost less than $3000 in base trim, and would sell to the tune of 350,000 units in its maiden year. "We think it will have the same kind of impact that the original Mustang did in 1964," said Ford Division general manager Ben Bidwell, who had just been promoted from general manager of Lincoln-Mercury Division. "I'm looking for a home run," he added. "I think the basic ingredients are there."

Daily press response to the car was generally enthusiastic, with positive comments on its ride, quietness and luxurious appointments and some negative ones about leisurely performance and lack of interior room. *Detroit News* syndicated auto columnist Bob Irvin set off on a 3000-mile jaunt from the San Diego preview site back to Detroit in a V-6, automatic notchback and reported after the first day that "Ford's new Mustang II is a unique little car which will go nearly 100 miles an hour and still get close to seventeen miles to a gallon..."

But Irvin's car developed a rear-axle noise problem on the second day, and when he stopped at Ford's Kingman, Arizona, Desert Proving Ground and had it looked at while he was interviewing some engineers there, he was told that a differential overheating problem existed with the V-6 engine and that they were already testing a larger axle as a mid-year fix. When Irvin duly reported this the next day, it touched off a controversy that had Ford executives denying any such problem and ultimately admitting that the larger axle under test was intended for use with a V-8-engined Mustang due in '75. It turned out that Irvin's cross-country test car had been equipped with a brand-new differential that had not been broken in, and his high-speed, hot-weather run through Death Valley and then through the mountains had burned the axle's lubricant and scored its gears.

The remainder of Irvin's trip was trouble-free and turned him into a big fan of the car even as some of the more enthusiast-oriented press started to criticize it. His reports of Mustang II's comfort on long trips, its near-nineteen-mpg average fuel economy and the enthusiastic response it drew from people he met along the way certainly served to enhance American car buyers' expectations as the mid-September public introduction approached. "People like the new Mustang—its looks, the expected price and the size," Irvin reported in September 3rd issues. "Almost unanimously, people said they were glad to see a small Mustang again."

But hopes for a repeat of the '65 version's triumphant introduction were soon dashed when the car landed on the U.S. market with what one writer termed a "resounding thud." People visiting dealerships looking for luxurious or sporty little Mustang II's near the $2895 advertised price were staggered to find nothing but top-line, heavily-optioned versions listing for $4000 to $4500—and most settled for cheaper Pintos, Mavericks, other products or nothing at all instead. Ford had predicted sales of over 31,000 units in the first month, but only some 18,000 materialized. An encouraging note, however, was that unfilled orders by mid-October totaled another 17,000-plus, and the factory started scrambling to change its production mix and meet this demand for less-expensive, less well-equipped cars.

Perhaps turned off by negative buff-book reports, prospective small-sporty-car buyers were resisting the fastback and Mach I models in large numbers. Though a spirited performer in Lincoln-Mercury's imported Capri, the 2.8-liter V-6 just didn't have the

Special paint treatment ideas for '77 (left) never made production. Though an improvement over Stallion I, the Stallion II package (right) didn't either.

"suds" to produce sufficiently exciting performance in the much-heavier Mustang II, and September-issue cover stories were not shy about voicing their collective disappointment.

"While the Mach I's general concept is enthusiast-oriented, its poor acceleration, wide-ratio transmission and overweight chassis leave too much of its undeniably sporting flavor unsupported by nourishment," said *Car and Driver*. "As usual with such a compromised design, the Mustang lacks the excitement of a more single-purpose car like the 240-Z or even the crisp European feel of its cousin the Capri," griped *Road & Track*. "The car in stock form is regrettably underpowered," complained *Car Craft*. "Looking at the Mach I from a performance standpoint, Ford will either have to lighten up the car or offer a V-8. We predict they'll do the latter." (Ford engineers, in fact, keenly aware of the problem even before introduction, were already rushing 302-cubic-inch V-8-powered Mustangs through the development process for introduction in the fall of 1974.)

Meanwhile, the promotional forces were still sailing at full steam in hopes of recapturing some of the "Mustang Generation" mania of a decade before. There was even a line of leisure-type merchandise, primarily golf, tennis and camping gear, being pushed at "below normal retail" to help create interest in the car and draw people into Ford showrooms. But the best Mustang II salesmen of all turned out to be a group of greedy Middle-Eastern oil barons in Arab garb who instantaneously created an insatiable small-car demand in this country by turning off their taps on October 18th, 1973.

As long lines formed at gas pumps throughout the country, U.S.-car dealers suddenly found they couldn't give away gas-hungry big cars and couldn't get enough Vegas, Pintos, Gremlins, Novas, Mavericks, Valiants ... and Mustang II's ... to satisfy a newly fuel-panicked public. Plants producing fuel-efficient small cars hummed on overtime while those making larger models curtailed output and even shut down for weeks at a time during the long, cold winter, while Washington imposed a "temporary" 55-mph speed limit and talked of weekend gas-station closings and rationing.

To make matters worse for the country's economy, inflationary pressures that had been pent up during President Nixon's wage and price freeze began creating substantial price hikes for everything from bread to steel, and automakers felt compelled to raise their prices as well. Ford cars and trucks went up an average of four percent (almost $200 at retail) in mid-December—all except the now hot-selling Mustang II, which as a new product was not yet eligible for a price increase under the government's "Phase IV" anti-inflation rules.

Road & Track came back with a full road test of a four-speed Mach I in its January issue, but the initial opinions hadn't changed. "It was too large, too heavy, too Detroit," said the magazine, "it seemed to miss the mark"—meaning it was unworthy competition for the sporty imports at which it was aimed—Toyota Celica, Opel Manta and Ford's own German-built Capri, which themselves had been inspired by the original Mustang concept. Other complaints involved the engine's lack of response, balky cold driveaway characteristics, and annoying part-throttle surge, luxurious but unsupporting seats without adjustable backrests, and the skinny, large-diameter plastic steering wheel, but *R&T* praised the car's inertia reel shoulder belts (an improvement that had come with the government-mandated seatbelt/ignition interlock system), full in-

Some super-macho King Cobras were produced in '78, but Motortown's mean-looking IMSA Cobra, inspired by Kemp racer, was never seriously considered.

strumentation, ventilation system and braking performance.

"The original Mustang didn't have a tachometer or a four-speed gearbox standard; Mustang II does," the magazine observed on a more positive note (forgetting the new car's standard front disc brakes). "And to replace an existing car with one of the same name (save the Roman numeral) that's far smaller and lighter has to be credited as a courageous, timely step for a big corporation like Ford to take." Zero-to-sixty and quarter-mile acceleration times were unimpressive at 13.8 and 19.4 seconds (and 70.5 mph), respectively, while handling with the "competition" suspension was deemed "reasonably good" despite the car's 58 percent front weight concentration. "It is solid, well-built, quiet and plush," ended the report, "—and not at all unpleasant to drive on the road as long as you don't ask too much of it."

As the oil embargo dragged on and Mustang II sales accelerated almost to the level originally expected (albeit at a seventy percent to thirty percent notchback-to-fastback ratio), Ford went ahead with plans to install the car at its San Jose, California plant in March, a month later than scheduled. And an unexpected (at least to outsiders) image boost came on January 16th when *Motor Trend* magazine named it "Car of the Year." Perhaps in anticipation of the award, *Motor Trend* had spoken more favorably of the car than most other magazines from the beginning, calling it "a total departure from the fat old horse of the recent past ... a rebirth of the Mustang of 1964-65—smaller and even more lithe in feel than the original pacesetter—a pony for the '70's."

On the occasion of this announcement, Iacocca noted that sales during the first ten days of January had totaled 7180 units, a 212 percent increase over the larger Mustang's performance during the same period the previous year. Thanks to the Arab oil embargo, the car's introduction, as *Motor Trend* noted, had truly been "one of the best-timed announcements in auto history."

The embargo finally ended on March 18th, and (due mainly to further steel price increases) Ford raised its car and truck prices twice again during 1974 (a total of 3.7 percent), and this time Mustang did not escape the boosts. With the second increase on July 2nd, the base notchback's sticker (now with standard radial tires) climbed to $3134 and the V-6-equipped Mach I rose to $3674; but sales nonetheless reached 296,041 by the model year's end.

With the '75 model came the expected 302 V-8 engine for a much-needed performance boost, but making it fit had been no easy task. "We had a very difficult time shoe-horning it into the car because there hadn't been provision made for it," recalls product development vice-president Harold MacDonald. "There just wasn't as much room as we would have liked, and we had to keep moving this and moving that. The hood had to be much longer for installation and a half-inch higher for clearance, we had to change the radiator support and move the radiator forward three inches, change things along the firewall, beef up the cross member and side rails and mount the engine differently on the cross member. It got to be a larger job than we thought it would be originally, but we didn't have to move the tread or change any suspension mounting points." Additionally, springs, brakes and other chassis components were upgraded throughout to accommodate the extra weight.

Externally, the most noticeable change was a larger eggcrate pattern in the grille, which was moved forward almost flush with the grille opening. Standard equipment now included radial tires and solid-state ignition, and the luxury Ghia notchback got an "opera" window with choice of a full or a half vinyl roof. A special Silver Luxury Group with cranberry velour interior, paint stripes and a Mustang II hood ornament was promoted as a sort of "mini-Mark IV," and new options included spoked cast aluminum wheels, a 3.5-gallon auxiliary fuel tank (standard with the V-8) and 195/70R13 steel-belted radial tires. The 302 V-8 was available only with automatic transmission, power steering and power brakes; and, interestingly, the promotional literature and photos drew direct comparisons between the 1975 Mustang II and the similarly-sized 1957 Thunderbird.

Road & Track's John Dinkle tested the new V-8 Mach I for the September 1974 issue and came away surprisingly impressed. "Rarely can an automobile company take a car designed for a four-or six-cylinder engine, stuff in a heavier, thirstier V-8 and have us liking, much less praising the results," said Dinkle. "But that's exactly what happened with the 302-equipped 1975 Mustang II....Surprise, it really handles. Besides the stiffer springs and bigger

anti-roll bars, all shock absorbers have been revalved to reduce porpoising of the front end over dips or during braking. In addition the three-way adjustable Gabriel shocks (standard with the competition and Rallye suspensions) have been rebalanced to make the car more neutral during transient maneuvers."

The first break the industry got from government regulators (Congress, actually, which overturned NHTSA's mandate) came when the hated seatbelt/ignition interlock rule was revoked on October 29th, 1974, but the annoying buzzers remained until replaced by a timed seat-belt reminder light and buzzer. Car sales remained slow, however, throughout the recession that followed the embargo-caused fuel shortage. By mid-winter, automakers were stripping standard equipment off of their products to keep prices low, reducing prices of other options and even offering cash rebates of up to $500 to buyers of slow-selling models.

As an indication of how dull and dreary U.S. cars had become due to fuel worries, safety, emissions and damageability requirements, high insurance rates and recession-caused unemployment, Ford rushed special high-mileage "MPG" versions of their small cars (including Mustang II) into production in mid-June. Powered by slightly modified 2.3-liter four-cylinder engines and 3.18:1 rear axles (versus the previous 3.40:1), these cars were EPA-rated at thirty-four mpg highway, twenty-three mpg city with four-speed transmission, and thirty mpg highway, twenty-one city with automatic. The MPG cars were launched with Ford's biggest-ever June advertising campaign and certainly found a fair number of fuel-conscious buyers, but it was a new low for the once-mighty Mustang's image.

Meanwhile, *Road & Track* had tested still another V-8 Mach I, this time comparing it with Chevrolet's new 262 V-8 Monza sporty

Above: Perhaps the best-looking custom Mustang II was the blue-on-yellow Monroe Handler built by Monroe Auto Equipment as show car and product demonstration vehicle; Hot Rod *made it the cover subject for its June 1977 issue. Below: 1977 Mustang II notchback; and the fastback featuring brushed-aluminum instrument panel appliqué, and optional hatch roof panels. Page opposite: The author tests a 1977 Cobra II on Waterford Hills race track in Michigan.*

coupe. While the magazine preferred the Monza's sleek good looks and agile handling, the Mustang scored much better in both performance and braking. At 10.5 and 17.9 seconds in zero-to-sixty and quarter-mile runs, respectively, the Mustang was 2.9 and 1.6 seconds faster than the Monza (both automatic-equipped) and sailed through the quarter-mile traps at 77.0 mph versus the Chevy's 72.5. "The Mustang is clearly the more capable car in acceleration, braking and pure cornering power on a smooth road," the article concluded; "it is virile in character too, a quality almost totally absent from this year's crop of domestic cars."

Changes were minimal for 1976 as Mustang II entered its third model year firmly in command of the domestic subcompact sporty-car market with sales of 199,199 '75 models...nothing to rave about, but still better than GM's Monza, Starfire and Skyhawk combined. There were fuel economy gains, catalytic converters (formerly only on MPG's and California V-8's) across the board, a few new dress-up and convenience options (windshield wiper controls had been moved to a steering column stalk in mid-'75, and an intermittent wiper option was added for '76), a four-speed manual option for the 302 V-8 engine, and—surprise!—two new youthful appearance packages.

The first, a heavy black-out treatment called "Stallion" (and shared with Pinto and Maverick) was a real yawner; but the second was a realistic attempt, in appearance at least, to recapture the Shelby GT excitement of the decade before. Called "Cobra II" and available in blue-on-white or gold-on-black, this striped, scooped and spoilered creation actually was the brainchild of Jim Wangers, whose Motortown firm manufactured the parts and applied them to stock Mustang 2+2's in a small plant near the Dearborn assembly facility. Wangers is credited with fathering the GTO idea when he was working for Pontiac's advertising agency in the early 1960's, and it looked like once again he had come up with a fresh (and affordable) concept to help lift the industry out of its two-year doldrums.

With the basic four-cylinder engine as standard equipment, the Cobra II at first was greeted with a loud chorus of laughter from the enthusiast press and righteous indignation from legitimate Shelby Mustang fans. But properly equipped, the thing actually performed pretty well by 1976 standards, and it slowly caught on and became increasingly acceptable as a modern mini-musclecar. It also helped when road racer Charlie Kemp built an all-out Cobra II-based IMSA GT machine and raced it competitively during the 1976 season. It had reliability problems and often didn't finish, but it went like Jack the Bear when it ran, and it gave Ford road racing fans something to cheer for again after a long dry spell.

Encouraging also was evidence that Ford designers were beginning to spend some time again on some interesting projects apart from ordinary production-car work. Although none ultimately reached production, there were special Mustang paint treatments, a second-generation (and much nicer) Stallion package called "Stallion II," and even a clean-looking restyle proposal using Monza-type soft front and rear end caps and integral bumpers. A hefty price increase (averaging $216 on base cars and $31 on options) also came with the '76 model year; and another $97 boost was effective January 5th, 1976...but was rescinded ten days later "to keep Ford products competitive in the marketplace and to sustain the sales successes we have experienced with our 1976 models," according to Ben Bidwell, who was now corporate sales vice-president. The base Mustang II notchback now was priced at $3535 and the Mach I listed for $4209.

While the industry as a whole recovered nicely in 1976, Mustang II sales fell to 178,541 for the model year. Clearly the car's popularity had peaked and was on its way down as buyers turned again to larger, more comfortable automobiles. Motortown's Cobra II, however, which most everyone had expected to fall on its pseudo-Shelby face,

Mustang II Ghia for '78, and Cobra II with bold, new paint design and optional white-spoked aluminum wheels. The King Cobra shown at press preview sported garish cowcatcher spoiler, later revised.

had proven so successful that Ford decided to take it away from Motortown and build it alongside other models at the Dearborn plant for '77. If scoops and stripes and spoilers are good, management reasoned, more of the same should be better...so Bordinat's designers were set to work on a super-macho "King Cobra" package for '78.

Not to be outdone, Motortown designed and built a street imitation of Kemp's flare-fendered IMSA racing Cobra called, appropriately, "IMSA Cobra," but was unsuccessful in selling it to the company for limited production. Possibly the best-looking custom Mustang II of the year, however, was done as a promotional exercise by Monroe Auto Equipment Company, makers of Monroe shocks and other products. Called the "Monroe Handler," this clean, lean and mean blue-on-yellow beauty toured the car-show circuit and was featured on the cover of the June 1977 *Hot Rod* magazine.

The more mundane Mustang II's, meanwhile, benefited from some new options (a Sports Group for the luxury Ghia, a flip-up or removable sunroof, twin removable roof hatches for the 2+2, and a four-way adjustable driver's seat—up and down and fore/aft—but *still* no adjustable seatback), additional standard equipment for the 2+2 fastback (sport steering wheel, styled steel wheels, white-letter tires, blacked-out grille, and brushed-aluminum instrument panel appliqués), and several money-saving optional equipment packages. Notchback models got a new horizontal-bar grille, Cobra II boasted two new paint schemes (red or green on white) and fastbacks acquired the Cobra II's front chin spoiler as a no-cost option. There was also a new-design, two-barrel, variable venturi carburetor for V-6 and V-8 California Mustangs that automatically adjusted its venturi openings to maintain high air velocity and constant air/fuel mixture for improved driveability at the tough California emissions levels.

Mustang II sales slipped to 161,654 for the '77 model year despite the addition of a discounted Limited Edition model in February, and about the most exciting thing that happened all year came as a result of Congressional foot-dragging. Both the Senate and the House passed separate bills to extend '77 emissions rules into '78, but then went on recess before acting on a measure agreeable to both, leaving the industry unable to legally produce and ship '78-model cars. Ford's solution was to build carryover '78 Pintos, Bobcats and Mustang II's and title them as '77's from late June through early August until Congress finally made up its mind.

When the real '78's did debut for their last season in the four-year-old body, there was little new except the King Cobra and a female-oriented Fashion accessory group for the base hardtop model. The optional power-assisted rack-and-pinion steering was variable ratio to improve road feel at speed, and a revised torque converter was used to squeeze more miles per gallon out of the V-6 automatic combination. All models got separate rear-seat cushions replacing the near-useless full-width rear seat, a handsome, white-painted spoked aluminum wheel option was introduced, and the Cobra II inherited a bold, new colored tape stripe and lettering treatment.

Biggest industry news was the government's strict corporate average fuel economy (CAFE) rules that would do more to change the size, weight, efficiency and character of American cars and trucks than any single factor in history. What it meant (in simplified terms) was that every vehicle sold with an EPA rating below the mandated average for a given year would have to be offset by another vehicle equivalently above it. The requirements were arbitrarily set at eighteen miles per gallon for the '78 model year, nineteen for '79, twenty for '80, twenty-two for '81 and on up to twenty-seven-and-a-half for '85, with heavy fines for noncompliance.

It was with this crucial and difficult challenge in mind that Ford engineers readied the exciting third-generation Mustangs for market as the '79 model year approached.

9. TODAY'S HOOFPRINTS

The 1979 Mustang story, ironically, begins in the summer of 1972, more than a year before the car it was to replace was publicly launched. It was then that the nation's coming fuel problems first began to telegraph themselves in the form of spot shortages in some parts of the country. Environmentalist actions had prevented the oil companies from constructing the new refining capacity they needed to keep up with mushrooming demand (most everyone wants refineries, but in someone else's back yard), and some areas began to feel the pinch in fuel supplies. By the end of the year, Ford executives already had formed a small committee to discuss the implications of more serious future shortages.

Early in 1973, Ford engineers and executives were writing papers and giving speeches on the need for more attention to fuel economy, and the decision was made to increase proposed production of the coming '74 Mustang II. April brought EPA's first round of passenger-car fuel economy ratings, and some management people began to suspect that gas mileage standards might not be too far down the road. There had been some home heating oil shortages over the winter, and the resulting conversion of more refining capacity to heating oil helped create more spot shortages of diesel fuel and gasoline during the summer. Then came the Arab-Israel conflict of October 1973, followed by the Arab oil embargo.

Almost overnight, fuel-efficient cars were in and gas-hogs were definitely out, maybe forever as far as anyone knew, and Detroit wasted little time in formulating future plans for a newly fuel-conscious America. Fitting neatly into these far-reaching plans at Ford Motor Company was a project codenamed "Fox" which had been conceived early in 1973 as a whole new family of small, fuel-stingy cars to be produced at Ford facilities throughout the world. Such a "world car" concept, it was reasoned, would greatly simplify Ford's international product lineup; and parts commonality between various countries' versions would save money and ease both planning and production complexity.

A new era, a new Mustang; the pioneer ponycar approaches the '80's.

Initial Fox objectives were to "develop a new corporate world-wide sport/family four/five-passenger sedan" with "imaginative packaging and component application" to replace the European Taunus/Cortina, the American Pinto/Mustang and potentially the Australian and South American Falcon/Corcel. "By March of 1973," recalls James Bruin, a principal staff engineer in Ford's Product Planning and Research group, "we were working on developing both a front-wheel-drive and a rear-wheel-drive car and the possibility of a rotary engine application — all of them Pinto or Taunus-sized cars."

By that summer, these plans had expanded and were beginning to solidify. "As the world-car concept began to jell," says Fox product planning director John Risk, "we actually worked on ideas for three (U.S.) cars — all of them dubbed Fox. One was a replacement for Pinto, one for Mustang and one for Maverick." Emphasized at first was the 100-inch-wheelbase Pinto-sized version because a true world car would have to be very small and fuel efficient (due to high gas prices in Europe and elsewhere) and because the Pinto and Taunus/Cortina would be aging and in need of replacement by the time it could be brought to market. When the fall energy crunch arrived and drove small-car demand through the ceiling, this direction seemed even more valid.

In development of the front-drive Fiesta minicar, Ford engineers had used a procedure they called the "best-ball" concept, which involved literally tearing apart the best competitive cars to pinpoint and study their desirable features, and then adapting or improving upon those features for the new Ford vehicle. The same effective method was used in developing early Fox prototypes, and in this case the "best ball" cars were Ford's German Taunus, Audi's 80 (Fox in the U.S.), GM's German Opel Manta, Toyota's Celica and Carina, Datsun's 610, BMW's 2002 and the American Pinto.

On October 8th, 1974, shortly after the Mustang II had belly-flopped into shark-infested U.S.-market waters, its eventual replacement was transferred from Product Planning and Research to Ford's North American Automotive Operations' Product Development Group. Fox was ready for the long development process into real, live, produceable and marketable passenger cars. Two months and three days later, Ford president Lee Iacocca gave the official go-ahead to work toward production by August 1977, for the '78 model year. The first Fox car would be either a Pinto or a Maverick replacement, while the proposed Fox Mustang derivative was put off for launch sometime after the '78 model year.

The world car concept eventually died due to complications

TURBO
FORD

involved in adapting the same platform to diverse safety and other standards throughout the industrialized world, plus differences in production techniques; and the rotary (Wankel) engine idea never got off the ground because of the powerplant's (then) reputation for poor fuel economy and emissions difficulties. But by April 1975, the U.S. program was committed toward introduction of a Maverick replacement in the fall of 1977, the Fox Pinto idea had been scrubbed and the Fox Mustang was set for the '79 model year. The decision to go with a compact-size car first was due to projected strong growth in that market segment, the profit potential of a new compact station wagon model, and the threat posed by General Motors' plan to launch a new family of downsized '78-model intermediate cars. A third Fox derivative, a downsized '80 Thunderbird specialty car, would follow the Mustang with introduction planned for the fall of 1979.

It's interesting to note that while the original Mustang was almost completely Falcon-based and the Mustang II was a Pinto spin-off with some shared components, the third generation ponycar was planned from the beginning as a unique product derived from a platform shared by two other very different cars. Powertrains, the basic chassis and some other parts would be largely common, yet each car would have its own very distinct appearance and character and a fair amount of unique pieces over and above obvious sheet metal differences. And, although the compact family-car versions (Ford Fairmont and Mercury Zephyr) would precede the new Mustang chronologically, the engineering and development program reportedly was tailored around the Mustang's needs as a sporty, agile, European-style product better by far than either previous try at the theme.

"With this one we had to do a little more planning and think a lot farther in advance," says light- and mid-size-car planning manager Gordon Riggs, who was put on special assignment for the Fox program. "We said, okay, we're going to have a series of cars off of a platform as yet undefined, and what should that platform be? We decided first-off that it was going to be a sporty platform, because we knew that the focal point of it was really Mustang. Anything we did to that platform to help the Mustang would probably benefit any other car that we took off of it. It was not planned just for the Mustang, but the whole platform was designed to accommodate it."

As the Fox progressed from paper to hardware, several key objectives were stressed. Efficiency in size, weight and fuel consumption were paramount, as were fixed and variable costs of producing the cars versus their profit potential for the company. But right on top of the Mustang objectives list were both styling and ride-and-handling. Gene Bordinat's Design Staff, of course, was charged with the former responsibility, while Product Development engineers tackled the second. Both found inspiration from "across the pond."

Early design concept sketches by light-car design manager Fritz Mayhew showed significant European sports-car influence, with low noses, slim pillars and large glass areas. Yet, as in the past, other studios were working on '79 Mustang ideas as well, many carrying over traditional Mustang design cues and some using more squared-off, sedan-like shapes inherited from the Fairmont/Zephyr program. "Even though these cars are done in separate studios," Mayhew explains, "the efforts are all orchestrated by Mr. Bordinat. Looking back, you can see that he was allowing several different directions to happen."

The '79 Mustang design process began during the summer of 1975 with some sketches and models done as spin-offs from the ongoing Fairmont program, but the inter-studio competition process really began early the following year. It was already underway when Jack Telnack, who had been design vice-president at Ford of Europe, returned to Dearborn as executive director, North American Light Car and Truck Design in April, and he wasted little time in putting his considerable European experience to use in coming up with a suitable new Mustang concept.

Actually, Telnack had gotten involved even before the official transfer. "Fritz and Bob Zokas had been talking to me on the telephone and sending photographs while I was still in Europe," he explains, "and I had made trips back and forth to talk to them about the car and the way it was developing."

Working independently around the basic "hard points" — length, width, height, wheelbase, tread, cowl height, etc. — three Design Center studios and Ford's Ghia Studio in Turin, Italy, now under Don DeLaRossa, were trying to decide what the definitive third-generation Mustang should look like. Most of these early models were notchbacks because it had been decided this time around to do the traditional notchback first and then adapt a fastback roofline to it — instead the reverse had occurred with the '74 Mustang II.

Almost immediately, Telnack's studio produced a new model that was radically different from the others. While the rest were basically straight-sided, flat-nosed, and had beltlines blending with the fenders, this one featured tuck-in fenders (viewed from above), a back-slanted nose with the hood sloping sharply down to it, and a substantially dropped beltline, for a very European — and aerodynamic — look.

To accomplish this, Telnack had violated one of the crucial hard points, which are normally "cast in stone" at that point in a program. "In order to get the hood down lower in front," he explains, "we had to change the package. We were supposed to hold the Fairmont cowl (at the windshield's base) and radiator support, which really stiffened the hood ... made it much straighter. Bob Alexander was in charge of engineering at the time, and he had just come back from Europe, too.

Page opposite: Early concept drawings by Fritz Mayhew emphasized ultra-low hoodlines, hidden headlamps, large glass areas; Mayhew shows Dave Rees some of the early '79 Mustang ideas. This page: Different studios had different ideas, some rounded and sporty, others more squared off. August 1975 model was obvious Fairmont derivative, February 1976 model showed Olds Cutlass influence.

Above: The model at the top shows rear roof and taillamp treatments similar to those eventually chosen, while attempts at a notchback profile with a rear hatch were rejected because the reach to close it would have been uncomfortably high. Below: The first two models with Jack Telnack influence stressed dropped beltlines, one with blunt nose and angled rear, the other with aerodynamic sloped nose. The latter, with minor changes, eventually became the '79 Mustang.

We had a lot of people who had just come back from Europe and who had a different feel for this type of car. One of the ideas we came up with was to pivot the hood around the air cleaner and actually raise the cowl to get the front end down. No Detroit designer ever asks to make anything higher, but we felt it was important aerodynamically to get the nose down lower. Of course, this would require a new radiator support, unique from the Fairmont's, which would add to the cost, but we felt it would be worth it; and Gene Bordinat said to go ahead and give it a try. Normally we get the package hard points and adhere to them, but we weren't accepting anything on this car as gospel." The lower nose also added some four-and-a-half feet of frontal visibility compared to the Mustang II.

Tucking in the fenders at both ends, which Telnack refers to as "giving it more plan view" (the plan view in an engineering drawing shows the top of an object), makes a car more aerodynamically efficient by slimming the nose to present a smaller, more slippery surface to the airstream and smoothing airflow along the sides. It also gives a wide-stance, high-performance appearance with the tires at the body's outer extremities, definitely in keeping with Mustang's sporty image. The low, European-style beltline and large glass area contributed to visibility, while the wrapped-around rear window (backlight) and louvered grille were other aerodynamic tricks picked up from European designs.

This model and several others favored by management (all notchbacks), as always, were surveyed in styling clinics to gauge public response to the various ideas. The usual procedure involved presenting these proposed designs, along with a number of competitive products, all in the same color and with identifying marks and badges removed, to a jury of from 250 to 500 people fitting a desired age, income, and car-ownership profile. Participants normally have no idea what company is conducting the survey (to avoid preconceived prejudices either pro or con) and are asked to rate individual parts of the cars on a one-to-ten scale and provide criticism on each design as a whole.

Tested against a Datsun 280-Z, a Mustang II, a German-built Mercury Capri and other small, sporty cars, the Telnack model faired well but was not an overwhelming winner among the '79 Mustang proposals. One thing that *was* proven in these early clinics, however, was a continuing fifty-fifty split in public preference for notchback versus fastback designs. There was no doubt that a fastback Mustang still would be needed to maximize the new car's market appeal.

The studios went to work on some fastback concepts, and by late August Telnack's group was comparing its now-finished notchback design with adaptations of it bearing both full-fastback and semi-fastback rooflines. The latter, they felt, was easily the better alternative. "One of the design objectives was to keep a 'coupey' look to the thing," says Mayhew. "It's a rather long package, and when we looked at a model with a true fastback we felt that it just didn't work visually."

"As soon as you make it a full fastback," Telnack adds, "the car begins to look 'over-greenhoused' ... it becomes a sedan. We wanted to lighten it, to make the car look light and airy, and we wanted good visibility. That full-fastback greenhouse really cut down on visibility."

It was after the semi-fastback version was added that Telnack's design became the clear favorite with Ford management and in public opinion clinics. The louvered grille (patterned after an innovative European Ford design that gives better high-speed engine cooling by directing more air through the radiator) did not survey especially well, but the rest of the car got high marks from a majority of clinic participants in the Midwest as well as on the West Coast.

It often happens that finished designs are made up of parts of several different models based on management preferences and clinic results — but not the '79 Mustang. Except for the addition of louvers on the C-pillar and substitution of an eggcrate-style grille for the less-favored louvered design, the finished model that was approved for production in September 1976 was almost totally unchanged from the initial concept created shortly after Telnack's transfer from Europe. "It was not a matter of selecting the front of one model, the roof of another and the rear of something else," says he with obvious pride. And, even more than the original Mustang, it remained unaltered right up through the start of production two years later.

"I think it's interesting that the approved design bears no resemblance to earlier Mustangs," says pre-production design executive Dave Rees. "In the other studios there was a definite attempt to capture Mustang cues and design evolutionary concepts, and those were rejected."

"Jack wanted this car to have the impact of the original Mustang, which was a very revolutionary car," adds Mayhew, "rather than have an ordinary feel; so we went off in a different direction trying to do a car that would look as different on the road as the original had. We felt, as management obviously did, that it was time for a change. We had done about as much as we could with those original design cues from 1964."

But it wasn't easy getting it past the production and feasibility engineers intact. "I can remember one engineer saying that when his group got through with it, we wouldn't recognize it, which is the typical approach that a body engineer has," complained one designer. Luckily, product development vice-president Bob Alexander had liked the design from the beginning. He told them to hold the design just the way it was; and if they couldn't make it work, he wanted to

More traditional shapes, many with evolutionary Mustang design cues, were coming from various studios, but so were further ideas with Continental influence. Above: The single-headlamp design with forward-facing air scoop and slanted nose was well liked by management, but the more European-looking Telnack car, now with C-pillar louvers, remained the favorite during the summer of '76. Below: Rear treatments were now mostly European in character.

know why not. Says Telnack, "I've never seen a car hold so closely in my life!"

One conflict that came up involved wrapping the sides of the hatchback's "third door" around into the pillar and rear deck. The designers had done it that way because it looked good and because several other contemporary hatchback cars had these "cutlines" on the side, but Ford engineers had never done a hatch like that before. "Our engineers and manufacturing said they couldn't do it without fit-and-finish problems," says Mayhew, "but we reminded them that the VW Scirocco, the Honda Accord and several others do it that way. We finally rammed it through, with excellent support from Bob Alexander and Al Guthrie in Body Engineering. They just stood on those guys and said 'you *will* make the car look like this!' "

Fox product planning chief Gordon Riggs also was strongly in favor of holding the approved design without the usual changes. "We spent a lot of time looking at a lot of alternatives on this car," says he, "and we did a lot of market research. Once we settled on a style, we decided we were not going to change it. Often you have to make a lot of changes to make a car feasible to manufacture after settling on a design, but with this one we wanted to avoid that as much as possible.

Above: Dearborn studios and Ghia working along different lines, car with front-fender louvers is Ghia's. Gary Haas touching up derivative of Mayhew-Telnack Cobra.

So the car that went into production was largely the same as what had been approved at the Design Center two years before. Styling was a very key objective of this program, and I think we were successful."

Telnack's expensive ($1.4 million) cowl and hoodline changes had soon proved their worth in the wind tunnel, as had the soundness of the entire basic design. "We had our package objectives to meet, but aerodynamics was uppermost in our minds," he explains. "I think that all the designers who worked on this project had enough background with aero, either here or in Europe, to apply it to this car, which really helped us. When we got it into the tunnel, it was just a matter of fine-tuning — no major changes — which is a nice way to do a car."

There was some management resistance to the wrapped backlight, both because it would be expensive to produce and because the Mustang had always had a more traditional flat backlight. But Jack Telnack thought the wrapped glass would be better aerodynamically, and when the car was tested with and without it, the wind tunnel indeed proved him right by a factor of six percent in aerodynamic drag.

"That was one of the unique aspects of this program," Telnack

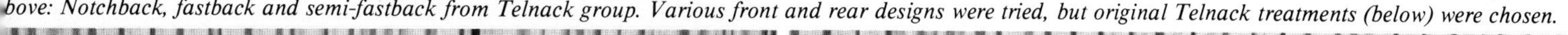

bove: Notchback, fastback and semi-fastback from Telnack group. Various front and rear designs were tried, but original Telnack treatments (below) were chosen.

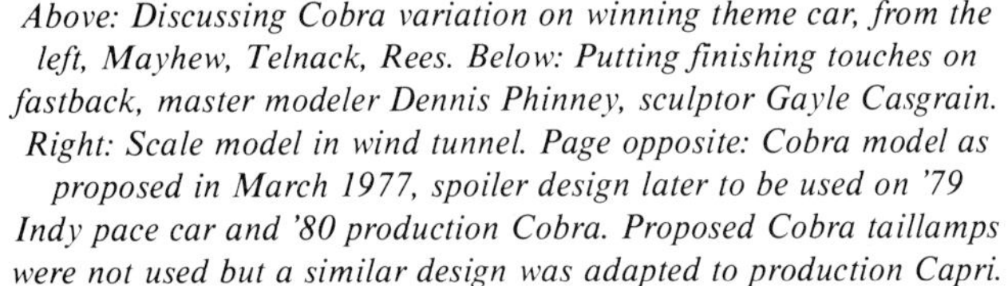
Above: Discussing Cobra variation on winning theme car, from the left, Mayhew, Telnack, Rees. Below: Putting finishing touches on fastback, master modeler Dennis Phinney, sculptor Gayle Casgrain. Right: Scale model in wind tunnel. Page opposite: Cobra model as proposed in March 1977, spoiler design later to be used on '79 Indy pace car and '80 production Cobra. Proposed Cobra taillamps were not used but a similar design was adapted to production Capri.

says. "It was probably one of the first U.S. programs that was so function-oriented, where design decisions were made by the wind tunnel rather than by the whim of the designer or management. We didn't look at this car and say we like this line because it flows well or it's graceful; we said, hey, we've got a six percent deterioration by going to a square corner on that, gentlemen. Here are the facts, now what do you want to do? And there was no contest."

Fox vehicle durability and development testing began in earnest when the first Fairmont/Zephyr mechanical prototype vehicles were completed in late January 1976. These mechanical prototypes are literally "glue and tape" approximations of the final vehicles in terms of overall size, weight and balance, but usually bear no resemblance in appearance. For instance, a Fairmont wagon mechanical prototype might have the rear end of a Pinto wagon grafted to the front section of a Maverick sedan, while underneath would be hand-fabricated versions of the Fairmont suspension, steering, underbody, fuel tanks and drivetrain components being tested. These cobbled-up cars may look funny, but they cost $60,000 or more apiece to build.

Several months after the earliest mechanical prototypes go on test, more-advanced engineering prototype vehicles are under construction. These look like very basic versions of the fledgling product being developed; but since no production body tooling yet exists, their sheet metal is hand-tooled and their price tags run to something like $150,000 each. Fairmont/Zephyr mechanical prototype testing had been underway for just seven months when the first three engineering prototypes arrived at the Experimental Garage, and this event enabled Mustang engineers to get an early start on their own development program.

"When you get your engineering prototypes, the value of the mechanical prototypes begins to fade," explains Howard Freers, who was chief powertrain and chassis engineer at that time. "So one of the first things we did to get the Mustang program underway was to convert some of the original Fairmont/Zephyr mechanical prototypes into Mustang prototypes. We cut them down in length and wheelbase and got the suspension wheel rates to where they'd be similar to the proposed Mustang and went to work, long before we'd normally have been able to."

As time goes on and more and more increasingly representative prototype vehicles are built and delivered, the engineering test program becomes as complex as it is intensive. "There are always minor problems with a new car," says Mustang development manager Glen Lyall. "If there weren't, you could take a car straight from paper to production. The whole idea behind vehicle development testing is a system of checks and balances to spot those problems and make sure that the best designs prove out in the real world."

There are as many tests involving specific components, both on the road in test cars and in the engineering laboratories, as there are on any car as a whole — air conditioning, defrosting, heating and ventilation; engine starting and performance under various conditions; chassis vibration; corrosion resistance; door and window mechanism durability; and electrical system reliability, to name just a few — not to mention exhaustive safety, damageability, emissions and fuel economy testing.

Instead of "babying" their expensive, hand-built prototypes, development engineers put them through all manner of abuse to find out what will fail or fall off and why. Hundreds of thousands of miles of vehicle durability testing is run throughout the program, on repetitive schedules where 26,000 miles equals 100,000 miles of normal driving and only 10,000 miles on the Proving Ground rough road course is equivalent to the usual lifetime of certain chassis parts. After completing their prescribed schedules, the test vehicles are completely disassembled and every part is inspected for defects.

Many prototypes and pre-production cars are destroyed in crash testing to satisfy Federal safety standards. Others run 50,000 miles of government-specified emissions and fuel economy certification testing; some are used for Federal bumper tests; some are unceremoniously shaken apart on road-simulator machines; some sacrificed to the salt bath for accelerated corrosion testing; and some more fortunate examples are spared for evaluation trips to and from Florida, Minnesota, the mountains of Kentucky, the deserts of Arizona or most anywhere else, depending on individual trip objectives.

A most important part of any vehicle's development involves location, analysis and elimination of as much noise, vibration and harshness (NVH) as possible. "Among other things," says Ray Schaffart, who supervised the Mustang NVH program, "we evaluate shock absorber and suspension bushing specifications to make sure the cars give satisfactory ride and vehicle control. We also draw up tire specifications and run powertrain balance, vibration and noise studies.

"So we get into very sophisticated and exact research using in-car instrumentation and facilities like Ford's computerized model analysis room or the company's 'quiet' chambers, where sound insulation is analyzed. But part of our evaluation is subjective, too. A car that feels fine to one engineer might feel bad to another; so we run several NVH test trips with various people involved to get a cross-section of opinion on the cars."

Adds Rod Alexander, manager for light-vehicle NVH: "The trips are very worthwhile in evaluating the cars. We have cold rooms and hot rooms in Dearborn; but the trips help in validating your test room findings, and there is really nothing that can match real-world testing under various road, wind, humidity and sun conditions — or ice and snow conditions, as the case may be. You want to expose a car to as many types of operating conditions as possible before it is released for production."

Much of the extensive component testing, of course, doesn't even have to wait for the first prototypes. "You try to test as many components as early as you can, before prototype vehicles are even built," says John Velte, chief chassis engineer in Powertrain and Chassis Engineering. "You can't wait until the last minute to test all the parts of a new car. For one thing, making major changes late in a program can foul up the whole government certification process. For another thing, the Pilot Plant has to have accurate specifications before it can build any engineering prototypes."

"To give you an idea of the extensive nature of our testing," Velte continues, "a list of the different kinds of tests for front disc brakes alone takes up six pages of standard typing paper. There are tests for weight distribution, city traffic braking, mountain braking, fatigue, fading, corrosion, spike stops, stone packing, ozone resistance — things most people never heard of."

Of course, one of the major Mustang development objectives was to take the basic, shortened Fox platform and create a car with truly outstanding handling performance and feel. "We had the hardware that came out of the '78 Fairmont/Zephyr program," explains chief powertrain and chassis engineer Howard Freers, "and from there on it became a relatively systematic program to just go through and adjust the spring rates, shock absorber valving, roll bar diameters, etc. Fairmont is a crisp-handling car, so when we took that base and applied it to the Mustang with a superior tire and wheel and then tuned the whole system to that particular set of characteristics, the program went very well."

Product planning manager Gordon Riggs points out that once the total Fox program was well down the road, specific Mustang development could focus on the handling, "and as part of that development we introduced the Michelin TRX tire and wheel. We'd been working with Michelin on that for some time, and then finally decided it was time to do it with the '79 Mustang. There were no major problems because the fundamental suspension had already been designed and was practically in production when we were finalizing the Mustang. The only real surprises were pleasant ones, and the most pleasant surprise was the handling with the TRX. It was even better than we'd expected."

Mustang development manager Glen Lyall, the former amateur road racer who was charged with the car's chassis development, however, relates one unpleasant surprise that came along late in the program. "Our initial position," he says, "was to have a plastic fuel tank and be first in the industry with that innovation. We had brought it along and had it ready, but then the decision was made by the company not to go with it because we could not get the government to say yes or no. From an engineering standpoint, we thought we had a good thing, but there's the problem of passing a government fire test ... how long will it stand up when exposed to flame ... and there was no accepted, recognized standard. So, not having an okay from the government, we had to back out of it.

"But when we went back to the steel tank, which happened in February 1978, just six months before production, it changed the entire rear structure of the car. To protect the steel tank adequately, we had to stiffen up the structure, and when we did that the car went to hell from a balance standpoint. We had the chassis all set, had just finished what we thought would be our final tuning for ride and handling, and then along came this change. The ride balance was gone and the handling was shot. We had to rework all the prototypes extensively, structure-wise, and then go back and do more ride-and-handling tuning work. But we turned it around, redid the entire car, in a period of about two months."

The challenge was to achieve good ride, especially in terms of impact harshness, combined with excellent handling in the base car, and then to work up from there through the optional "handling" suspension to the ultimate TRX package. The base suspension was optimized with the standard bias-ply tires, the intermediate package tuned to the radials that would come with it and the TRX chassis, of course, developed around the special high-pressure, low-profile Michelin tires and wheels. Well-known sports and sporty cars such as the Pontiac Trans Am, the Chevy Corvette, the Datsun 280-Z and the Porsche 924 were used as "bogeys" to meet or beat with the TRX Mustang; and all but one was beaten ... the Trans Am turned out to be just a bit quicker through a test slalom course mainly due to its greater engine power.

Modified European-style MacPherson struts (with the coil springs mounted separately inboard instead of integrally around the strut towers) had been chosen as the best ride-and-handling compromise for the Fox front suspension, and they proved equal to Lyall's Mustang chassis objectives in spite of Ford's initial inexperience with them. "As we progressed on the program," he explains, "both the people working on the Fairmont and the people working on the Mustang were learning more and more about the strut-type shock absorbers. We even went so far as to make a tour of the European shock manufacturers to examine their ways of producing them; and we came back and tried to apply the best of what we had learned there, as well as going beyond that and improving some of the internal pieces. But we had to change the company's thinking on shock absorbers in many ways, and that proved to be a difficult task."

Lyall might have preferred to tune the suspension for "neutral" handling at the limit, where the car slides sideways when its tires can develop no more traction, instead of front-first (understeer) or back-first (oversteer). The company philosophy, however, is to have the car understeer at the limit because management feels that it's safer for the inexperienced and unskilled driver. And so it is that every Ford product, like most other American cars, is tuned to understeer rather than behave neutrally when traction is lost. As before, the V-8-equipped Mustang was the worst-understeering variation because of its more nose-heavy weight distribution, but even the base suspension's cornering limits were so high that few but the skilled and brave would ever exceed them.

One way to reduce excessive understeer characteristics is to add a rear stabilizer bar, and the V-8 Mustang was one of few domestic cars to include this extra-cost item as part of its standard suspension

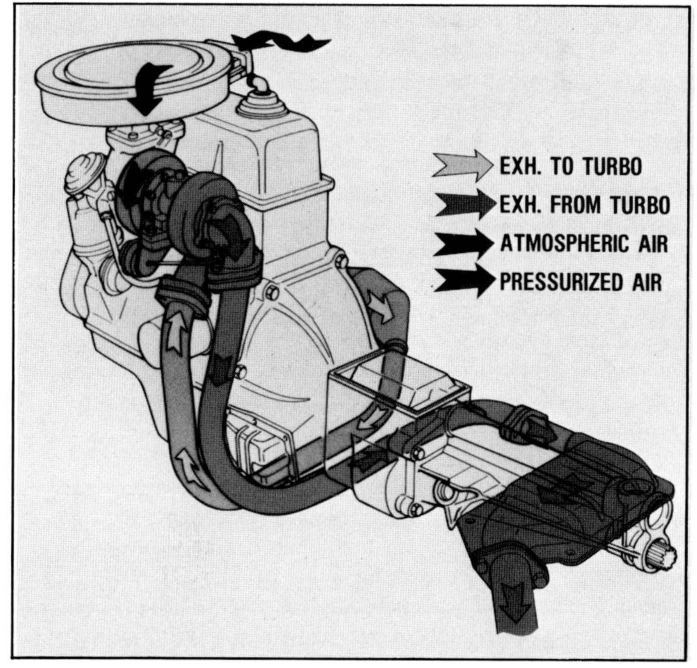

Testing the results of chassis development, the turbocharged engine.

package. Lyall's group even developed rear "sway" bars of two slightly different sizes to fine-tune each Mustang's rear suspension to its own powertrain and option load. "I have to say that I was pretty much given a free hand on how the cars were set up," says he. "Normally we forgo a rear bar on standard suspension packages, but I felt that a car with that weight distribution and that much power really needs one, and it was not challenged. I think part of that was because Mr. Rivard's feelings on the matter are pretty much like mine." (Lyall's immediate boss on the program was executive engineer, light vehicle development Dan Rivard.)

"In the vehicle development end of the business," Lyall continues, "one of the main goals is to make sure a car's image level is satisfied by the hardware and the way it's set up. Generally speaking, unless you run into an unusual amount of cost pressure, you usually can do that. In this case I'd say that we were more interested in image than in cost, compared to some other cars. I had the personal goal," he adds, "of taking this existing platform and making it something I could be proud of from the standpoint of what my background is. Given all the compromises you have to make, I'm very satisfied with the end result."

There were plenty of other areas in which extra money was spent to make the new Mustang the car it was intended to be. Although increased interior room and other objectives resulted in 4.1 inches of added length on a 4.2-inch-longer wheelbase, the '79 Mustang weighed some 200 pounds less than the '78. This weight savings, which contributed significantly to fuel economy, was accomplished primarily through the addition of strategic lightening holes in the body structure, a new soft-fascia front end, thinner doors and glass and the redesigned suspension systems. The strut-type front and the front-bar link rear suspension with coil springs were not only lighter than the previous designs, they also contributed to interior package efficiency.

An innovative serpentine "V"-ribbed belt on the optional 5.0-liter V-8 drove all six engine accessories — alternator, water pump, cooling, fan, emissions air pump, air conditioning compressor and power steering pump — for longer belt life, improved serviceability, increased fuel economy and a reduction in weight and complexity compared to the three-belt system previously used. The V-8 engine also got a nostalgic-sounding, low-restriction exhaust system and a new, standard, single-rail, four-speed overdrive manual transmission. A slick "fluidic" windshield washer worked like a massaging showerhead to coat the entire windshield from a single nozzle for better and faster cleaning action, using less fluid in the process.

Extensive wind-tunnel refinement of the already slippery Telnack exterior design made the '79 Mustang one of our industry's most aerodynamic cars with drag coefficients (Cd) of 0.44 for the fastback and 0.46 for the notchback — the latter figure representing a full twenty-five percent improvement over the '78 notchback for a one-mile-per-gallon gain in average fuel economy.

A number of "tricks" in both front and rear suspension systems (voided rubber and "tri-rate" bushings, pre-loaded ball joints, coil spring insulators and dampers) helped reduce impact harshness and noise transmission while providing very good control of suspension movement in jounce and rebound. The front "scrub radius" (distance between the turning axis and the tire contact-patch centerline) was close to zero for extra stability in uneven-surface braking. Thirteen-inch bias-ply tires were standard, with various fourteen-inch radials optional as well as the Michelin TRX metric low-profile tires on special forged aluminum wheels.

Ford was the first and (for 1979) only domestic automaker to get these super-handling tires and wheels, and possibly for that reason GM actually filed a complaint with the Department of Transportation trying to throw a monkey-wrench into the deal. "We almost lost that tire right before production," says design manager Fritz Mayhew. "GM said it could be a safety problem because a workman on the line might inadvertently try to mount one on the wrong rim. You'd have to be awfully stupid to try it, and you couldn't do it anyway because it won't fit on any other rim ... it's a 15.4-inch-diameter, 5.9-inch-wide metric wheel, and there's just no way to mix them up. We have an exclusive on that tire, and GM was a little nervous about that." The beautiful wheel may look like an Italian design, but it was done by Nehemiah Amaker, a young designer in Telnack's studio; "and we're very proud of it," says Telnack.

The Michelin TRX is available on certain exotic European cars, including the European Ford Granada, so Ford was already experienced with it and knew how good it was. The Mustang TRX package included a special suspension system with spring and shock rates tuned to the tire's characteristics, a larger front sway bar and one of three different rear bars depending on the engine size.

Additional chassis features worthy of note were the variable-ratio rack-and-pinion steering (with optional power-assist) introduced in 1978, a new, smaller, lighter-weight case center rear axle assembly, and a high-strength light-alloy (HSLA) steel rear engine cross member mounted on voided bushings to absorb engine vibrations. Other significant lightweight material applications included the soft urethane plastic bumper coverings and HSLA steel rear suspension arms, plus the aluminum front and rear bumpers on some four-cylinder- and V-8-equipped models.

Serviceability engineers also were hard at work reducing scheduled maintenance operations to only twenty-nine in the first 50,000 miles at an estimated cost of $158, compared to 125 procedures at $541 for the '74 Mustang II. Windshield washer fluid and coolant overflow bottles, as well as the battery case, were made transparent for quick visual checking, and the instrument cluster trim cover was designed to be easily removable for access to all instruments and the heater/air conditioner controls. Front disc brake pads were given audible wear indicators, and visual wear indicators were built into the front ball joints. Many other features such as the inboard front coil springs (separate from the suspension struts) and the V-8 engine's single-belt accessory drive were incorporated specifically with easy service in mind.

Inside the sleek new body was a lot more passenger and cargo room compared to the Mustang II — fourteen and sixteen cubic feet more in the notchback and hatchback, respectively. Unfortunately, much of the five-inch rear legroom gain came at the expense of limited front seat travel that shortchanged taller drivers and passengers. And, incredibly, Ford product planners still hadn't discovered adjustable front seatbacks (standard or optional in virtually all imported cars), which allow fatigue-relieving driving position changes. Limited front seat travel and fixed seatbacks were among the complaints about the first Mustang in 1964, and it's unbelievable that Ford hadn't learned about driver comfort and convenience in fifteen years!

On the positive side, the Fairmont-based instrument panel featured a full collection of useful gauges as standard equipment, the climate-control system was much-improved, and an optional console sported both a digital clock and a slick graphic warning system for low fuel, low washer fluid, and headlamp, taillamp and brakelight failures. Cruise control was available for the first time with the floor-mounted automatic or four-speed transmission, but the controls for it were on a wimpy, skinny, plastic "deluxe" four-spoke steering wheel that had no place in sporty versions of the car. Three other Mustang firsts for '79 were an optional tilt steering wheel, optional rear-window wiper/washer for the hatchback and standard steering column stalk controls for turn signals, headlamp dimmer, horn and windshield wiper/washer ... a nice European touch except that they're too far away from the wheel for convenient fingertip operation.

Aside from the few rough edges mentioned, it's obvious that a lot of careful thought, planning and engineering development went into the '79 program to make it what everyone involved wanted it to be — the best Mustang yet. As the August 1978 production date neared, most everything was progressing on schedule and engineers were "signing off" on their various responsibilities, confident that the best possible job had been done. A number of "sign off" and evaluation vehicles are kept up-to-date primarily for that purpose.

"The evaluation vehicles are used to meet a definite and strict set of Ford criteria," executive development engineer Dan Rivard explains.

Mustang for '79: Two-door notchback, three-door hatchback, Cobra, with beautiful forged aluminum wheels designed by Nehemiah Amaker.

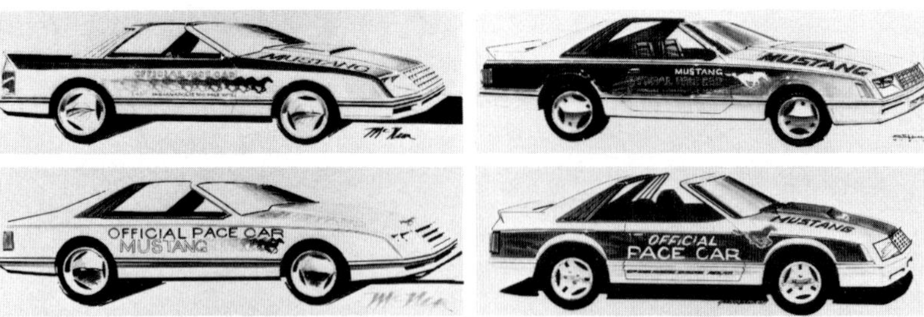

Sketches leading to design of the Mustang which would pace the Indianapolis 500 in 1979, and of which 11,000 pace-car replicas would be built.

"Doors have to close with a certain pound-force; they have to pass leakage tests; the brake pedal and accelerator have to operate with only a certain amount of driver foot pressure; the defroster has to clear the windshield within a specified time, and so on."

But while the body, chassis and component engineers were happily signing off on their last few items, some of the engine people were still struggling with what they hoped would be the '79 Mustang's most exciting new option — a turbocharged version of the 2.3-liter overhead-cam four-cylinder engine. Both Swedish automaker Saab and GM's Buick Division had joined Porsche in offering production turbocharged engines in the U.S. market in 1978, and Ford had decided late in the Mustang program that a turbo version would be just the ticket to enhance their new small sporty car's image.

Pressed for time, the engineers started dynamometer testing with unmodified turbo'd engines "just to see what would break," and then worked from there, eventually upgrading nearly every internal part. Turbocharging involves using an exhaust-driven turbine connected to a booster pump to pressurize the air/fuel mixture and shove more of it into the cylinders for combustion. Except for initial cost, it's almost a "something for nothing" system because the exhaust energy that powers it would be otherwise wasted; but it does create its own special problems.

"Boosted" combustion causes extra-high temperatures in the cylinders that have to be controlled to avoid engine-damaging detonation, so a two-stage retardation process was designed into the electronic ignition to retard the spark six degrees at one p.s.i. and another three degrees (six in California) at four p.s.i. boost pressure. A "wastegate" safety valve was incorporated to limit total boost to five and one-half p.s.i.; a large, cross-flow radiator contributed extra cooling capacity; a beefed clutch and heavy-duty 3.45:1 rear axle handled the added torque and power; and a 2.25-inch-diameter exhaust system and low-restriction muffler kept backpressure to a minimum.

Internally, the cylinder-head gasket, valves, valve-stem seals, oil pump and lubrication system, main and rod bearings and water pump all were upgraded to near-racing quality to cope with the turbo's higher loads, pressures and temperatures. Forged aluminum pistons with special-material piston rings, increased bore clearance and other modifications replaced the 2.3's cast-aluminum pistons and conventional rings. The turbocharger itself, a Garrett AiResearch unit that spins at 20,000 rpm at idle and up to 110,000 rpm at maximum boost, was fitted to a special intake manifold below the conventional two-barrel carburetor.

The idea of turbocharging is to make a small, otherwise economical engine think it's much bigger when the driver wants it to. At low engine speeds it contributes nothing and has little effect on fuel economy, but when you put your foot into it and the exhaust temperature and velocity start rapidly increasing, the turbo comes to life and kicks in with a bunch of extra power. Then chief powertrain and chassis engineer Howard Freers called it "one of the best ways known to combine V-8 power and I-4 fuel economy," and a few weeks before introduction he was predicting 147 horsepower and 154 pound-feet of torque from the turbo four, compared to the ordinary 2.3's 101 hp and 122 pound-feet. "This new option," he said, "will give the car enthusiast the kind of driving excitement he or she probably thought was gone forever from the American road."

But Freers couldn't have known at the time that his engine people, worried about possible reliability and warranty problems, would have it de-tuned to about 132 hp and 145 pound-feet of torque by the time it was released for production. "We started a little late in development," explains Mustang planner Gordon Riggs, "and we had some problems. We did not have a lot of experience with turbocharged engines, and our engineers felt they had to be a bit conservative. We would rather go out with a reliable engine instead of one that performed better but wasn't as reliable." At least the turbo team deserves credit for getting their job done on time when mid-summer predictions were that the package might be a couple of months late.

As before, selected media were invited to advanced briefings and given the opportunity to test prototype Mustangs as early as May 1978, so that articles could be prepared for August and September issues. Following nearly a year of "sneak" photos and leaked information in various publications, *Motor Trend*'s July issue featured accurate drawings of the Mustang notchback and its new sister-ship Mercury Capri (the German Capri had not been imported here since 1977) on its cover and the complete design story inside, plus an accompanying piece on the coming turbocharged engine.

The next month saw Mustang/Capri cover stories in both *Car and Driver* and *Road & Track* as well as a TRX Mustang test in *Motor Trend. Car and Driver*'s Don Sherman called the '79 Mustang "a piece of Detroit iron ready and able to over-rev your pulse rate," raved about its performance and handling and complained about the overdrive four-speed's wide gear ratios, the seats' lack of side support, the pedal's poor spacing for heel-and-toe downshifting, and the brakes' uneven balance. Nevertheless, he loved the way it drove: "Musclecar mavens who long ago abandoned the Mustang faith when the 'II' was added may now rejoin the flock. Wide gear ratios and tall axles will take a little getting used to, but there are compensations. In terms of sheer roadability, the new Mustang is the best thing that's happened in America since Trans Ams got sway bars."

Road & Track's John Dinkle was not quite so complimentary. "Conspicuous by their absence from the option list," he complained, "are reclining seatbacks. In a car aimed at the enthusiast this is an unforgiveable sin." He was disappointed with the amount of axle tramp under hard acceleration: "The rear wheels hopped and hopped when I engaged the clutch. Bringing the revs up to 3000 resulted in initial wheelspin followed by severe axle tramp when the wheels regained traction." Dinkle also griped about the front-heavy weight distribution (about sixty percent front, forty rear with the V-8), the brake balance (too much rear bias) and the lack of an available four-speed with the optional V-6; but he, too, loved the TRX's handling capabilities, calling it "nothing short of phenomenal."

Similar praises and criticism came from *Motor Trend*'s John Etheridge: "The general feel of the suspension," said he, "is what we would call 'natural,' meaning that it exhibits no quirks or surprises, and we felt comfortable driving the car fast right from the start." As for go-power, "the five-liter engine in this lightweight chassis produces very lively performance, the likes of which have been almost totally missing from Detroit products for many years. The TRX tires get a good bite for standing-start acceleration, but wheelspin is still a problem because there's more torque available than they can handle."

Etheridge clocked the four-speed, V-8 TRX Mustang at 8.7 seconds zero-to-sixty compared to Sherman's 8.3- and Dinkle's identical 8.7-second time. Quarter-mile elapsed times and speeds were reported as 16.7 seconds at 82 mph by *Motor Trend* and 17.0 seconds at 84.8 mph by *Car and Driver. R & T*'s Dinkle also put a watch on V-8 automatic and (2.8-liter) V-6 automatic versions, getting zero-to-sixty times of 8.6 and 12.9 seconds, respectively.

The September introduction was carried out with great enthusiasm from the public relations forces and comments like "one of the most exciting new cars ever introduced by Ford," from Ford Division general manager Walt Walla. Calling it "sportier, roomier and quicker," with "more handling and performance features" than its predecessors, Walla predicted that "the 1979 Mustang will continue and enhance the enthusiasm first generated by the original 1965 Mustang."

"The New Breed Mustang is dedicated to the proposition that all men and women believe that owning and driving a car should be fun," trumpeted the introduction issue of *Ford Times,* the Ford Division owners' magazine. "The all-new 1979 Mustang has been created for such men and women, for people who think that looking at their cars should give them pleasure, that riding in them should give them comfort and joy and that operating and maintaining them should be as easy as possible."

It wasn't exactly a repeat of April 17th, 1964; but neither was it the debacle of September 1973. Spurred by the advanced publicity and mostly favorable press reports, people did come out to see the new Mustang in significant numbers and some of them bought or ordered on the spot. Mustang sales in September and October ran about 150 percent of what Mustang II deliveries had been the year before, and by April the new car was outselling the old by nearly two-to-one ... 31,202 for the month versus Mustang II's 16,662 in April 1978. Ironically, small cars were getting some of the same sort of boost they had during the 1973-1974 fuel crisis due to widely publicized gas shortages in California and predictions of a similar fate for the whole country by summer.

More magazine stories followed the initial blitz. An October-issue driving impression by *Car and Driver* managing editor Mike Knepper compared the four different engines, calling the standard 2.3-liter four-cylinder "rough and buzzy as it is goes about its business of not producing much power." Knepper recommended the V-6 (later to become available with a four-speed manual) as the best performance/handling compromise, since "it isn't a heavy chunk of cast iron, like the V-8, sitting up front to screw up weight distribution and therefore handling," and reported that the turbo four turned in a respectable zero-to-sixty time of 9.1 seconds and did the quarter-mile

in 17.4 seconds at 82 mph ... just a tad slower than the V-8.

On the other hand, *Road & Track* came back with a full road test of the turbocharged Mustang and once again was less than impressed. The Turbo's performance was disappointing (10.4 seconds, zero-to-sixty), as was its gas mileage (19.5 mpg in a standard *R&T* economy test); and there were other complaints — poor driveability, too much noise and vibration, and above-average oil consumption, to name three. The article rated Mustang's turbo engine as "marginally acceptable in its present state of development." To make matters worse publicity-wise, some Turbos already in customers' hands started developing oil leaks in the Garrett-supplied turbine lubrication system. They were quickly recalled and fixed, and Turbo Mustang production halted until the problem had been taken care of.

Back on the positive side, *Car and Driver*'s annual readers' choice poll, reported in the April issue, had selected the third-generation Mustang from a group of twelve domestic models as "America's most significant new car." "We were pleased to learn that the 1979 Mustang had received the highest number of votes cast for a domestic automobile in the history of the *Car and Driver* poll, which began in 1964," said division manager Walt Walla on the occasion. "Our 2.6 million monthly readers are much more sophisticated about cars than the typical automotive buyer," crowed editor/publisher David E. Davis in return. "They are the ones who buy the cars and should do the voting. With the readers'-choice poll, they are speaking out loud."

History was repeated on Memorial Day weekend when a specially-modified 1979 Mustang paced the Indianapolis 500, just as the original had six weeks after its tumultuous introduction in 1964. This marked the eleventh time a Ford Motor Company product had paced the race, but only the second Mustang and the first Ford since 1968.

Under development since the previous July by Glen Lyall's chassis group, the pace car's TRX suspension used stock componentry but was stiffened and slightly retuned for the Goodyear Wingfoot tires it wore on race day due to the track's promotional tie-in with Goodyear. Externally, it carried special aerodynamic spoilers front and rear, a non-production T-roof, a louvered grille and hood scoop (similar to those drawn by Fritz Mayhew for the original Cobra proposal), a set of multi-adjustable Recaro bucket seats, and plenty of orange, red and black decal decorations on a black-and-pewter paint job.

Ford chose well-known engine builder Jack Roush to modify the 302 V-8 engine for 125-mph pace-car duty (the turbo four wasn't considered ready for such an assignment) and to oversee the whole project, while Detroit-based Cars and Concepts took care of the structurally-difficult T-top, the graphics, spoilers, scoop and modified grille. Roush dipped deeply into Ford engine history to come up with 351 (Windsor) cylinder heads, oversized racing valves, 1970 Boss 302 forged steel crankshafts and connecting rods, high-performance four-barrel carburetors and a high-rise aluminum intake manifold to arm the 302 with some 260 horsepower compared to the stock engine's 140 or so. Brakes, too, were beefed up for the heavy-duty job, and a modified and strengthened automatic transmission was coupled to the muscular little engine to handle the shifting duties.

A few weeks before the race, 11,000 pace-car replicas with the neat seats, scoop, spoilers and graphics, sunroofs (instead of the hard-to-produce T-tops), stock 302 V-8 or turbo four engines and four-speed manual transmissions were built and distributed to dealers throughout the country. These cars should be worth their price for the excellent

Mustang for 1980. Left: The three-door fastback, the notchback with two doors and ersatz convertible-top vinyl roof. Above and below: The Cobra, with front and rear spoilers, grille, louvered hood scoop and graphics from the 1979 Indianapolis pace car, which in turn had originated from '77 Cobra styling proposal. "Snake" decal is optional.

seats alone and are sure-fire collectors' items. And, as part of the whole pace-car promotion, Ford hired former World Driving Champion and heavy-duty salesman Jackie Stewart to test-drive one of the real examples on the Indy track. "It seemed very stable," said the alto-voiced Scot. "It's more of a high-performance vehicle than the Porsche 924. And I think it is also a darn good-looking motor car."

When the '80-model Mustangs were rolled out in the fall of 1979, there was a beautiful new Cobra version with the pace-car nose, hood and rear spoiler treatment and (finally!) optional Recaro buckets with both thigh-support and backrest adjustments. Maybe someday Ford will have designed an inexpensive reclining seat of its own, but the nice (but pricey) Recaros were definitely a step in the right direction. Other new options were a simulated and scarcely to be admired convertible top for the notchback model, a roof-mounted luggage rack, a cargo cover for the hatchback, an analog digital clock and a new "accent" tape-stripe treatment.

The gutsy 5.0-liter V-8 was unfortunately replaced by a more fuel-stingy 4.2-liter optional engine (with automatic only) while the old boat-anchor 3.3-liter in-line six (a mid-year 1979 addition) replaced the nice but hard-to-get German V-6. Automatic transmission became available with the Turbo package, a self-adjusting clutch came standard with the manual gearbox, a maintenance-free battery joined the standard-equipment list, a travelers' advisory band was added to all radios, and (perhaps most important) new high-pressure "P" metric radial tires became standard on all models. In the cockpit, the inner door handles were moved up to a more convenient location, the "luxury" steering wheel got a slightly-modified appearance and replaced the "sport" wheel on high-line Ghia cars, and a few other minor trim variations were made for the sake of variety.

As this is written, Mustang sales are continuing to accelerate and are presently at a volume unequalled since the happy, halcyon days of 1965-1967. America's ponycar pioneer has had its ups and downs, its good times and its not so good. It has progressed from an attractively-modified economy Falcon to a macho muscle-machine to an overstuffed sedan to a mini-Mark IV shrunken luxury liner and finally to its rightful placc as a smoothly-designed, lithe-muscled member of a whole new family of efficient, European-inspired cars at the forefront of Ford's fast-changing model lineup.

Mustang in its early years created a brand-new class of car for a newly youthful and fun-seeking buying public, attracted a loyal following of Mustang Generation men and women, led them into the Seventies and then lost them with eight straight years of size and image misdirection. Entering the uncertain Eighties, the Mustang Generation has matured and so has its car; but the right size and the image and the fun are back. Long may it live!

MUSTANG: A COLOR PORTFOLIO

Car Portraits by Richard Brown: 1966 Shelby G.T. 350,
1966 Mustang Convertible GT, 1967 Mustang Fastback 2+2 GTA, 1969 Mustang Hardtop, 1970 Mustang Convertible.
Car Portraits by Stan Grayson: 1967 Shelby G.T. 500, 1969 Shelby G.T. 350, 1974 Mustang II Notchback.
Car Portraits by Rick Lenz: 1965 Mustang Convertible, 1965 Mustang Fastback 2+2,
1965 Shelby G.T. 350, 1967 Mustang Hardtop, 1967 Mustang Fastback 2+2, 1968 Mustang Hardtop GT/CS,
1969 Mustang Mach I, 1971 Mustang Boss 351, 1972 Mustang Convertible, 1973 Mustang Grandé,
1974 Mustang Mach I, 1975 Mustang Notchback, 1976 Mustang II Ghia,
1977 Mustang II Cobra II, 1977 Mustang II Ghia, 1978 Mustang 2+2 T-Roof, 1978 Mustang II King Cobra.
Car Portraits by Roy Query: 1962 Mustang I Prototype,
1963 Mustang II Pre-Production Show Car, 1964½ Mustang Convertible, 1965 Mustang Hardtop, 1966 Mustang Hardtop,
1967 Mustang Convertible, 1968 Shelby GT500KR, 1970 Mustang Boss 302,
1973 Mustang Convertibles, 1979 Mustang Turbo Cobra, 1979½ Mustang Indianapolis 500 Pace Car.
Car Portrait by Don Vorderman: 1968 Mustang Hardtop.
Note: The 1962 Mustang I Prototype is owned, as indicated, by Greenfield Village and the Henry Ford Museum.
It is not, however, now on display, nor will it be for some time.
Regulations for the museum dictate that cars on exhibition must be twenty-five years or older.

1962 Mustang I Prototype • Collections of Greenfield Village and the Henry Ford Museum | Below: 1963 Mustang II Pre-Production Show Car • Detroit Historical Museum

HORSE SHOEING & GENERAL BLACKSMITHING
3-664

Above: 1965 Mustang Convertible • Owner: Ed Beaumont | Below: 1965 Mustang Fastback 2+2 • California Mustang Sales
Left: 1964½ Mustang Convertible, Serial Number 000001 • Collections of Greenfield Village and the Henry Ford Museum

Above: 1965 Shelby G.T. 350 • Owner: Robert Key | *Below: 1965 Mustang Hardtop*

Above: 1966 Mustang Hardtop • Owners: Dave and Maureen Bart | *Below: 1966 Shelby G.T. 350 • Owners: Tom and Caroline Shepherd*

MUSTANG

Above: 1967 Mustang • Convertible, owners, Jerry and Carolyn Shaw; Hardtop, owner, Ray Dunn
Left: 1966 Mustang Convertible GT • Owner: Brent Danneman | Below: 1967 Mustang Fastback 2+2 GTA • Owner: Bonnie Hart

MUSTANG
MUSTANG
VHG 975

Above: 1968 Shelby GT500KR • Owners: Taryl and Barbara Lamb
Left: 1967 Mustang Fastback 2+2 • Owner: Ed Beaumont | Below: 1967 Shelby G.T. 500 • Owners: Henry and Linda Busch

1968 Mustang Hardtop
Owner: Grace Perrin Kimes

1968 Mustang Hardtop GT/CS
Owner: Stuart Miles

1969 Mustang Hardtop • Owner: Debra Sheridan | Below: 1969 Shelby G.T. 350 • Owner: Raymond F. Hofmann, Jr. | Right: 1969 Mustang Mach I • California Mustang Pa

mach 1
ZNN 662

BOSS
302
GOODYEAR

Left: 1970 Mustang Boss 302 • Owner: John Stewart | 1970 Mustang Convertible • Owner: W. T. Hatfield | Below: 1971 Mustang Boss 351 • Special Interest Fords

Above: 1972 Mustang Convertible • Owner: Jim Dimico | Below: 1973 Mustang Grandé • Owner: L.L. Adams

Above: 1973 Mustang Convertible • Owner: Herb Hasenclever | Below: 1973 Mustang Convertible • Owner: Bob Palma

1974 Mustang II Notchback
Ford Motor Company

1974 Mustang Mach I
Owner: Bob Parkerson

Mustang

Left: 1975 Mustang Notchback • Lange & Runkel, Inc. | *1976 Mustang II Ghia • Owner: Toni Garcia* | *Below: 1977 Mustang II Cobra II • L.J. Snow Ford*

1978 Mustang 2+2 T-Roof • Owner: Linda Beaumont | Below: 1977 Mustang II Ghia • Owner: Jim Snow | Right: 1978 Mustang II King Cobra • Warren Anderson For

5.0
KING COBRA
STEEL RADIAL 721

Above: 1979 Mustang Turbo Cobra • Ford Motor Company | *Below: 1979½ Mustang Indianapolis 500 Pace Car • Ford Motor Company*

BIBLIOGRAPHY

Bailey, L. Scott, "Bertone Builds a Mustang." *Automobile Quarterly,* Volume IV, Number 2, Fall 1965.

Boyd, Maxwell, "New U.S. Sports Car." *London Sunday Times,* September 30th, 1962.

Gilbert, John, "Mustangs for 1971 to Grow Out of 'Pony Car' League." *Minneapolis Tribune,* August 9th, 1970.

Gill, Barrie, byline article. *London Daily Herald,* September 29th, 1962.

Howell, Grant W., "Knudsen Boss in Most Surprising Auto Exec Shift Ever." *Daily Tribune,* Royal Oak, Michigan, February 7th, 1968.

Irvin, Robert W., "Ben Bidwell's Embarrassing Success." *Washington Star News,* February 8th, 1974.

Lamm, Michael, *The Great Camaro.* Stockton, California: Lamm-Morada Publishing Company, 1978.

Levine, Leo, *Ford: The Dust and the Glory, A Racing History.* New York: The Macmillan Company, 1968.

Ludvigsen, Karl E., *The Inside Story of the Fastest Fords.* Torino, Italy: Style Auto Editrice, 1970.

Lunn, Roy C., "The Mustang, Ford's Experimental Sports Car." SAE Paper, Detroit, Michigan, January 14th-18th, 1963.

McCarthy, Joe, *Mustang.* New York: Sports Car Press, 1973.

Mateja, James, "Mustang II Reverses 'Goof', Awaits Buyer Stampede." *Chicago Tribune,* January 6th, 1974.

Miller, Ray, *Mustang Does It.* Oceanside, California: Evergreen Press, 1978.

"Mustang, The--A New Breed Out of Detroit." *Newsweek,* April 20th, 1964.

"Mustang Experimentals Given to Detroit Museums." *Old Cars,* December 2nd, 1975.

Noble, William T., "Mustang." *The Sunday News Magazine,* Detroit, Michigan, September 2nd, 1973.

Oldham, Joe, "Striped Lightning--The Shelby Mustangs." *Automobile Quarterly,* Volume XVI, Number 3, Third Quarter 1978.

Plegue, Jim, "Automotive Gestation: Designing the New Mustang." *Autoweek,* May 21st, 1979.

Stone, William S, "The Ford Mustang." Surrey, England: Profile Publications Ltd., 1966.

Storer, Jay, "Mustang—Breeding Improves the Race." *The Complete Ford Book.* Los Angeles: Petersen Publishing Company, circa 1971.

Witzenburg, Gary, "The Trans-Am Years: Great Fun While It Lasted." *Autoweek,* December 20th, 1975.

______, "U.S. Racing's Brightest Day." *Autoweek,* December 13th, 1975.

Yamaguchi, Jack, "Ford Mustang/Capri: Marriage of Design and Engineering." *Car Styling,* Issue #25, 1979 Quarterly, Winter.

NEWSPAPERS AND MAGAZINES

Car and Driver, Mustang articles and tests. December 1962, January 1963, May 1964, October 1964, November 1966, May 1967, July 1968, June 1969, June 1971, March 1972, August 1978, October 1978.

Car Life, Mustang articles and tests. December 1962, May 1964, September 1964, January 1967, February 1969, March 1969, September 1969, September 1970.

Consumer Reports, Mustang tests. July 1964, August 1964, July 1965.

Detroit Free Press, various articles. February 26th, 1966; April 17th, 1973; September 1st, 1973; October 13th, 1973; October 31st, 1973; June 10th, 1975; June 20th, 1977.

Detroit News, various articles. October 16th, 1966; August 25th, 1968; September 12th, 1969; September 21st, 1969; July 25th, 1973; August 14th, 1973; August 26th, 1973; August 28th, 1973; August 30th, 1973; August 31st, 1973; September 1st, 1973; September 2nd, 1973; September 3rd, 1973; September 4th, 1973; September 10th, 1973.

Ford Times, Mustang articles. November 1978, and others.

Motor Trend, Mustang articles and tests. January 1963, May 1964, August 1964, December 1966, May 1967, August 1968, November 1977, July 1978, August 1978, January 1979.

Road & Track, Mustang articles and tests. May 1964, August 1964, March 1967, January 1971, September 1973, January 1974, September 1974, January 1975, August 1978, January 1979.

Sports Car Graphic, Mustang articles and tests. May 1964, September 1964.

APPENDICES

MUSTANG PRODUCTION AND SALES

	Model Year Sales*	Model Year Production				Calendar Year Production
		Hardtop	Convertible	Fastback	Total	
1964	—	—	—	—	—	303,408
1965	499,242	409,260	73,112	77,079	559,451	580,187
1966	547,512	499,751	72,119	35,698	607,568	580,767
1967	442,686	356,271	44,808	71,042	472,121	394,482
1968	299,061	249,447	25,376	42,581	317,404	345,194
1969	293,338	150,640	14,746	134,438	299,824	275,391
1970	170,003	96,150	7,673	86,904	190,727	165,414
1971	139,942	83,102	6,121	60,455	149,678	130,488
1972	119,920	75,395	6,401	43,297	125,093	118,972
1973	123,402	76,754	11,853	46,260	134,867	193,129
1974	296,041	267,148	—	118,845	385,993	338,136
1975	199,199	137,475	—	51,100	188,575	187,554
1976	178,541	116,023	—	71,544	187,567	183,369
1977	161,654	97,293	—	55,880	153,173	170,315
1978	179,039	116,034	—	76,376	192,410	240,162

*Figures reflect sales in the United States only and do not include cars sold in Canada, Mexico and overseas.

MUSTANG ENGINES

	Cu.In.	Bore & Stroke	Carb.	C.R.	BHP @ RPM	Model Years
SIXES	170	3.50 x 2.94	1V	8.7	101 @ 4400	64½
	200	3.68 x 3.13	1V	9.2	120 @ 4400	65, 66, 67
	200	3.68 x 3.13	1V	8.8	115 @ 3800	68, 69
	250	3.68 x 3.91	1V	9.0	155 @ 4000	68, 69, 70
	200	3.68 x 3.13	1V	8.7	120 @ 4000	70
SMALL BLOCK V-8's	260	3.80 x 2.87	2V	8.8	164 @ 4400	64½
	289	4.00 x 2.87	4V	9.0	210 @ 4400	64½, 65
	289 (HP)	4.00 x 2.87	4V	10.5	271 @ 6000	64½, 65, 66
	289	4.00 x 2.87	4V	10.5	306 @ 6000	65, 66 (GT-350)
	289	4.00 x 2.87	4V	10.0	225 @ 4800	65, 66
	289	4.00 x 2.87	2V	9.3	200 @ 4400	65, 66, 67
SMALL BLOCK V-8's	289	4.00 x 2.87	4V	9.8	225 @ 4800	67
	289	4.00 x 2.87	4V	10.0	271 @ 6000	67
	289	4.00 x 2.87	2V	8.7	195 @ 4600	68
	302	4.00 x 3.00	4V	10.0	230 @ 4800	68
	302	4.00 x 3.00	4V	10.5	250 @ 4800	68 (GT-350)
	302	4.00 x 3.00	2V	9.5	220 @ 4600	69, 70
	351	4.00 x 3.50	2V	9.5	250 @ 4600	69, 70
	351	4.00 x 3.50	4V	10.7	290 @ 4800	69
	302	4.00 x 3.00	4V	10.6	290 @ 5800	69½, 70
	351	4.00 x 3.50	4V	11.0	300 @ 5400	70
LARGE BLOCK V-8's	390	4.05 x 3.78	4V	10.5	320 @ 4800	67, 69
	428	4.13 x 3.98	4V	10.5	355 @ 5400	67 (GT-500)
	390	4.05 x 3.78	4V	10.5	325 @ 4800	68
	427	4.23 x 3.78	4V	10.9	390 @ 5600	68
	390	4.05 x 3.78	2V	10.5	280 @ 4400	68
	428	4.13 x 3.98	4V	11.6	360 @ 5400	68 (GT-500)
	428 (&CJ)	4.13 x 3.98	4V	10.6	335 @ 5400	68½, 69, 70
	429 (HO)	4.36 x 3.59	4V	10.5	375 @ 5000	69½, 70
SIXES	250	3.68 x 3.91	1V	9.0	145 @ 4000	71
	250	3.68 x 3.91	1V	8.0	95*	72, 73
SMALL & LARGE-BLOCK V-8's	302	4.00 x 3.00	2V	9.0	210 @ 4600	71
	351	4.00 x 3.50	2V	9.0	240 @ 4600	71
	351	4.00 x 3.50	4V	10.7	285 @ 5400	71
	351 (HO)	4.00 x 3.50	4V	11.0	330 @ 5400	71
	351 (CJ)	4.00 x 3.50	4V	8.6	280 @ 5800	71½
	302	4.00 x 3.00	2V	8.5	136*	72, 73
	351	4.00 x 3.50	2V	8.6	168	72, 73
	351	4.00 x 3.50	4V	8.8	N.A.	72
	351 (HO)	4.00 x 3.50	4V	8.6	275 @ 6000	72½
	429 (CJ)	4.36 x 3.59	4V	11.3	370 @ 5400	71
	429 (CJ-RA)	4.36 x 3.59	4V	11.3	370 @ 5400	71
	429 (SCJ)	4.36 x 3.59	4V	11.3	375 @ 5600	71
FOURS	140	3.78 x 3.13	2V	8.4	88 @ 4800	74, 75, 76, 77, 78, 79, 80
	140 (Turbo)	3.78 x 3.13	2V	9.0	131 @ 5400	79, 80
SIXES	200	3.68 x 3.13	1V	8.5	85 @ 3600	79½, 80
V-6's	171	3.66 x 2.70	2V	8.7	109 @ 4800	74, 75, 76, 77, 78, 79
V-8's	302	4.00 x 3.00	2V	8.0	133 @ 3600	75, 76
	302	4.00 x 3.00	2V	8.4	140 @ 3600	77, 78, 79
	255	3.68 x 3.00	2V	N.A.	N.A.	80

*Beginning with model year 1972, horsepower figures are unreliable and were often unreported. Those available are SAE net, measured at the transmission output, with all engine accessories installed and operating.

BIBLIOGRAPHY

Bailey, L. Scott, "Bertone Builds a Mustang." *Automobile Quarterly,* Volume IV, Number 2, Fall 1965.

Boyd, Maxwell, "New U.S. Sports Car." *London Sunday Times,* September 30th, 1962.

Gilbert, John, "Mustangs for 1971 to Grow Out of 'Pony Car' League." *Minneapolis Tribune,* August 9th, 1970.

Gill, Barrie, byline article. *London Daily Herald,* September 29th, 1962.

Howell, Grant W., "Knudsen Boss in Most Surprising Auto Exec Shift Ever." *Daily Tribune,* Royal Oak, Michigan, February 7th, 1968.

Irvin, Robert W., "Ben Bidwell's Embarrassing Success." *Washington Star News,* February 8th, 1974.

Lamm, Michael, *The Great Camaro.* Stockton, California: Lamm-Morada Publishing Company, 1978.

Levine, Leo, *Ford: The Dust and the Glory, A Racing History.* New York: The Macmillan Company, 1968.

Ludvigsen, Karl E., *The Inside Story of the Fastest Fords.* Torino, Italy: Style Auto Editrice, 1970.

Lunn, Roy C., "The Mustang, Ford's Experimental Sports Car." SAE Paper, Detroit, Michigan, January 14th-18th, 1963.

McCarthy, Joe, *Mustang.* New York: Sports Car Press, 1973.

Mateja, James, "Mustang II Reverses 'Goof', Awaits Buyer Stampede." *Chicago Tribune,* January 6th, 1974.

Miller, Ray, *Mustang Does It.* Oceanside, California: Evergreen Press, 1978.

"Mustang, The--A New Breed Out of Detroit." *Newsweek,* April 20th, 1964.

"Mustang Experimentals Given to Detroit Museums." *Old Cars,* December 2nd, 1975.

Noble, William T., "Mustang." *The Sunday News Magazine,* Detroit, Michigan, September 2nd, 1973.

Oldham, Joe, "Striped Lightning--The Shelby Mustangs." *Automobile Quarterly,* Volume XVI, Number 3, Third Quarter 1978.

Plegue, Jim, "Automotive Gestation: Designing the New Mustang." *Autoweek,* May 21st, 1979.

Stone, William S, "The Ford Mustang." Surrey, England: Profile Publications Ltd., 1966.

Storer, Jay, "Mustang—Breeding Improves the Race." *The Complete Ford Book.* Los Angeles: Petersen Publishing Company, circa 1971.

Witzenburg, Gary, "The Trans-Am Years: Great Fun While It Lasted." *Autoweek,* December 20th, 1975.

______, "U.S. Racing's Brightest Day." *Autoweek,* December 13th, 1975.

Yamaguchi, Jack, "Ford Mustang/Capri: Marriage of Design and Engineering." *Car Styling,* Issue #25, 1979 Quarterly, Winter.

NEWSPAPERS AND MAGAZINES

Car and Driver, Mustang articles and tests. December 1962, January 1963, May 1964, October 1964, November 1966, May 1967, July 1968, June 1969, June 1971, March 1972, August 1978, October 1978.

Car Life, Mustang articles and tests. December 1962, May 1964, September 1964, January 1967, February 1969, March 1969, September 1969, September 1970.

Consumer Reports, Mustang tests. July 1964, August 1964, July 1965.

Detroit Free Press, various articles. February 26th, 1966; April 17th, 1973; September 1st, 1973; October 13th, 1973; October 31st, 1973; June 10th, 1975; June 20th, 1977.

Detroit News, various articles. October 16th, 1966; August 25th, 1968; September 12th, 1969; September 21st, 1969; July 25th, 1973; August 14th, 1973; August 26th, 1973; August 28th, 1973; August 30th, 1973; August 31st, 1973; September 1st, 1973; September 2nd, 1973; September 3rd, 1973; September 4th, 1973; September 10th, 1973.

Ford Times, Mustang articles. November 1978, and others.

Motor Trend, Mustang articles and tests. January 1963, May 1964, August 1964, December 1966, May 1967, August 1968, November 1977, July 1978, August 1978, January 1979.

Road & Track, Mustang articles and tests. May 1964, August 1964, March 1967, January 1971, September 1973, January 1974, September 1974, January 1975, August 1978, January 1979.

Sports Car Graphic, Mustang articles and tests. May 1964, September 1964.

APPENDICES

MUSTANG PRODUCTION AND SALES

	Model Year Sales*	Model Year Production Hardtop	Convertible	Fastback	Total	Calendar Year Production
1964	—	—	—	—	—	303,408
1965	499,242	409,260	73,112	77,079	559,451	580,187
1966	547,512	499,751	72,119	35,698	607,568	580,767
1967	442,686	356,271	44,808	71,042	472,121	394,482
1968	299,061	249,447	25,376	42,581	317,404	345,194
1969	293,338	150,640	14,746	134,438	299,824	275,391
1970	170,003	96,150	7,673	86,904	190,727	165,414
1971	139,942	83,102	6,121	60,455	149,678	130,488
1972	119,920	75,395	6,401	43,297	125,093	118,972
1973	123,402	76,754	11,853	46,260	134,867	193,129
1974	296,041	267,148	—	118,845	385,993	338,136
1975	199,199	137,475	—	51,100	188,575	187,554
1976	178,541	116,023	—	71,544	187,567	183,369
1977	161,654	97,293	—	55,880	153,173	170,315
1978	179,039	116,034	—	76,376	192,410	240,162

*Figures reflect sales in the United States only and do not include cars sold in Canada, Mexico and overseas.

MUSTANG ENGINES

	Cu.In.	Bore & Stroke	Carb.	C.R.	BHP @ RPM	Model Years
SIXES	170	3.50 x 2.94	1V	8.7	101 @ 4400	64½
	200	3.68 x 3.13	1V	9.2	120 @ 4400	65, 66, 67
	200	3.68 x 3.13	1V	8.8	115 @ 3800	68, 69
	250	3.68 x 3.91	1V	9.0	155 @ 4000	68, 69, 70
	200	3.68 x 3.13	1V	8.7	120 @ 4000	70
SMALL BLOCK V-8's	260	3.80 x 2.87	2V	8.8	164 @ 4400	64½
	289	4.00 x 2.87	4V	9.0	210 @ 4400	64½, 65
	289 (HP)	4.00 x 2.87	4V	10.5	271 @ 6000	64½, 65, 66
	289	4.00 x 2.87	4V	10.5	306 @ 6000	65, 66 (GT-350)
	289	4.00 x 2.87	4V	10.0	225 @ 4800	65, 66
	289	4.00 x 2.87	2V	9.3	200 @ 4400	65, 66, 67
SMALL BLOCK V-8's	289	4.00 x 2.87	4V	9.8	225 @ 4800	67
	289	4.00 x 2.87	4V	10.0	271 @ 6000	67
	289	4.00 x 2.87	2V	8.7	195 @ 4600	68
	302	4.00 x 3.00	4V	10.0	230 @ 4800	68
	302	4.00 x 3.00	4V	10.5	250 @ 4800	68 (GT-350)
	302	4.00 x 3.00	2V	9.5	220 @ 4600	69, 70
	351	4.00 x 3.50	2V	9.5	250 @ 4600	69, 70
	351	4.00 x 3.50	4V	10.7	290 @ 4800	69
	302	4.00 x 3.00	4V	10.6	290 @ 5800	69½, 70
	351	4.00 x 3.50	4V	11.0	300 @ 5400	70
LARGE BLOCK V-8's	390	4.05 x 3.78	4V	10.5	320 @ 4800	67, 69
	428	4.13 x 3.98	4V	10.5	355 @ 5400	67 (GT-500)
	390	4.05 x 3.78	4V	10.5	325 @ 4800	68
	427	4.23 x 3.78	4V	10.9	390 @ 5600	68
	390	4.05 x 3.78	2V	10.5	280 @ 4400	68
	428	4.13 x 3.98	4V	11.6	360 @ 5400	68 (GT-500)
	428 (&CJ)	4.13 x 3.98	4V	10.6	335 @ 5400	68½, 69, 70
	429 (HO)	4.36 x 3.59	4V	10.5	375 @ 5000	69½, 70
SIXES	250	3.68 x 3.91	1V	9.0	145 @ 4000	71
	250	3.68 x 3.91	1V	8.0	95*	72, 73
SMALL & LARGE-BLOCK V-8's	302	4.00 x 3.00	2V	9.0	210 @ 4600	71
	351	4.00 x 3.50	2V	9.0	240 @ 4600	71
	351	4.00 x 3.50	4V	10.7	285 @ 5400	71
	351 (HO)	4.00 x 3.50	4V	11.0	330 @ 5400	71
	351 (CJ)	4.00 x 3.50	4V	8.6	280 @ 5800	71½
	302	4.00 x 3.00	2V	8.5	136*	72, 73
	351	4.00 x 3.50	2V	8.6	168	72, 73
	351	4.00 x 3.50	4V	8.8	N.A.	72
	351 (HO)	4.00 x 3.50	4V	8.6	275 @ 6000	72½
	429 (CJ)	4.36 x 3.59	4V	11.3	370 @ 5400	71
	429 (CJ-RA)	4.36 x 3.59	4V	11.3	370 @ 5400	71
	429 (SCJ)	4.36 x 3.59	4V	11.3	375 @ 5600	71
FOURS	140	3.78 x 3.13	2V	8.4	88 @ 4800	74, 75, 76, 77, 78, 79, 80
	140 (Turbo)	3.78 x 3.13	2V	9.0	131 @ 5400	79, 80
SIXES	200	3.68 x 3.13	1V	8.5	85 @ 3600	79½, 80
V-6's	171	3.66 x 2.70	2V	8.7	109 @ 4800	74, 75, 76, 77, 78, 79
V-8's	302	4.00 x 3.00	2V	8.0	133 @ 3600	75, 76
	302	4.00 x 3.00	2V	8.4	140 @ 3600	77, 78, 79
	255	3.68 x 3.00	2V	N.A.	N.A.	80

*Beginning with model year 1972, horsepower figures are unreliable and were often unreported. Those available are SAE net, measured at the transmission output, with all engine accessories installed and operating.

MUSTANG OPTIONAL EQUIPMENT INSTALLATION (PERCENTAGE)

	1965	1966	1967	1968	1969	1970	1971	1972	1973	1974	1975	1976	1977	1978	1979
Engine, V-8	64.0	58.3	70.0	70.7	81.6	85.0	90.2	92.3	94.2	—	25.1	17.6	25.6	17.9	19.2
Engine, Six-Cylinder	35.6	41.7	30.0	29.3	18.4	15.0	9.8	7.7	5.8	44.1	23.4	29.1	23.6	32.9	18.5
Engine, Four-Cylinder	—	—	—	—	—	—	—	—	—	55.9	51.5	53.3	50.8	49.2	62.3
Transmission, Automatic	53.6	62.8	67.8	71.8	71.1	74.6	83.9	90.4	90.4	59.4	56.5	57.8	67.2	63.5	69.8
Transmission, Four-Speed	14.5	7.1	7.3	6.1	11.7	11.2	5.3	2.7	2.9	40.2	43.5	45.2	32.8	36.5	30.2
Transmission, Three-Speed	31.9	30.1	24.9	22.1	17.2	14.2	10.8	6.9	6.7	—	—	—	—	—	—
Power Brakes	4.3	3.3	13.0	13.1	30.5	36.2	40.9	54.9	77.9	35.0	38.7	71.4	87.2	89.4	75.2
Front Disc Brakes*	6.7	6.7	13.0	13.1	30.5	36.2	40.9	54.9	77.9	100.0	100.0	100.0	100.0	100.0	100.0
Power Steering	24.9	28.9	43.9	51.8	65.9	73.2	85.7	90.2	92.9	57.6	67.0	74.8	83.2	84.5	89.4
Limited-Slip Differential	2.0	2.6	4.8	3.7	8.6	10.6	5.9	4.2	4.3	2.1	3.9	6.5	—	—	—
Tinted Windows	9.0	7.3	34.2	31.7	38.3	37.9	45.8	55.7	61.6	47.7	60.9	55.7	60.1	64.1	71.5
Air Conditioning	9.1	9.5	15.8	17.5	23.2	28.2	40.5	48.5	56.2	37.7	37.6	39.6	42.8	46.6	58.9
Bucket Seats	97.0	99.0	98.0	97.4	98.4	100.0	100.0	100.0	100.0	100.0	100.0	100.0	100.0	100.0	100.0
Cruise Control	—	—	—	0.2	0.2	0.2	0.3	—	—	—	—	—	—	—	11.1
Adjustable Steering Column	—	—	2.7	2.7	3.2	2.5	3.3	3.9	5.6	—	—	—	—	—	14.0
Power Windows	—	—	—	—	—	—	1.9	2.0	3.2	—	—	—	—	—	—
Vinyl Top	8.1	9.5	14.7	18.0	16.1	19.1	29.0	32.3	43.5	38.1	37.0	23.3	28.9	25.2	16.4
Radial Tires	—	—	—	—	—	—	N.A.	N.A.	5.3	65.9	96.2	65.7	58.5	62.7	70.2

*Front disc brakes were available without power assist in the 1965 and 1966 model years, but beginning in 1967 front discs were included with and offered only in combination with power assist. NOTE: A dash indicates the item was not offered; N.A. indicates the item was offered but installation percentages were not available.

MUSTANG ROAD TEST PERFORMANCE

Publication	Issue Date	Year/Model	Engine	Transmission	Rear Axle	0-60 (sec)	Quarter-Mile (sec)	Quarter-Mile (mph)	Top Speed (mph)
Car and Driver	January 1963	1962 mid-engine two-seat prototype	1.5L/90 hp four	four-speed	3.30:1	10.0	16.6	79	115
Car Life	May 1964	1965 convertible	289/210 hp	four-speed	3.00:1	8.9	17.0	85	111
Road & Track	May 1964	1965 Hardtop	260/164 hp	automatic	3.00:1	11.2	18.8	78	—
Sports Car Graphic	September 1964	1965 Hardtop	289/271 hp	four-speed	4.11:1	7.5	15.7	89	117
Car and Driver	November 1966	1967 GT 2+2	390/320 hp	automatic	3.00:1	7.3	15.2	91	124
Road & Track	March 1967	1967 Hardtop	289/225 hp	four-speed	3.00:1	9.7	17.4	84	110
Motor Trend	May 1967	1967 GT 2+2	390/320 hp	four-speed	3.00:1	7.4	15.6	94	—
Car Life	March 1969	1969 Mach I	428/335 hp	automatic	3.50:1	5.5	13.9	103	121
Car Life	September 1969	1969 Boss 302	302/290 hp	four-speed	3.91:1	6.9	14.9	96	118
Road & Track	January 1971	1970 Boss 302 Trans-Am Racer	302/460 hp	four-speed	4.33:1	5.5	12.9	110	151
Car and Driver	March 1972	1972 fastback	351 HO/275 hp	four-speed	3.91:1	6.6	15.1	96	120
Road & Track	January 1974	1974 Mach I	2.8L/119 hp V-6	four-speed	3.55:1	13.8	19.4	70.5	99
Road & Track	January 1975	1975 2+2	302/133 hp	automatic	3.00:1	10.5	17.9	77	106
Motor Trend	August 1978	1979 Hardtop	302/140 hp	four-speed	3.08:1	8.7	16.7	82	118

MUSTANG COLORS

1964½

Company Code		Ditzler	R/M	Acme	Dupont
A	Raven Black	9000	A-946, P-403	3000	88
B	Pagoda Green	12851	1628	9359	4495
D	Dynasty Green	12853	1629	9349	--
F	Guardsman Blue	12832	1630	8867	4483
H	Caspian Blue	12752	--	9094	4289
J	Rangoon Red	71243	1440	9079	4294
K	Silversmoke Gray	32377	1632	9345	4482
M	Wimbledon White	8378	1633	9343	4480
3	Poppy Red	60449	-	9604	-
P	Prairie Bronze	22438	1693	9605	--
V	Sunlight Yellow	81467	1692	9603	--
X	Vintage Burgundy	50657	1636	9354	4490
Y	Skylight Blue	12850	1637	9347	4484
Z	Chantilly Beige	22393	1638	9352	4488
S	Cascade Green	42925	1645	9072	4287

1965

Company Code		Ditzler	R/M	Acme	Dupont
A	Raven Black	9000, 9300	A-946, P-403	3000	88
B	Midnight Turquoise	--	--	9069	4284
C	Honey Gold	22581	1739	9643	4612
D	Dynasty Green	12853	1629	9349	4486
H	Caspian Blue	12547	1770	9731	4693
I	Champagne Beige	22436	1735	9644	4613
J	Rangoon Red	71243	1440	9079	4294
K	Silversmoke Gray	32377	1632	9345	4482
M	Wimbledon White	8378	1633	9343	4480
O	Tropical Turquoise	12852	1737	9640	4608
P	Prairie Bronze	22438	1693	9605	4603
R	Ivy Green	43337	1738	9650	4611
V	Sunlight Yellow	--	1692	--	--
X	Vintage Burgundy	50657	1636	9354	4490
Y	Silver Blue	12164	1734	8880	4692
3	Poppy Red	60449	1774	9604	4602

1966

Company Code		Ditzler	R/M	Acme	Dupont
A	Raven Black	9000, 9300	A-946, P-403	3000	88
F	Light Blue	12854*	1223[1]	8867[1]	4070
H	Light Beige	22528	1779[2]	5052[2]	4740
K	Dark Blue Metallic	13076	1780[3]	5047[4]	4734
M	Wimbledon White	8378	1633	9343	4480
P	Medium Palomino Met.	22603	1781[5]	5050[5]	4738
R	Dark Green Metallic	43408	1738[6]	9650[7]	4611
T	Candyapple Red	71528	1782	5056	4737
U	Med. Turquoise Met.	12745	1231	8742[8]	4299
V	Emberglo Metallic	22610	1777	9855	4700
X	Maroon Metallic	50669	1636[9]	9354[9]	4490
Y	Light Blue Metallic	13045	1734**	8880[10]	4692
Z	Med. Sage Metallic; Gold Metallic	43433	1783[11]	5053[12]	4742
4	Med. Silver Metallic	32520	1784[13]	5046[13]	4733
5	Signalflare Red	71529	1791	5100	4741
8	Springtime Yellow	81510*	1776	9856	4699

*Also 1965 Spring colors; **not on charts, assumed to be same as 1965.

[1]Arcadian Blue, [2]Sahara Beige, [3]Nightmist Blue, [4]Nightmist Blue Metallic, [5]Antique Bronze, [6]Ivy Green Metallic,[7]Ivy Green, [8]Tahoe Turquoise Metallic, [9]Vintage Burgundy, [10]Silver Blue Metallic, [11]Sauterne Gold Metallic, [12]Sauterne Gold, [13]Silver Frost.

1967

Company Code		Ditzler	R/M	Acme	Dupont
A	Raven Black	9000, 9300	A-946, P-403	3000	88
B	Frost Turquoise	12876	1741	9642	4610
D	Acapulco Blue	13357	--	--	4851
F	Arcadian Blue	12854	1223	5450	4070
I	Lime Gold	43576	1882	8867	4790
K	Nightmist Blue	13076	1780	5264	4780
M	Wimbledon White	8734, 8378	1633	5047	4480
Q	Brittany Blue	12843	1643	5567[1]	4813
T	Candyapple Red	71528	1782	5056	4737
V	Burnt Amber	22749	1881	5263	4793
W	Clearwater Aqua	13073	1889	5257	4787
X	Vintage Burgundy	50669	1636	9354	4490
Y	Dark Moss Green	43567	1879	5258	4788
Z	Sauterne Gold	43433	1783	5053	4742
6	Pebble Beige	22249	1635	9353	4489
8	Springtime Yellow	81510	1776	9856	4699

[1]Medium Blue Metallic

Special colors for 1967:
H Diamond Green - Ditzler 43575
N Diamond Blue - Ditzler 11683
S Dusk Rose - Ditzler 50470
Mix No. 707908, Playboy Pink - Ditzler 71617

Mix No. 709377, Anniversary Gold #1 - Ditzler 22157
Mix No. 709431, Anniversary Gold #2 - Ditzler 23072
Mix No. 709571, Anniversary Gold #3 - Ditzler 23073

"High Country" Mustang colors for 1967:
Mix No. 700852, Columbine Blue - Ditzler 11666
Mix No. 708815, Aspen Gold - Ditzler 81434

Mix No. 7001297, Blue Bonnet - Ditzler 13660
Mix No. 7041278, Timberline Green - Ditzler 42750
Also...Lavender - Ditzler 50802; and Red - Ditzler 71697

1968

A	Raven Black	9000, 9300	A-946, P-403	3000	88
B	Royal Maroon	50746	1941	5459	4864
D	Acapulco Blue	13357	1935	5450	4857
F	Gulfstream Aqua	13329	—	5462	4868
I	Lime Gold	43576	1882	5264	4790
M	Wimbledon White	8734, 8378	1633	5047	4775
N	Diamond Blue	11683	1238	8530	4950
O	Sea Foam Green	43529	1885	5259	4789
Q	Brittany Blue	13619	1643	5567	4951
R	Highland Green	43644	1946	5463	4869
T	Candyapple Red	71528	1782	—	4737
U	Tahoe Turquoise	12745	1231	8742	4876
X	Presidential Blue	13356	1950	5460	4866
W	Meadowlark Yellow	81584	1949	5467	4878
Y	Sunlit Gold	22833	1951	5454	4874
6	Pebble Beige	22249	1635	9353	4489

1969

A	Raven Black	9000, 9300	A-946, P-403	3000	99
B	Royal Maroon	50746	1941	5459	4864
C	Black Jade	2037	2038	5565	5050
D*	Pastel Grey	2038	2033	5675	5053
E	Aztec Aqua	2039	2036	5585	4967
F	Gulfstream Aqua	13329	1942	5462	4868
I	Lime Gold	2054	1882	5264	4790
M	Wimbledon White	8378, 8734	1633	5047	4775
P	Winter Blue	2042	2035	5582	4965
S	Champagne Gold	2044	2044	5589	4970
T	Candyapple Red	71528	1728	5056	4737
W	Meadowlark Yellow	81584	1949	5467	4878
Y	Indian Fire	2046	2045	5591	4972
2	New Lime	2047	2037	5583	4976
4	Silver Jade	2048	2040	5595	4975
6*	Acapulco Blue	13357	1935	5450	4858

*One chart shows D as Acapulco Blue and 6 as Pastel Grey, but all other color charts show the reverse.

1970

A	Black	9000, 9300	A-946, P-403	3000	99
C	Dark Ivy Green Met.	2146	2308	5753	5099
D	Bright Yellow	2214	2309	11078[1]	5194
G	Medium Lime Metallic	2152	2311	5760	5176
K	Bright Gold Metallic	2156	2198	5756	5101
M	White	8378	1633	9343	4775
N	Pastel Blue	11683	1238	8530	4950
Q	Medium Blue Metallic	2138	2316	5750	5097
S	Medium Gold Metallic	2044	2044	5889	4970
T	Red	71528	1728	5056	4737
1	Vermillion	—	1774	9604	4602
2	Light Ivy Yellow	2047	2037	5583	4976
6	Bright Blue Metallic	13357	1935	5450	4857
J9	Grabber Blue	—	2313	11089	5205
U9	Grabber Orange	—	2318	11088	5208
Z9	Grabber Green	—	2328	11090	5206

[1] Yellow

1971

A	Black	9000, 9300	A-946, P-403	3000	99
M	White	8378	1633	9343	4775
3	Bright Red	2296	2433	11124	5229
B	Maroon Metallic	2295	2423	11125	5230
V	Light Pewter Metallic	2287	2430	11135	5318
6	Bright Blue Metallic	13357	2367	5450	5330
N	Pastel Blue	11683	1238	8530	4950
P	Medium Green Metallic	2289	2365	11128	5233
C	Dark Green Metallic	2291	2424	11127	5235
5	Medium Brown Metallic	2371	2481	11259	5344
I	Grabber Lime	2294	2427	11132	5231
8	Light Gold	2043	2043	5588	5969
D	Grabber Yellow	2214	2309	11078	5194
E	Medium Yellow Gold	2299	2371	11133	5238
Z	Grabber Green Metallic	2293	2370	11131	5234
J	Grabber Blue	2230	2313	11089	5205

1972

9A	White	8378	1633	9343	4775
2B	Bright Red	2296	2433	11124	5229
2J	Maroon	50746*	1914	5459	4864
3J	Bright Blue Metallic	13357	2367	5450	5330
3F	Grabber Blue	2230	2313	11089	5205
3B	Light Blue	2403	2516	11316	5366
4Q	Dark Green Metallic	2291	2424	11127	5235
4P	Medium Green Metallic	2289	2365	11128	5233
4F	Medium Lime Metallic	2412	2521	11323	5361
4E	Bright Lime	2385	2497	11322	5362

5H	Medium Brown Metallic	2371, 2482	2481	11259	5344
6C	Medium Yellow Gold	2299	2371	11133	5238
6E	Medium Bright Yellow	2414	2524	11330	5374
5A	Light Pewter Metallic	2287	2430	11135	5318
4C	Ivy Glow	2362	2477	11240	5334
6F	Gold Glow	2415	2525[1]	11331[2]	5373

*Also 1971 Spring color

[1]Gold Glamour Iridescent
[2]Bright Yellow Gold Metallic

1973

9A	White	8378	1633	9343	4775
2B	Bright Red	2296	2433	11124	5229
3B	Light Blue	2403	2516	11316	5366
3D	Medium Blue Metallic	2404	2517	11317	5377
3K	Blue Glow	2499	2661	11395	5535
4B	Bright Green Gold Met.	2406	2520	11321	5364
4C	Ivy Glow	2362	2477	11240	—
4N	Medium Aqua	2507	2664	11398	5532
4P	Medium Green Metallic	2289	2365	11128	5233
4Q	Dark Green Metallic	2291	2424	11127	5235
5T	Saddle Bronze Metallic	2575	2691	11153	—
5H	Medium Brown Metallic	2482	2592	11394	5386[1]
5M	Medium Copper Metallic	2504	2668	11402[2]	5530[3]
6C	Medium Yellow Gold	2299	—	11133	—
6E	Medium Bright Yellow	2414	2524	11330	5374
6F	Gold Glow	2415	2525	11332[4]	5373

[1]Ginger Metallic
[2]Medium Chestnut Metallic
[3]Medium Chestnut
[4]Gold Fire Metallic

1974

9C	Pearl White	2512	—	11472	5414
1G	Silver Metallic	2593	2727	11557	5580
2B	Bright Red	2296	2433	11124	5229
2M	Dark Red	2609	2728	11616	42829
3B	Light Blue	2403	2516	11316	5366
3N	Med. Bright Blue Met.	2611	2730	11564	42836
4B	Bright Green Gold Met.	2406	2520	11321	5364
4W	Medium Lime Yellow	2615	2735	11565	42833
5M	Medium Copper Metallic	2504	2668	11402	5530
5T	Saddle Bronze Metallic	2575	2691	11553	5582
6C	Medium Yellow Gold	2299	2371	11133	5238
4T	Green Glow	2666	2733	11399	42834
5J	Ginger Glow	2363	2478	11239	5333
5U	Tan Glow	2618	2738	11559	42846

1975

1C	Black	9000	A-946, P-403	4950, 3000	99
1G	Silver Metallic	2593	2727	11557	5580
2B	Bright Red	2296	2433	11124	5229
2M	Dark Red	2609	2728	11616	42829
3E	Bright Blue Metallic	2610	2729	11563	42832
3M	Silver Blue Glow	2501	2663	11397	5541
3Q	Pastel Blue	2613	2732	11602	42873
4T	Green Glow	2666	2733	11399	42834
4V	Dark Yellow Green Met.	2614	2734	11558	42838
47	Light Green	2726	2834	11787	43522
5M	Med. Copper Metallic	2504	2668	11402	5530[1]
5Q	Dark Brown Metallic	2616	2736	11566	42840
5U	Tan Glow	2618	2738	11559	42846
6E	Bright Yellow	2414	2524	11330	5374
9D	Polar White	2684	2785	11707	43326

[1]Medium Chestnut

1976

Basically the same as 1975, with the following modifications: Pastel Blue was dropped, 5Q in Acme paint became 25153, 5M became Medium Chestnut Metallic, 4T became Medium Ivy Bronze Metallic in Ditzler and Medium Green Metallic in Rinshed/Mason.

1977

1C	Black	9000	A-946, P-403	4950, 3000	99
1G	Silver Metallic	2593	2727	11557	5580
2R	Bright Red	2830	2949	25046	44103
5Q	Dark Brown Metallic	2616	2997	25153	44174
6E	Bright Yellow	2414	2524	11330	5374
6P	Creme	2790	2923	25043	43938
6V	Golden Glow	2837	2956	25079	44153
7H	Bright Aqua Glow	2910	8717	25241	44751
7Q	Light Aqua Metallic	2887	8570	25176	44185
7S	Medium Emerald Glow	2913	8720	25239	44756
8G	Orange	2915	8722	25203	44746
8H	Tan	2916	8723	25202	44748
8K	Bright Saddle Metallic	2918	8725	25249	44754
9D	Polar White	2684	2785	11707	43326

1978

1C	Black	9000	A-946, P-403	4950, 3000	99
1G	Silver Metallic	2593	2727	11557	5580

MUSTANG COLOR NOTES: R/M indicates Rinshed/Mason. Footnoted colors indicate varying color designations of paint

2R	Bright Red	2830	2949	25046	44103
3A	Dark Midnight Blue	3035	9515	25423	45116
46	Dark Jade Metallic	2725	2833	11792	43517
5M	Med. Chestnut Met.	2504	2668	11402	5530
5Q	Dark Brown Metallic	2616	2997	25153	44174
6E	Bright Yellow	2414	2524	11330	5374
7H	Aqua Glow	2910	8717	25241	44751
7Q	Aqua Metallic	2887	8570	25176	44185
8W	Chamois Glow	2923	8730	25232	44757
83	Light Chamois	3057	8782	25364	45155
85	Tangerine	3058	9534	25363	45154
9D	Polar White	2684*	2785*	11707	43326

*Former Polar White now White

1979

1C	Black	9000	A-946, P-403	3000	99
1G	Silver Metallic	2593	2727	11557	5580
2H	Red Glow	3168	9824	30033	45761
2P	Bright Red	3169	9825	30217	45787
3F	Light Medium Blue	3170	9826	30038	45762
3H	Medium Blue Glow	3184	9827	30040	45763
3J	Bright Blue	3176	9828	30039	45764
46	Dark Jade Metallic	2725	2833	11792	43517
5M	Med. Chestnut Met.	2504	2668	11402	5530
5W	Med. Vaquero Gold	3174	9836	30034	45770
64	Bright Yellow	3063	9541	25414	45174
83	Light Chamois	3057	8782	25364	45155
85	Tangerine	3058	9534	25363	45154
1P	Medium Grey Metallic	2967	8778	25244	44783
9D	Polar White	2684	2785	11707	43326

MUSTANG RACING RECORD

Sports Car Club of America: National Championships

Class A Sedan: John McComb, 1967
Warren Tope, 1971
Class B Production: Jerry Titus, 1965
Walter Hane, 1966
Fred Van Beuren, 1967

Sports Car Club of America: Trans-Am Sedan Championship Victories

1966: Tom Yeager/Bob Johnson, Mid-America Raceway, Missouri
Tom Yeager/Bob Johnson, Virginia International Raceway
John McComb/Brad Brooker, Green Valley Raceway, Texas
Jerry Titus, Riverside International Raceway, California
(won four of six races for Manufacturers' Championship)

1967: Jerry Titus, Sebring Air Terminal, Florida
Jerry Titus, Mid-Ohio Sports Car Course
Jerry Titus, Continental Divide Raceway, Colorado
Jerry Titus, Modesto Naval Air Station, California
(won four of twelve races for Manufacturers' Championship)

1968: Jerry Titus/Ron Bucknum, Daytona International Speedway, Florida
Jerry Titus, Watkins Glen Grand Prix Course, New York
Horst Kwech, Riverside International Raceway, California
(won three of thirteen races)

1969: Parnelli Jones, Michigan International Speedway
Sam Posey, Lime Rock Park, Connecticut
George Follmer, Bridgehampton Race Circuit, New York
Parnelli Jones, Donnybrooke International Speedway, Minnesota
(won four of twelve races)

1970: Parnelli Jones, Laguna Seca Raceway, California
Parnelli Jones, Lime Rock Park, Connecticut
George Follmer, Bryar Motorsport Park, New Hampshire
Parnelli Jones, Mid-Ohio Sports Car Course
Parnelli Jones, Seattle International Raceway, Washington
Parnelli Jones, Riverside International Raceway, California
(won six of eleven races for Manufacturers' Championship)

1971: George Follmer, Bryar Motorsport Park, New Hampshire
George Follmer, Mid-Ohio Sports Car Course
(won two of ten races)

1972: Warren Tope, Road America, Wisconsin
Warren Tope, Sanair Internationale, Quebec, Canada
(won two of seven races)

MUSTANG BASIC SPECIFICATIONS*

Major Mustang Model Series	1965 to 1966	1967 to 1968	1969 to 1970	1971 to 1973	1974 to 1978	1979 to 1980
Overall length, ins.	181.6	183.6	187.4	189.5	175.0	179.1
Overall width, ins.	68.2	70.9	71.3	74.1	70.2	69.1
Overall height, ins.	51.1	51.6	51.3	50.8	49.9	51.5
Wheelbase, ins.	108.0	108.0	108.0	109.0	96.2	100.4
Front track, ins.	55.4	58.0	58.5	61.5	55.5	56.6
Rear track, ins.	56.0	58.0	58.5	61.0	55.6	57.0
Curb weight, lbs.	2562	2695	2832	3087	2679	2516
Usable trunk room, ft^3	8.9	9.2	9.8	9.5	6.7	10.0
Fuel capacity, gal.	16.0	17.0	20.0	20.0	13.0	12.5

*Specifications for base two-door hardtop

suppliers. When there are two numbers for the same color, the first indicates enamel, the second lacquer.

GENERAL INDEX

INDEX OF ILLUSTRATIONS

Note: Page numbers in bold refer to photographs in color.

PHOTO CREDITS

24 below right, 48 right: Courtesy of *Road & Track* magazine. 22 right: Courtesy of Jacque Passino. 48 above left, 69, 90 above and below: Photographs by Dave Arnold. 60 right: Courtesy of Gail Halderman. All other photographs and illustrations courtesy of the Ford Motor Company—with special thanks to the staff people of Ford Photo Media and Ford Design Center Photographic—or from the archives of *Automobile Quarterly* magazine.